Women in Trade Unions

By
BARBARA DRAKE

TRADE UNION SERIES
No. 6.

PUBLISHED BY THE LABOUR RESEARCH DEPARTMENT, 34 ECCLESTON SQUARE, S.W.; AND BY GEORGE ALLEN AND UNWIN, LIMITED, 40 MUSEUM ST., LONDON, W.C.1.

Barbara Drake

Labour Research Department

34, ECCLESTON SQUARE, LONDON, S.W. 1

Chairman : W H HUTCHINSON   *Vice-Chairman*   C. M LLOYD

Treasurer   A L BACHARACH

Hon Secretary · G D. H. COLE.   *Secretary*   R. PAGE ARNOT

THE LABOUR RESEARCH DEPARTMENT is an independent organization, supported by the three Trades Union Congresses of England, Scotland and Ireland, by the Labour Party, the *Daily Herald*, and the Co-operative Union, and by a number of Trade Unions, Trades Councils, Co-operative Societies, and other Labour organizations. It exists in order to conduct research and inquiries into all social and industrial questions affecting Labour from a Labour standpoint, to publish books, pamphlets and periodicals on these subjects, and to provide information for answers to inquiries. For this purpose the Department has accumulated, and is still collecting, a unique collection of Trade Union and Labour documents of all kinds, a Press-cutting system covering the whole Labour field (including Labour abroad), and a library of Government documents   Committees of Inquiry have been set up to deal with Trades Councils and Local Labour Parties, the organization of capital and its effects on prices, profits, and the position of Labour, and many other subjects.   The results of the work of all these committees will be available for the use of affiliated societies. A special section deals with Local Government, another with International matters, and there is a Legal Advisory Committee which gives advice on legal matters   Monthly, the information collected by the Department is summarized as far as possible and published in the *Monthly Circular*, a copy of which is sent free to every affiliated society   The *Circular* contains sections dealing with Trade Union news, Co-operative News, the policy and actions of the Government, profits and other capitalist activities, legal cases affecting Labour, and an International Supplement   Terms of affiliation can be had on application to the Secretary

Some recent publications of the Labour Research Department .

FACTS FROM THE COAL COMMISSION, by R Page Arnot   6d each.

FURTHER FACTS FROM THE COAL COMMISSION, by R. Page Arnot.   6d. each.

THE TWO INTERNATIONALS, by R. Palme Dutt   Paper, 1s 6d. , cloth, 2s. 6d

EGYPT, by E M. Forster   6d

A HISTORY OF TRADES COUNCILS (1860-1875), by Cicely Richards, with an Introduction by G. D H Cole   1s.

TRADE UNIONISM IN RUSSIA   1s 6d.

THE BRITISH LABOUR MOVEMENT   a historical introduction.   By G. D. H. Cole.   1s.

PREFACE

THE following Report on Women in Trade Unions is the result of an Enquiry made by a Joint-Committee of the Labour Research Department and the Fabian Women's Group. The Report was unanimously adopted by the Committee, but the opinions expressed in it do not necessarily represent the views of the members, either individually or collectively, and only those of the writer. The thanks of the Committee are especially due to Miss Lilian Dawson, who was responsible for the main burden of secretarial work involved by the Enquiry, and for the preparation of the clerks' section of the Report. Also to Miss Kaye and Miss Young, who undertook the preparation of the wood-working and pottery sections They are further due to Mr. and Mrs. Sidney Webb, Mr. and Mrs. G. D. H. Cole, Miss B L. Hutchins, Mrs. Barton, Miss Madeleine Symons and Miss Wilkinson for valuable criticism and corrections, and to Miss Mary McLaren for the revision of the draft. The Committee has also to express its great indebtedness to the many trade union officials, without whose generous assistance the Enquiry would have been impossible to carry out. The early reports and journals of the Women's Trade Union League and of some of the older trade unions form the main sources of information for the historical chapters; whilst the facts relating to to-day have been taken from the latest trade union documents or given by officials and members in written or verbal evidence.

BARBARA DRAKE,
Chairman of the Joint-Committee

CONTENTS

PART I

THE WOMEN'S TRADE UNION MOVEMENT

CHAP   PAGE
I. THE EARLY APPEARANCE OF WOMEN IN TRADE UNIONS (18TH
    CENTURY—1874) - - - 3
II. THE WOMEN'S TRADE UNION LEAGUE AND THE FORMING OF
    WOMEN'S SOCIETIES (1874—1886) - 10
III. THE OPENING OF THE MEN'S TRADE UNIONS TO WOMEN
    (1886—1906) - - 26
IV. THE NATIONAL FEDERATION OF WOMEN WORKERS AND THE
    MODERN TRADE UNION MOVEMENT (1906—1914) - 44
V. THE CRISIS OF THE GREAT WAR (1914—1918) - - 68

PART II

SURVEY OF WOMEN'S ORGANIZATIONS

I. WOMEN'S UNIONS IN GENERAL - III
II. MINERS' UNIONS - 114
III. METAL UNIONS - - 115
IV. TEXTILE UNIONS - - 118
V. CLOTHING UNIONS - 141
VI. TRANSPORT UNIONS - - 147
VII. PRINTING AND KINDRED UNIONS - 150
VIII. WOOD WORKING AND FURNISHING UNIONS - 157
IX. CHEMICAL AND POTTERY TRADES - 159
X. FOOD AND TOBACCO TRADES - - 162
XI. DISTRIBUTIVE UNIONS - 164
XII. CLERICAL UNIONS - - - 171
XIII. VARIOUS UNIONS - - - 180
XIV. GENERAL LABOUR UNIONS - - - 181

PART III

PROBLEMS OF WOMEN IN TRADE UNIONS

I. WOMAN'S PLACE IN INDUSTRY - 189
II. OBSTACLES TO ORGANIZATION - - 198
III. TYPES OF WOMEN'S ORGANIZATIONS - 203
IV. THE WOMEN'S SECTION WITHIN THE JOINT-ORGANIZATION - 210
V. TRADE UNION RESTRICTIONS ON FEMALE LABOUR - 220
VI. "EQUAL PAY FOR EQUAL WORK" - 227

TABLES

I. FEMALE MEMBERSHIP OF ALL TRADE UNIONS (1876—1918)
II. ANALYSIS OF PRINCIPAL TRADE UNIONS - - between pp
III. STATE OF EMPLOYMENT IN THE UNITED KINGDOM (1914-19) 237-239

GENERAL INDEX - 239
INDEX OF TRADE UNIONS - - - - 241

PART I
⸙ THE WOMEN'S TRADE UNION MOVEMENT

CHAPTER I.

THE EARLY APPEARANCE OF WOMEN IN TRADE UNIONS.

18th Century—1874.

COMBINATION was not unknown amongst the "female poor" even as early as the 18th century and the beginning of the 19th. At Leicester in 1788, an informal union of hand-spinners, known as the "sisterhood," stirred up their men-folk to riot against the use of machinery. "The Humble Petition of the Poor Spinners," their protest ran, "which on a very moderate calculation consists of eighteen thousand five hundred, employed in the town and country aforesaid, showeth that the business of spinning, in all its branches, hath ever been time out of mind the peculiar employment of women; in so much that every single woman is called in law a *spinster*. . . . It is therefore with great concern your petitioners see that this ancient employment is likely to be taken from them—an employment so consistent with civil liberty, so full of domestic comfort and so favourable to a religious life. This we apprehend will be the consequence of so many spinning mills, now erecting after the model of the cotton mills. The work of the poor will be done by these engines and they will be left without employment."* At Loughborough, in 1811, a parson magistrate was much alarmed by the conduct of some women lace workers, who showed "a spirit of combination to dictate to their employers and to raise the price of their wages." These daring women not only held meetings but sent emissaries to organize and collect funds in the neighbouring towns, leading the parson to issue a warning that all such proceedings were a breach of the law.†

Combination was, however, casual. The aristocratic and exclusive craft unions of the 18th century and the beginning of

* Leicester, 1788   British Museum Tracts   (Appendix to *Women in Modern Industry*   B L Hutchins)
† *The Town Labourer*. J L. and B Hammond.   Page 262

3

the 19th were not open to women. The modest wife or daughter, working as the unpaid assistant of her husband or father, was hardly qualified to claim membership of his union, but the men's trade unions were not altogether unconcerned by the problem of female labour. In 1811, the Company of Master Tailors complained "that the journeymen's rules precluded the wife and children from earning one shilling in the way in which the husband and father can best instruct them." In a later address, the Journeymen Tailors' Society put forward its defence " Have not women been unfairly driven from their proper sphere in the social scale, unfeelingly torn from the maternal duties of a parent and unjustly encouraged to compete with men in ruining the money-value of labour? The *Times* lies when it says that the Tailors of the Metropolis have struck against these poor creatures, with whose sufferings and privations the Committee deeply sympathize, and the terms under which they obtain employment are too gross for the public ear. The crafty time-serving slave would fain turn our mothers and sisters against us to assist his masters the aristocracy in their ignorant opposition to our class, ungratefully forgetting how much they owe to the tailor for their personal dignity."*

The struggling unions of factory operatives, which sprang up with the growth of the "great industry," had a less exclusive policy. The Manchester Spinners' and the Manchester Small Ware Weavers' Societies are known to have had women members in the 18th century. During the spinners' strike of 1818, men and women drew equal strike pay, but, owing it would seem to their failure to observe trade union conditions, the women were afterwards excluded At least one employer, in giving evidence before the Committee on Combinations of Workmen in 1838, boasted of using females as strike breakers Women were condemned by men as blacklegs. At the great meeting of 1829, inaugurating the " Grand General Union of the United Kingdom," the cotton spinners laid down, "that the union shall include only *male* spinners and piecers," and urged the women and girls to form separate unions.† The Glasgow Spinners' Association advised the women, however, in the intricate business of reckoning up the piece-rate and in trade disputes. Members started a campaign in the early thirties, in order to secure equal rates of pay for men and women; but employers protested that women turned out an inferior quality and quantity of work, and persistently refused to pay men's rate of wages The agitation failed. A representative of the Association, in his evidence before the 1838 Committee on the Combinations of Workmen, stated that

* *The Tailoring Trade.* F W Galton. Pages 103 and 191
† *History of Trade Unionism.* B. and S. Webb Page 105

the object of his union was not that the employment of women should cease, although the members were " not fond of seeing women at such severe employment," but the protection of women against being " paid at an under rate of wages if possible.''*

The cotton weavers' unions, on the other hand, included women from the start.   The reluctance of the hand-loom weaver to enter the power-loom factory left the door open to his wife and children,† whom his own failure to earn a living had forced into wage-earning.   Women had an equal, if not a prior, claim to the machines.   Both sexes received the same rate of wages and neither saw any reason to exclude the other from the union.   The power-loom weaver earned, however, the barest living.   The standard was, perhaps, set by the women, or else by the hand-loom weaver, whose wages had been forced down to an indefinitely low level by the pitiless competition of machinery.   At Stockport in 1817, the average earnings of power-loom weavers were estimated at 8s. for a week of 82 hours.   Until the repeal of the Combination Act in 1824, indeed, the workers were almost completely at the mercy of their employers.   The same year, eleven men and twelve women weavers, from whose meagre wages the employer had deducted a charge of 6d. to 9d. a week for artificial light, came out on strike.   " They were taken before a magistrate, who sent them into a yard to deliberate whether they would go to work or prison; they refused to return at the reduced price and were given a month's imprisonment, the women at Middlewich and the men at Chester."‡

No conspicuous part was, however, played by women in trade unions until the great conflagration of 1833-4.   The Grand National Consolidated Trades Union of Great Britain and Ireland, which united half-a-million workers, and struck terror into the hearts of rulers from one end of the kingdom to the other, included " female lodges," together with lodges of shop assistants, chimney-sweeps, shearmen and ploughmen   The Grand Lodge of the Women of Great Britain and Ireland vied in activity with the Grand Lodge of Operative Bonnet Makers.   The " Ancient Virgins " distinguished themselves in the Oldham riots, and joined with the men in their clamour for a ten-hour day.   The " Female Gardeners " gained an equal notoriety.   Nor were women without a programme of their own.   The Lodge of Female Tailors asked indignantly " whether the Tailors' Order was really going to prohibit women from making waistcoats,"

---

* *Women in Modern Industry*   B. L. Hutchins.   Page 94.

† The hand-loom weavers refused to admit women to their unions, and issued a memorandum in 1823, praying " for a tax to be laid on power-looms, which are now transferring labour from men to children and girls and from cottages to factories."

‡ *The Town Labourer*.   By J L and B. Hammond.   Page 130.

while the Grand Lodge of Operative Bonnet Makers complained
" that the heroes returning from the fighting of 1815 had invaded
the straw bonnet trade and lowered the price of female labour."

After the collapse of the Grand National Consolidated Trades
Council in 1834, women relapsed into silence.   Little was heard
of them except an occasional protest by men trade unionists
against " unfair female competition," as the introduction of a
new machine or subdivision of labour brought one trade after
another within reach of a less qualified or robust class of worker.
In 1845, the potters' unions were to be found expostulating with
the women employed for the first time on the new " flat-press "
machines. " To maidens, mothers, and wives," their appeal stated,
" we say machinery is your deadliest enemy.   Of all the sufferers
by mechanical improvements you will be the worst.   It is a
systemized process of slow murder for you.   It will destroy your
natural claims to home and domestic duties, and will immure
you and your toiling little ones in over-heated and dirty shops,
there to weep and toil and pine and die." The " potters' scourge "
had yet to levy its full toll of suffering on women and children,
and the potter had every cause to dread the dire effects of their
employment   As the employer of his wife or daughter it is,
however, probable that he also resented her removal from the
home to the factory, her exploitation by his own oppressor, and
her competition with himself, driving him from employment by
her willingness to accept about one-half his rate of wages.

More rare was the example of the London Union of Journeymen
Bookbinders, whose members championed the women's cause
along with their own during the famous dispute in the thirties
and forties between the Union and the Bible Societies.   Women
were not members of the Union, although employed as " folders
and sewers " since the 18th century *   The dispute began in
1825 when the Union charged the Society for Promoting Christian
Knowledge with unfair reductions of wages.   The matter was
settled at the time, but reopened in 1834, when a similar charge
was brought against the British and Foreign Bible Society.
" Your memorialists beg leave to state that there are a number
of females (about 200) employed in binding the books of your
Society, the whole of whose wages have been reduced in consequence of the late alteration in the prices of these books.   Their
wages were before very low   Your memorialists respectfully
submit that the making it more difficult and in some cases
impossible for females to earn an honest subsistence by their
labour, is in the same proportion to give potency to the seducers
of female virtue."   According to a statement by the Bible Society,
" competent and industrious women earned 8/- to 10/- a week and

* *Women in the Printing Trades* J. R Macdonald.   Pages 33-35

upwards," while men "in the same description" earned 6d. an hour or 30/- a week. Mr. Dunning, secretary of the union, however, disputed the facts, estimating the average earnings of twenty-four women at not more than 5/11 a week. An agreement was reached in 1843, and the five firms patronized by the Bible Society promised to pay the women a time-rate of 7/6 to 15/- a week, and not to exceed a ten-hour day, but the Bible Society apparently was unable or unwilling to enforce these terms, and the dispute was revived in 1849 One employer, Miss Watkins, having secured a monopoly of binding, had introduced piece-work contrary to the practice of the trade, and paid excessively low rates. Mr. Dunning estimated the average wages of ninety-seven female "folders" and "sewers" at 6/2½ a week of sixty-four hours. The women were, moreover, subject to unaccustomed fines, while "learners" were discharged so soon as they claimed an adult wage. "Females often have not the power to plead their own cause in such matters, and being helpless in many respects where their wages are concerned, they are trodden down until a state of things such as described in the ' Song of the Shirt ' appals the mind with the enormity of their injuries, their suffering and their moral conditions" Miss Watkins, denying the correctness of Mr. Dunning's estimate, placed the earnings of female "folders" and "sewers" at 10/- a week of sixty hours, and ordered the women to sign a statement to the effect "that they were perfectly satisfied." Thereupon, the indignant men advised the women to strike, and drew up on their behalf the following demands :

(1) That prices should be raised to the standard paid by the S.P.C K.*
(2) That fines should be abolished.
(3) That the women should have access to cold water as well as hot for tea.
(4) That after the learners then employed had completed their apprenticeship, not more than twenty learners should be employed at one time

The women took the men's advice and left work, and the Union organized a strike fund, but Miss Watkins was as obdurate as before, and the workers were too weak to enforce their demands. The strike failed, and the women were obliged either to seek work elsewhere, or else to return to the old conditions. Mr. Dunning claimed no other success for the movement than that " it arrested a downward tendency in prices and wages." Incidentally, the

* The prices paid by the Society for Promoting Christian Knowledge worked out at 7s. 6d to 8s. 4d. a week of sixty hours. Miss Watkins' refusal to adopt even this modest standard hardly coincided with her statement that the women already earned 10s a week.

dispute cost the Union £146, in addition to £650 collected by the
" strike committee." " Finishers," alone amongst men bookbinders, were opposed to this generous policy towards unorganized
women, and their section to the number of 150 members was in
consequence expelled from the union. Of the women's leader,
the youthful Mary Zugg, nothing is known beyond the tribute
paid to her by Mr. Dunning in the *Bookbinders' Trade Circular*
after her death from consumption in November 1861. " Nothing
could exceed the temper, moderation and firmness she displayed.
Possessing great energy, strong sense, of great acuteness of per-
ception, detecting at a glance pretence from reality, she was not
what was termed a strong-minded woman, commanding great
respect but little affection, for her goodness of heart and great
regard for the feelings and welfare of others endeared her to all."
The chivalrous and disinterested action of the London Union of
Journeymen Bookbinders brightens one at least of the dark pages
which record the early history of working-women.

The same year—1849—marked the appearance of an Edinburgh
Society of Women in the Printing Trades, but there was not the
same good feeling between the sexes. More than one printing-
house had been overrun by women compositors since the middle
of the century,* and the Typographical Societies had no intention
of supporting a women's movement The efforts of Miss Emily
Faithfull in the 'sixties to open the trade to women, and to establish " women's printing societies " at London and Edinburgh,
met with a like resistance. " The compositor trades should be
in the hands of women only,"† wrote Miss Emily Faithfull in her
enthusiasm, but the men replied in scorn, " Women compositors
will die off like birds in winter." The comparatively low rates
of wages paid by the women's printing societies‡ did not allay
the suspicions of men trade unionists, who saw the usual threat
to their standard of living from " unfair female competition."

During the middle part of the 19th century, whilst the great
craft unions were consolidating their position and building up
substantial reserve funds, it was only the Lancashire cotton unions
which made a serious effort to organize women.§ The weavers'

* As early as 1792, Thomas Beddoes, " struck with the opening which the
printing trades seemed to offer to women," gave his *Alexander's Expedition*
to be set up by a woman of his village. " I know not," he wrote, " if
women be commonly employed in printing, but their nimble and delicate
fingers seem extremely well adapted to the office of compositors, and it will be
readily granted that employment of females is amongst the greatest *desiderata*
of Society " But the case was exceptional (*Women in the Printing Trades*
J. R. Macdonald Pages 24-25) † *Englishman's Journal*, 1860.
‡ The London Women's Printing Society, established about 1874, still continues in existence, employing about a score of women compositors.
§ The Society of Cordwainers amended its rules in 1872 in order to admit
female members; but the experiment failed, and no women joined the union.

associations, which grew into sound and stable organizations during the 'fifties and 'sixties, had 15,000* women members in 1876, women forming nearly one-half of the membership. The less advanced associations of card and blowing-room operatives began a similar campaign to organize women in the early seventies. Women, however, took apparently no active part in the trade union agitation in support of the Short Hours Bill of 1872, which proposed to extend existing legal restrictions on female labour. The spinners' associations, to whose initiative the movement was due, did not even include women members, and the agitation would only seem to have reflected the desire of the adult male spinner for a shorter day. Men had learned the dependence of their own hours of work on those of women and children employed in the same mills, and fought a battle for themselves from " behind the women's petticoats." The agitation was viewed by the " feminists " of the day as an unwarranted attack by working-men on the personal liberties of working-women; and the Women's Suffrage Society joined hands with Mr. Fawcett in obtaining the defeat of the Bill.

The failure to combine was, however, not confined to women. Semi-skilled and unskilled men, who belonged to the same class as women, and were equally ineligible for the craft unions of the early period of organization, similarly failed to form societies of their own. Trade unionism was still mainly reserved to apprenticed tradesmen, amongst whom women were not generally included; but a fresh wave of labour unrest swept over the country in 1872, and the workers once more were inspired by a sense of labour solidarity. The skilled tradesman stretched out his hand to the unskilled labourer and helped him to form a union. In the three years between 1872 and 1875, the number of organized workers nearly doubled. New unions sprang up like mushrooms. A Society of Agricultural Labourers enrolled 100,000 members in a few months, although only to lose them within as brief a period. The same excitement found its echo amongst women, and paved the way for the advent of the Women's Trade Union League.

* Estimate by Mr. Birtwistle, Secretary of the Accrington Weavers' Association.

CHAPTER II

THE WOMEN'S TRADE UNION LEAGUE AND THE FORMING OF WOMEN'S SOCIETIES.*

1874—1886.

—Mrs. Emma Paterson, founder of the Women's Trade Union League, was born in St George's Parish, Westminster, in 1848. She was the daughter of Thomas Smith, a schoolmaster, and married a cabinet-maker, by name Thomas Paterson Miss Smith served a short apprenticeship as a bookbinder; she afterwards taught as a governess, but soon devoted her whole attention to social work. At the early age of 18, she was appointed assistant-secretary of the Working Men's Club and Institute, of which Thomas Paterson was honorary secretary, and also acted as secretary of the Women's Suffrage Association, assisting Miss Emily Faithfull in her campaign for promoting " women's printing societies " She married in the year 1873 Mr. Paterson was possessed of small private means, and he and his wife now visited America, where Mrs. Paterson was much impressed by " some successful unions in New York consisting of and managed by working-women, of which the two largest were the Parasol and Umbrella Makers' Union and the Women's Typographical Society." Her faith in the ability of working-women to help themselves and play an active part in trade unions was confirmed. On returning to England in 1874, she at once started on her mission, and published a series of articles in the *Labour News* in which she exposed the " sweated " conditions of female labour and urged women to form trade unions " Not only are women frequently paid half or less than half for doing work as well and as quickly as men," but " skilled women whose labour requires delicacy of touch, the result of long training as well as thoughtfulness, receive from 11/- to 16/- or 17/- a week, whilst the roughest unskilled labour of a man is worth at least 18/- " The earnings of the Leicester " seamers " and " stitchers," or of the Black Country metal workers, were said to be as low as 3/- and 4/- a week " So long as women are unprotected by any kind of combination, and are consequently wholly at the mercy of employers for the rate of their wages and the length of their

* The facts given in this and the following chapter are largely taken from old numbers of *The Women's Trade Union Journal*, and Annual Reports of the Women's Trade Union League

working hours, working-men not unnaturally look with suspicion on their employment in trades, in some branches of which men are engaged. The fear that women will lower wages has led them to pass rules in many of their trade societies positively forbidding their members to work with women. They have also carried on, and are still continuing, an agitation to limit the hours of women in factories and workshops. Women more than ever need the protection afforded by combination; for at the present the women affected by the proposed restrictions have no means of making known their collective opinions. . . Working-men might invite women to join their trade unions, or assist them to form similar societies There is no provision for the admission of women as the members of the men's societies (with some few exceptions in the North of England) Nor would women be able to avail themselves of such provision, as they could not pay the same subscription.'' Moreover, the '' mixed '' cotton unions were held by Mrs. Paterson to be unsatisfactory, for '' the women paid only half-contributions and were excluded from management.''*

Mrs. Paterson followed up these articles in July, 1874, by calling together in London a conference of '' sympathetic ladies and gentlemen,'' the outcome of which was the formation of the '' Women's Protective and Provident League,'' afterwards taking the name of the '' Women's Trade Union League.'' Its members included the Hon. Auberon Herbert, Canon Kingsley, Mr. Arnold Toynbee, Mr Henry Crompton, Rev. Stewart Headlam, Mr. and Mrs. Hodgson Pratt, Miss Harriet Martineau, Miss Anna Swanwick, Mr. F. W. Verney, and other well-known philanthropists, together with two influential trade unionists, Mr King, secretary of the London Society of Journeymen Bookbinders, and Mr. George Shipton, secretary of the London Trades Council Mrs. Paterson was appointed honorary secretary

The main object of the League was to promote trade unionism amongst working-women, but its policy was by no means hostile to employers Members were '' anxious to disclaim any views of antagonism towards employers of female labour as such,'' and aimed less at obtaining advances than at resisting reductions of wages. The '' strike '' was deprecated as '' rash and mistaken action.'' The prevention of strikes and the promotion of arbitration were noted amongst the chief advantages of combination. The League was prepared to undertake the preliminary expenses of organization, '' to provide office accommodation at a moderate charge,'' and '' to induce persons having leisure to act as pro-

---

* It should be explained that the rules of the cotton weavers' unions imposed no sex disabilities ; the women were only excluded from management as low-scale or 1d contributors

visional secretaries." In other respects the women's unions were to be independent and self-supporting. The original proposal was to form a " National Union of Working Women," which would act "as a convenient centre," and also "afford excellent facilities for the formation of separate unions, while those women who were tolerably well paid would assist those who were very badly paid" A society was established on these lines at Bristol, and survived some twenty years with a membership of about 100 women, but the original plan was modified in London, and the League decided to form a separate union for each trade.

Mrs. Paterson turned her attention first of all to her fellow-tradeswomen, and in September, 1874, the League formed a Society of Women Employed in Bookbinding, with the assistance of Mr. King, secretary of the London Society of Journeymen Bookbinders. Mrs Paterson was appointed provisional honorary secretary. Nor was this first experiment of the League among the least successful. Some 300 women joined the union at once, proving themselves to be reliable " paying members." The Society also was fortunate in the person of its secretary, Miss Whyte, a working book-folder, who succeeded Mrs. Paterson in April, 1875, and held office until a few months before her death in 1913, when the Society was dissolved. The membership, on the other hand, remained almost stationary, and the policy was unprogressive, so that men trade unionists came afterwards to regard the women's union as a mere "friendly" society and not a genuine trade union A "Society of Dressmakers, Milliners and Mantlemakers," followed in February 1875. Some dressmakers, hearing of the new movement, approached the League with a request for assistance. An enthusiastic meeting was held in the Co-operative Institute, and attended by 400 working-women. The Society was launched with every appearance of success; but the dressmakers, unlike the bookbinders, did not prove to be stable members, leaving the union almost as quickly as they had joined it. The Society became rapidly insolvent, and presently succumbed. A third venture was the "Society of Women Employed in Binding, Sewing, and Trimming Men's Hats," which was formed in the same February, but was equally unfortunate The difficulties were said to be exceptional, "owing to the antagonism shown by the employers" A "Society of Upholstresses," established in the following April, had more success Mrs Paterson reported that "the encouragement given by the ' Upholsterers' Society ' to the efforts of the women has been most gratifying." The membership rose to several hundred, and the women elected their committee and officers entirely from amongst themselves. The Society remained in existence until 1894. A fifth venture—the "Society of Shirt and Collar

Makers "—completed the record of the first year's work in London. A sympathetic employer took part in the preliminary proceedings, and "cordially welcomed the women's movement." Nevertheless, the Society languished and survived only a few years. These five societies were all formed on one plan. A committee of the League drew up a model constitution, which included the following objects :

1. To protect the trade interests of the members by endeavouring where necessary to prevent the undue depression of wages and to equalize the hours of work.

2. To provide a fund from which members may obtain an allowance weekly, in sickness or while out of employment

3. To arrange for the registration of employment notices so that trouble in searching for work may be avoided, and to collect useful information.

4. To promote arbitration in cases of dispute between employer and employed.

All women over the age of sixteen employed in the trade were eligible for membership; but after the first six months of working an applicant required a voucher from two members, testifying to her competency as a work-woman. The contribution was 2d. or 3d. a week, according to the trade, with an entrance fee of 1/- or 2/-; whilst benefits, which included sickness and out-of-work, were payable after one year's membership, and amounted to 5/- a week for not longer than eight weeks in any one year. No mention was made of " strike " or " lock-out " pay. The secretaries, or provisional secretaries, of the London societies were *ex-officio* members of the executive committee of the League.

In the provinces, the year's achievement was even more encouraging Some Dewsbury woollen weavers, whose wages had been reduced by 10 per cent. at the instigation of the newly-formed Masters' Association, had come out on strike. The women were unorganized, but a " friend " of the League advanced £10 to form a women's union, and some local " sympathizers " raised a further fund of £150 in aid of the strikers. The movement took hold at once, and nearly a thousand women joined the union. The contribution was 1d. per week. In each mill members elected a committee, and these committees in turn elected a central council. Mrs. Ellis, a working weaver, was appointed secretary, and soon developed brilliant qualities as leader. The strike lasted eight weeks; and, at the end of this time, the strikers returned to work in triumph, whilst the Masters' Association broke up in disorder The Dewsbury and District Heavy Woollen Weavers formed later two branches at Batley and Bingley. The women would, indeed, seem to have achieved a more successful local organization than the men, some of whom afterwards were

B

admitted to the women's union, but "took no part in the management." After the collapse of the Masters' Association, there was less enthusiasm; and, in 1882, some 700 women decided to join the men's Huddersfield and District Power Loom Weavers' Association, afterwards the General Union of Textile Workers. Mrs. Ellis kept her post for a time as secretary of the Dewsbury Branch, but a too fiery speech at a public meeting led to her discharge by her employer. Compelled to leave her trade, she carried her proud spirit into domestic service at Brighton. In grateful acknowledgment of her services to the Union, she was presented by members with a " purse of gold," and from time to time she returned to speak at a meeting; but the women's self-confidence would seem to have failed them with the loss of their leader, and the tendency was to leave the conduct of affairs more and more in the hands of men.

The Leicester " Society of Seamers and Stitchers " promised equally well. " Some town councillors and other gentlemen of the neighbourhood," seeing with concern the depressed conditions of female labour in the Leicester hosiery trade, appealed to the League for assistance. A meeting was held in the Town Hall, when the women formed a union. They went on a deputation to the employers, and at once secured an advance of 25 per cent. on wages. Members threw themselves with extraordinary ardour into the movement, conducting the whole of the business themselves. Many women earned less than 5/- a week; and enthusiastic members of the committee, although middle-aged or elderly married women, would walk ten or twenty miles in order to collect contributions, or to interview employers. Mrs. Mason, a working " seamer," was appointed secretary, and rivalled Mrs. Ellis in devotion. The contribution was 1d. per week, and the membership rose in a year to nearly 3,000 women. The "menders" and " worsted spinners " followed the example, and formed two small societies, which were able not only to resist reductions of wages, but to secure advances amounting to from 2/- to 5/- a week. The women were jealous of their independence. At a meeting of the " Seamers' and Stitchers' Society " in 1877, when some inquisitive members of the men's society came to listen to the proceedings, they were turned away from the door, and none permitted to enter except the president of the Leicester Trades Council. Mrs. Mason represented her union at the Trades Union Congress of 1877, and was the first woman to serve on a local trades council; but the spirit wore out the flesh. In the year 1880, she died. The membership at once fell to about one-third, and the unions became insolvent. The secretary of the men's society reported to the League that " the women have become indifferent to their union." He gave in excuse the long distances to be covered by home-workers in order to pay a contribution or attend a meeting. Two years later the " Society of Seamers and Stitchers " took refuge in the men's trade union, out of which amalgamation grew the present Leicester Amalgamated Hosiery Union. Women formed the majority of the members, numbering over 1,000 out of 1,800 in 1886, but the old animation was gone. " It is impossible to get a woman to serve on the executive committee," complained the secretary to the League, " so accustomed are they to have everything done for them." At an important members' meeting in 1886, in order to protest against a proposed relaxation of the Factory and Workshops Act in regard to female labour—essentially a woman's question—the few women present were said to have sat in a gallery apart, and to have kept silent throughout the proceedings.

The women's societies now sent their delegates to the Trades Union Congress. For three years in succession the president had refused a request by " some middle-class ladies " for permission to attend the Congress and represent the interests of working women. According to the rules of the Congress, no person was eligible as a delegate unless he or she represented a *bonâ fide* trade union or trades council, and the refusal was not unreasonable. During the Liverpool Congress of 1875, Mrs. Paterson wrote again calling the attention of the delegates to the increasing employment of women in various trades, and the urgency of combination, if only to ensure " a fair day's work for a fair day's pay." Some delegates were sceptical as to the ability of workingwomen to combine, or suspicious of " middle-class championship," but the letter received on the whole a " sympathetic hearing." The National Union of Working Women, which had been formed by the League at Bristol, was immediately affiliated as a *bonâ fide* trade union, Mr. Whetstone (Engineers) only demurring at the anomaly of a " gentleman delegate " from a " ladies' union." The ice was broken, and Mrs. Paterson and Miss Simcox, representing the three London Societies of Bookbinders, Upholstresses, and Shirt and Collar Makers, took their places as of right at the Glasgow Congress of 1876. The women received a most courteous reception, a portion of the fifth day being allotted to the discussion of women's questions. Miss Simcox read a paper on the " Organization of Women's Labour," upon which Mr. Shipton (London Trades Council) proposed, and Mr. Hayes (Darlington Trades Council) seconded, a formal resolution that " the members regard with much satisfaction the development of the self-relying trade union movement among women employed in the various industries, and pledge themselves to assist in promoting it in their various localities." The resolution was carried unanimously.

The Leicester Congress of 1877 witnessed the first breach in the harmony between the sexes, when the three women delegates opposed a resolution of the cotton unions in favour of extending restrictions on female labour under the new Factory and Workshops Bill. Mrs. Paterson, who led the opposition, gave the women's point of view " It was becoming more and more exceptional legislation for women, whereas the first Factory Acts applied to men and women alike. They might perhaps now leave children to the care of school boards, and dispense with the legal regulations of working hours altogether, but even if continued for children, women did protest against legislation for them. She was somewhat startled the preceding day to hear three delegates declare that when they got this Bill passed they would next try to get a Bill to remove women from certain branches of work (agriculture and chain-making) altogether. When Mr. and Mrs Fawcett some time ago had said that trade union men wished to turn women out of work, great indignation had been expressed, and a strict denial given to the charge. She (Mrs. Paterson) had been glad to accept the denial. She asked them to help women by combination to increase their wages, and not to attempt to drive them from work altogether." Mrs. Mason, representing 3,000 " seamers " and " stitchers," objected to the resolution on similar grounds. " She was placed in a position of being compelled to earn a few shillings because her husband was not able to support the whole of the family. . . . As a working-woman she would like to do her best the same as every woman should do to support the house. . . . Sometimes there were orders in hand which required to be completed, but if there came an advance in wages there would not be any necessity for this extra labour. She repeated that it would be as reasonable to pass a law to enable inspectors to visit their houses, and see that their husbands were out of bed, instead of laying there until what they called luncheon time, as to have these laws for inspecting the work of women " Mr. Broadhurst (secretary of the Parliamentary Committee) was, however, not convinced. " They knew it was very natural for ladies to be impatient of restraint at any time, and therefore they might imagine the uneasiness which would be created when the law of the factory prescribed rules and regulations. They (the men) had the future of their country and children to consider, and it was their duty as men and husbands to use their utmost efforts to bring about a condition of things, where their wives should be in their proper sphere at home, instead of being dragged into competition for livelihood against the great and strong men of the world." The resolution was carried by an overwhelming majority of men delegates.

In the same year of 1877, the League at Leicester began its

custom of inviting the delegates to a "women's conference" or "social," during the annual Congress week, a function which soon attained to a high degree of popularity under the gracious presidency of Lady Dilke, and afterwards of her niece, Miss Gertrude Tuckwell. The first conference was attended by no fewer than eighty delegates, and there followed a lively discussion. Mrs. Paterson opened the debate. "The meeting," she said, "had not been called in consequence of the slightest disposition on the part of the Congress to refuse an opportunity for a discussion on women's questions, but because the women felt it would not be fair to overcrowd the Congress programme. She was afraid that her remarks during the Congress discussion on the Factory and Workshops Act had been somewhat misunderstood. Nothing was further from her desire than that women should work for an indefinite number of hours in factories and workshops. The difference of opinion was only as to the best mode of securing the much-needed shortening of the working hours—combination or legislation. If the work were better paid, women would be glad enough to work for shorter hours. What she dreaded was too much reliance being placed on legislation. Women were accused of 'impatience.' She only wished that they would show themselves a little more impatient than they do of restraint upon their wages, and not meekly go on trying upon how small a pittance they could live, or rather just exist. She thought it was the duty of men, especially of working-men, who must know so well the hardships and privations the women of their class had to endure owing to bad payment, to arouse them out of the state of torpor which long years of grinding down had produced. It was to the interest of men, too, that women should be better paid; but selfish considerations apart, mere ordinary human sympathy must make men wish for a change to be brought about. She would conclude by urging every gentleman present to give his best consideration to the subject, and to the question of how he could forward the good work in his own neighbourhood." The Rev. Page Hopps, another member of the League, deprecated the arbitrary prohibition of female labour by a men's trade union. "The conduct of the doctors which, he was sorry to say, had caused physical riots in the streets, he considered most reprehensible"

Mr. Birtwistle (Accrington Cotton Weavers) then described the successful experience of the Lancashire cotton associations. "In his union, the women (9,000) rather outnumbered the men, but the business was principally conducted by men. They always found the women willing to assist, and very ready and regular in their payments" Mr. Buckley (Oldham Cotton Weavers), on the other hand, spoke of the special difficulties in organizing women. "Parents wanted to take all their daughters' earnings, and grudged even the small amount of their contribution to the union. As many of the fathers were engineers, he hoped that Mr. John Burnett (Engineers), whom he was glad to see present, would give them a hint in this matter." Mr. Ackrill (London Shoemakers) said that "his society had made special laws in order to admit women into their unions, but the women had not availed themselves of the facilities thrown into their way because of their unfortunate tendency to lean for advice upon males." Mr. Withers (Cigar Makers) spoke to the same effect. "It was a difficult matter for men to set about organizing women. He and some co-workers attempted it in the cigar trade in 1872, but there was a fear on the part of the women that the men wanted to turn them out of work. They would probably have succeeded better had they been able to find women who would speak in favour of the proposal. . . . In many cases, female labour was introduced into workshops under the cloak of philanthropy, but really to lessen the cost of production. Men very naturally objected to such competition as this, but if women would demand fair payment the objection would be removed." Mr. Richardson agreed. "What the men objected to was to allow the women to manufacture the same articles as the men at half the cost. They were willing to allow women to enter any trade, and produce any article, as long as they did not work for a lower wage than the men." Only Mr. Sedgwick (Birmingham Metal Workers) was definitely opposed to organizing women. "Whenever female labour in his trade had been introduced the wages of the men had been reduced by one-half. He refused to support a movement which would make such a result more general." In trade union philosophy, "to organize" was "to recognize," and men metal workers were not prepared to recognize those presumptuous women who "turned at the lathe and filed at the vice" in Birmingham, incidentally driving their own men-folk from employment. The consensus of opinion was, however, in favour of forming women's societies, and a resolution to this effect was moved by Mr. King, secretary of the London Society of Journeymen Bookbinders, and carried without opposition.

The Factory and Workshops Bill became law before the Congress of 1878, and the women delegates turned their attention forthwith to the appointment of women factory inspectors. A resolution was before the meeting, which laid down that "practical persons (i.e. workers) shall be appointed as factory inspectors"; but these terms were too ambiguous for Mrs. Paterson, who moved to amend *practical persons* by *practical men and women*. She was taunted by the president with a change of front. The delegates jeered at the mere idea of a "female factory inspector." The ladies truly had strange ambitions!

The amendment was carried by a majority of forty-six against thirty-three votes, but the matter was not so easily settled. At twelve consecutive Trade Union Congresses, the men moved the same resolution, to which the women moved the same amendment, and carried their point each time, until the president himself expostulated at " feminine unreasonableness and obstinacy." At the Congress of 1892, however, the resolution took at last the form of the amendment. It was carried unanimously, and the first woman factory inspector was appointed in the following year. The delegates were not definitely antagonistic, but only indifferent to the women's point of view; and the president feared to prejudice an important resolution by a contentious amendment.

During the 'eighties, there were many similar disputes between the League and the men's trade unions. Thus, in 1882, Mr. Broadhurst, M.P., secretary of the Parliamentary Committee, acting on the instigation of the Black Country metal unions, had introduced a Bill into Parliament, which prohibited young girls from acting as blacksmiths under the age of fourteen. The Bill referred only to children, but the women at once suspected a trap, and charged the Bill with being the thin end of the wedge. The law, they urged, ought at least to apply to boys and girls alike. Employers made common cause with the League, and each side appealed for support to the Press. According to men trade unionists, " the women working side by side with the men were exposed to the grossest possible language and conduct," to which women replied that " the statement was a libel on the men and no reflection on their sex." A chain-maker wrote to complain that " when he himself was thoroughly exhausted, his daughter could still go on," but women remained unimpressed even by this exhibition of feminine indelicacy. The men drew attention to the shocking conditions under which the women worked, and the League undertook an investigation. " The girls were found singing hymns, and strong and healthy. The work was less injurious to the women's health than in the Lancashire weaving sheds." The investigators were, however, obliged to admit the charge of cutting men's wages. They deplored the low rates of 3/- and 4/- a week, which undermined the men's standard; but they attributed these evils mainly to the absence of women's unions, and advised men to assist women in organizing rather than to exclude them from employment. The men were not convinced, and rival meetings were held in the Black Country. Mr. Hill, secretary of the Oldswinford Nailers, tried to arrange a compromise. The men's object was only to " restrict females to certain classes of labour, but not to stop them from working." He suggested that " if women would only keep to the proper size of nails as suggested in the Report of the Government Commission, and not make above size *one*, they would not want legislation." He further advised women, who were thrown out of work in this way, to enter domestic service. The women were equally unconvinced The practice varied, moreover, with each district, and local societies differed between themselves as to which size of nail could, or could not, be safely entrusted to women. The matter was referred to the Trades Union Congress of 1882, when a report by Mr Juggins, secretary of the Nut and Bolt Makers, was adopted by the Parliamentary Committee. "We have no hesitation," the report stated, "in saying that the condition of things described is a disgrace to the nation, and that the statement of the half-nude women engaged in company, with men in the same state of undress is supported by the evidence given before the Royal Commission of 1875 " Mr. Juggins moved a resolution " to proceed with the Bill," and he implored the delegates " to stand out against the iniquitous system of female labour. He knew he would have the opposition of the females. One female had even said that ' women had a perfect right to compete with men ' " (Cries of " Shame," and a voice " I wish my wife would try it.") The resolution was carried by an overwhelming majority of the delegates, but the Bill was thrown out by Parliament Sir Charles Dilke, meanwhile, gave his support to the League, and on each side the agitation continued. At the Congress of 1887, Mr. Juggins, representing the newly-formed Midlands Trades Federation, finally threw off the mask, and moved " to introduce such amendments to the Factory and Workshops Act as shall prevent the employment of females in the making of chains, nails, rivets, bolts, etc., such work not being adapted to their constitution " Only the two women delegates voted against the resolution, but they were not prepared to accept defeat. The next year saw a compromise, and Miss Clementina Black (Women's Trades Council) moved, and Mr. Juggins seconded a resolution that, " where women do the same work as men, they shall receive equal pay." This resolution struck at the root of the trouble; and Mr. Juggins explained " that he had come to the conclusion that nothing but better pay for women could cure the evil, and they had therefore resolved to organize women as soon as possible." The resolution was carried unanimously, and Mr. Juggins immediately claimed the assistance of the League in forming a women's union at Cradley Heath—the first in a long series of campaigns which achieved no substantial results until the passing of the Trade Boards Act twenty years afterwards.

The action of the Miners' Federation in promoting the Coal Mines Regulation (Amendment) Act of 1885, with a view to removing the 4,450 women employed at the pit-heads, and again the strike of the Kidderminster Carpet Weavers, who paraded the streets, wheeling infants in perambulators, displaying placards of men cooking and turning mangles, and trying by means of ridicule to persuade the women from employment, brought forth similar protests from the League, whose action gained in each case the powerful support of employers. Women were suspicious of every form of restriction. They were even opposed to protection for working mothers At the Congress of 1883, Mrs. Ellis, representing 700 woollen weavers, many of them married women, strongly criticized a resolution "to prevent the employment of women with young children in factories and workshops." She attributed the inequality in the piece-rates paid to men and women woollen weavers partly to existing restrictions in regard to overtime and night-work; and she secured by her eloquence at least the postponement of the motion until after further investigation.

The number of women delegates rose to ten at the London Congress of 1881, and this figure remained the record until the Bristol Congress of 1915. A more active part in Congress debates has at no time been taken by women delegates than during the 'seventies and 'eighties. Nor has any speaker, advocating an unpopular cause, received a fairer hearing than Mrs. Paterson, Miss Whyte, Mrs. Ellis or Mrs. Mason.

Meanwhile, the pledge given by the Trades Union Congress of 1876, "to promote the self-relying trade union movement among women," bore fruit in action; and, during the next ten years, the League enjoyed the active co-operation of a number of important trade unions and trades councils, including the London Journeymen Bookbinders, the London Upholsterers, the Scottish Operative Tailors, the Amalgamated Society of Tailors, the United Hat Makers, the Hanley Hot Pressers and the Scottish Mill and Factory Workers. At a meeting of the Amalgamated Society of Tailors in 1877, when the time-honoured motion, that "the Society would use its strength against the increasing employment of women in the tailoring trade," came up as usual, members, "instead of complying with so unjust a request, resolved that the work of women must be recognized and the time had now arrived when it should be organized and properly remunerated." Nine societies of tailoresses were established in ten years, including societies in Soho, Pimlico, Whitechapel, Woolwich, Liverpool, Manchester, Leeds, Glasgow and Dublin. The Society of Royal Army Clothing Factory Tailoresses even grew to some size and importance. During the winter of 1878-79, grave disaffection had been caused in the factory by a reduction of 15 per cent. to 20 per cent. on piece-rates. The management defended its action on the ground of accelerated production due to certain improvements in machinery, but the women denied any increase in earnings and appealed for support to the League. A meeting was arranged in Pimlico; and 800 indignant tailoresses formed a union and marched to the House of Commons. The Government was sufficiently impressed to appoint a Departmental Committee of Enquiry, and, in spite of long delay, a large part of the women's demands was eventually granted. The Union afterwards fell to pieces, members losing their interest with the redress of their grievances; but, during the Egyptian war of 1886, the threat of a further reduction on piece-rates, following a period of prolonged overtime and speeding-up, gave a fresh impulse to organization The authorities, ignoring the cause of the women's discontent, invited a missionary to read to the workers on Sundays! The Society sprang instantly into life, and the women's demands were again substantially conceded, including the prohibition of home-work after factory hours. The Royal Army Clothing Tailoresses Society continued an intermittent existence, members falling away in times of quiet and coming together in times of trouble, until in 1907 women joined with men in forming the present society of Royal Army Clothing Department Employees

Between 1874 and 1886, the League established in England and Scotland between thirty and forty women's societies, of which eight were composed of dressmakers and milliners, and one was a general labour union at Oxford. The latter was partly composed of domestic servants and—by a miracle—continued to exist until 1913. Not many societies, however, counted more than a few hundred members or survived longer than a few years. The early promise failed of fulfilment and success was mostly shortlived. Members grew discouraged and left the union Some societies broke up on losing a popular leader, and others fell into insolvency, notwithstanding the " honourable behaviour of the women in the matter of medical benefit." About one-half succumbed within a year. The most successful, such as the Dewsbury Woollen Weavers and the Leicester Seamers and Stitchers, joined the men's trade unions. In 1886, the combined membership of women's societies was probably less than 2,500 women, of whom at least one-half belonged to the London district. During the same period, the female membership of the cotton unions, in spite of the passive part apparently played by women, steadily rose from 15,000 in 1876 to 30,000* in 1886, and women shared with men in the progressive advance of wages.

The success of the cotton unions had long been remarked by

---

* Estimate made by a cotton union official in the *Women's Union Journal.*

Mrs. Paterson. "Such unions," she declared in the early days of the League, "seem to be very desirable, but there appears to be a danger in them that the women either will not or are not invited to take a proper share of work." It was for this reason that she had advocated the forming of independent women's societies, but her point of view was afterwards modified. She wrote later that "wherever practicable, and the men desire it, we are strongly in favour of mixed societies, consisting of men and women in the same trade," but she made the reservation that "the women should not lose their separate identity."

There grew up at the same time a new understanding between the League and the men's trade unions. "The men's jealousy of the work of women," wrote Mrs. Paterson in the 'seventies, "had undoubtedly arisen from the fact that the women had allowed themselves to be used as a means of bringing down wages far below the market price" She saw a remedy in organization; but, after twelve years of experience, members of the League had grown cautious in advising men trade unionists to withdraw their restrictions on female labour, without sufficient security that women would be strong enough to observe trade union conditions and not allow themselves to be used as black-legs. Thus, three women had been introduced as "mule spinners" into the Lostock cotton mill, receiving, as usual, women's rates of wages. The local spinners' union, whose rules prohibited women from employment as "mule-spinners," there-upon had passed a resolution "to bind its members not to teach the trade any more" to women "piecers" or assistants. A correspondent of the League wrote to complain of the gross injustice done to women. For half-a-century, the Lostock women had been employed as "piecers." Owing to their delicacy of touch, women's work was even superior to men's. Women "piecers" had not only been recognized by men piecers, but actually admitted to their union. And now, forsooth, the spinners' union had ordered women "piecers" to cease work because, "the surroundings were totally unsuited to maintaining that feminine modesty of thought and behaviour which it is the duty of everyone to encourage and protect!" It was, however, recognized by the League that the woman "piecer" was only a scapegoat for the sin of the woman spinner in cutting men's rates of wages, and members hesitated to interfere.

The new understanding between the League and men trade unionists, on the other hand, gave rise to a certain alienation between the League and employers. Mrs. Paterson, addressing a middle-class audience at Oxford in 1883, observed that people liked the word "provident," but not the word "protective." "Rich people were always ready to urge women to be provident on 7/- a week." The League turned from such philanthropic schemes as the "halfpenny bank," the "women's labour exchange," the "workers' restaurant," the "seaside house," the "swimming club," the "circulating library," the "co-operative store," or the "co-operators' society of shirt-makers," to concentrate its activities on the "protective" side of its work. At its annual meeting of 1886, it was moved by the Rev. Stewart Headlam that "the best way to extend the work of the League is to lay stress on its *protective* as distinct from its *provident* element, and further for the League to use its influence to support all other modes of action which may tend to bring about a better distribution of wealth "; whilst other members declared that the League was in bad repute with working men as a "goody-goody" society, and deprecated "the air of patronage." The resolution was carried, but Mrs. Paterson, true to her individualist principles and distrusting the socialist theories of some members, bitterly opposed the second clause. From this time forward, the "entente cordiale" between capital and labour ceased to be applauded at annual meetings. The rules of the women's societies were even amended so as to include "dispute pay." A few years later, the League changed its name from the *Women's Provident and Protective League* to the *Women's Provident Trade Union League* and eventually the word *provident* was dropped.

Mrs. Paterson had it in her mind before she died to emancipate completely the women's societies from the middle-class tutelage of the League. Some assistance at the outset from "persons of wealth and leisure," she regarded as indispensable. During her twelve years of office, five local councils of "sympathetic persons" were established in Bristol, Glasgow, Oxford, Liverpool and Manchester, but she dreamed of future independence for her protégées. In 1882, with the view of supplanting the League, she formed a *women's trades council,* composed solely of representatives of *bonâ fide* women's trade unions, but this—her last venture—did not come to maturity The women's trades council only survived her two years.

Was the women's trade union movement a success or failure? This question was already being asked by friends of the League before Mrs. Paterson's death in 1886. Her own achievement, however, has a value which lies beyond any success or failure of the women's societies. She was not in the strict sense of the word an *industrial* woman, but she had served an apprenticeship in industry and from her youth had thrown in her lot with the workers She enjoyed the confidence and voiced the opinions of at least a section of thinking and intelligent working-women of her day, and she succeeded in making these opinions heard in the councils of organized men. Her views on protective legislation were afterwards discredited, and other policies were adopted by the League; but her faith in the high capacity of working-women to help themselves and not rely for support on another sex or class, inspires women trade unionists to-day. The indomitable spirit looks out from the fragile face whose portrait hangs in the present offices of the Women's Trade Union League.*

* Mr W J Davis, secretary of the Amalgamated Union of Brass Workers and Metal Mechanics, and chief opponent of the " feminist " policy of the League, in his *History and Recollections of the Trades Union Congress,* thus records Mrs Paterson's death " This able and amiable lady has died after a short illness, and at her funeral the Congress was represented by Mr Broadhurst, M.P Mrs. Paterson's views on restrictions of women's work were always unpopular, but she expressed them fearlessly, and no lady delegate was ever more respected."

Chapter III

THE OPENING OF MEN'S TRADE UNIONS TO WOMEN, 1886-1906.

In 1888-9, the country once more was swept by a wave of industrial unrest, and a new crop of societies sprang up in unskilled and women's trades. The strike of the East End matchmakers began the movement in London. These women had been mercilessly exploited by their employers; and low wages, coupled with long hours of work, were aggravated by petty persecution and exorbitant fines. The patient endurance of working-women seemed to have no limit, when the great London Dock Strike—the rebellion of 10,000 casual labourers almost as helpless as themselves—broke the spell at last. The men claimed 6d. an hour. For ten weeks they held up the Port of London, and won their case in the end Suddenly the apathy of despair gave way to the excitement of hope. A fiery article by Mrs. Besant in the *Link* gave the signal for revolt, and seven hundred women matchmakers marched out on strike. The outraged firm vowed to import blacklegs from Glasgow, to remove the factory from London to Norway, to starve out the wretched women whose avarice threatened to ruin a great national industry. The *Times* was alarmed, describing the strike as " the result of the class war which the body of Socialists have brought into action "; but the contrast between wages of 4/- to 8/- a week and dividends of 22 per cent. startled even an indifferent middle-class public into sympathy with the workers. The Women's Trade Union League appealed for funds in aid of the strikers, and raised a sum of £400; while the London Trades Council, acting on behalf of the women, opened negotiations with the firm. The unexpected forces arrayed on the side of the matchmakers caused the firm hurriedly to give way, and the strikers gained practically the whole of their demands. The London Trades Council further urged that, in order to keep their advantage, the women should organize and so " mark their appreciation of the assistance given to them." The League arranged a meeting, the outcome of which was a "Society of Matchmakers," with Mr. Herbert Burrows as honorary secretary. Miss Clementina Black, who had succeeded Mrs. Paterson as secretary of the League, wrote in her report that " the great success of the movement was due to the discipline, unity and steadiness of the girls themselves." The " Society of Matchmakers " included practically the whole body of women employed by the firm, and survived until 1903, but members drifted away as the excitement of the strike died down.

In the same year, 1889, a dozen little societies of women workers sprang up in London, and as many in the provinces. The strike of the Leeds tailoresses swelled the ranks of a local Society of Workwomen in a few weeks from a mere handful to 2,000 women. Earnings were by no means high, averaging about 10/- or 11/- a week, but the immediate cause of unrest was the arbitrary deductions from wages made by the firm, together with forced subscriptions to charities. Passive discontent again turned into active rebellion. The Society of Workwomen opened its doors at once, and the strikers poured into the union. The League and the Leeds Trades Council came to the rescue. A mass meeting was held in Town Hall Square, and attended by 5,000 workers. The strikers formed a committee, and raised a sum of £800, the Leeds Co-operative Store further contributing a gift of 50 lbs. of meat a week This time, however, the strike was doomed to failure. The sympathies of the general public were practically untouched, and the firm refused even to negotiate. One by one the tailoresses came back to the old conditions, or left the district, and the Society of Workwomen relapsed into oblivion

The brilliant campaign of the laundresses followed in the early nineties, and marked the radical change in the policy of the League with regard to protective legislation A further experience of legal restrictions had taught women to appreciate the new leisure assured by a compulsory working-day; and they saw no reason to regret the old " freedom " which allowed them to work every hour of the day, or night, as nature, or their employer might ordain. Nor had the handicap on women's labour proved as serious as was at first anticipated The usual result, as the cotton operatives had soon discovered, was to bring men into line with women, to the benefit of both alike. The League, whose policy about this time came under the influence of Sir Charles Dilke, turned its attention accordingly to extending the Factory and Workshops Act to new classes of workers. The failure to include laundresses in the Factory and Workshops Bill of 1891 brought an immediate protest The hours of work in laundries were appallingly long, amounting to fourteen and sixteen hours a day, and the issue was not obscured in this case by the agitation of a men's trade union to exclude women from employment. The men's support was clearly disinterested, and the women's voice was practically unanimous. A canvass of 67,500 laundresses, organized by the League, showed a majority of 66,000 votes in favour of extending the Bill to laundries An Amalgamated Society of Laundresses was formed out of the remnants of earlier societies. It counted almost at once 3,000 members, and eight branches in the London and Brighton districts. A deputation from the Society waited on the Home Secretary, and members put their case before him The London Trades Council organized a giant women's demonstration in Hyde Park—a novel sight in the early nineties; whilst the League arranged a similar meeting of 4,000 women at Brighton. The matter was taken up at the Trades Union Congress, and a motion in favour of the women's amendment to the Bill was carried unanimously. The Government was sufficiently impressed by the agitation to insert a new clause into the Bill which embodied practically the whole of the women's demands Unfortunately, however, the Irish Party, scared by the prospect of an inspection of convent laundries, withdrew its support at the last moment, and the Bill fell through. Disappointment was acute, and brought in its train a collapse of the women's society. Nevertheless, the campaign had achieved a large part of its object, and Mr. Asquith, then Home Secretary, provided for the inclusion of laundries in the Factories and Workshops Act of 1895

Amongst the " sweated " workers of East London, organization began under most unpromising circumstances. Mrs. Hicks, a member of the League, started a campaign amongst women rope-makers. Their wages were from 8/- to 10/- a week, and apparently the subject of constant friction with their employers. Mrs. Hicks was warned that she would find " a rough, wild, and even desperate class of women " She invited them to a meeting, but they were too much afraid of their employer to come. Eventually they were persuaded by Mrs Hicks to come all together. " A room was hired, and about 90 to 100 women walked there in a body, a proceeding which greatly alarmed the inhabitants, some of whom fled into their houses and barred the doors." A small but active union was formed, which remained in existence for ten years. Mrs Hicks and Miss James, the latter representing a small confectioners' union, succeeded, after repeated applications, in giving evidence before the Labour Commission of 1893. Not only did they reveal appallingly insanitary conditions of work, but " cases were known of the women being locked in the factory, and in at least one instance a fire occurred which was fatal to the unfortunate women locked in " In spite of this shocking treatment, few women dared to join the union for fear of dismissal.*

In the twenty years, 1886-1906, a fresh crop of women's societies—little unions of dressmakers, upholstresses, bookbinders, purse and pocket-makers, artificial flower-makers, feather

* The account of the Ropemakers' and Confectioners' Unions are taken from *Women in Modern Industry*, by Miss B L Hutchins, to whom the story was told by Mrs. Hicks herself.

dressers, shawl-makers, lace-makers, brick-makers, paper-makers, box-makers, bag-makers, glass workers, tobacco workers, jam and pickle workers, rag pickers, small metal workers, munition workers, shop assistants, typists, domestic servants—in all some eighty or ninety societies sprang up once more for brief years of existence. About sixty of these societies were established by the League, and others by local "women's trade union councils," which pursued similar campaigns in Manchester and elsewhere.

More important, however, about this time was the opening of men's trade unions to women. The early success of the cotton weavers' associations in organizing women, and the later efforts of the card and blowing-room operatives have already been described. The spinners' unions still continued their policy of prohibiting female labour, and had practically succeeded in preventing women's employment in mule-spinning. In one or two districts, where young men and boys were attracted by high wages to mines and foundries, women were recognized as " piecers " or assistants, and in this case were permitted or even compelled by the spinner who employed them to join his union; but " piecers " of either sex only ranked as minors and had no rights of membership. Ring-spinning was introduced about 1880, and was recognized by the spinners' unions as a women's process, but no attempt was made to organize ring-spinners The new machines were no doubt of a comparatively simple type and not adapted except to the coarser counts of yarn; but the fact remains that it was the sex of the ring-spinner and not her inferior skill which mainly decided the policy of the spinners' unions. Ring-spinners remained unorganized until about the end of the century, when they were admitted to the associations of card and blowing-room operatives. Apart from the cotton associations, only the Huddersfield and District Woollen Weavers and the Leicester Hosiery Amalgamation had women members before the middle 'eighties, but about this time a general movement to organize women began in the textile trades. The Dundee and District Mill and Factory Workers, founded by the Rev. Henry Wilkinson in 1885, aimed especially at organizing women and girls, " because women and girls were the only kind of workers who came out on strike and threw a whole town out of employment." The Scottish Mill and Factory Workers' Association, established in 1889, similarly opened its doors to women. The Textile Operatives of Ireland, formed under the auspices of the League in 1893, was practically a women's union. Men numbered barely 5 per cent. out of about 1,000 members. The Bolton Amalgamation of Dyers, and the small unions of silk workers belonging to the Leek district, also began to organize

c

women in the 'nineties. Of men's societies outside the textile trades, the first to admit women to membership was the National Union of Boot and Shoe Operatives, a few women joining the union in 1884. The Society of Journeymen Felt Hatters, as an alternative policy, formed an allied women's society in 1886. Women were said to be reluctant to join a men's trade union, and to prefer at least the formality of an independent organization. During the 'nineties, one union after another—the old-established Amalgamated Society of Tailors, the modern Amalgamated Union of Clothiers' Operatives, the conservative London Society of Compositors, the progressive National Union of Printers' Warehousemen and Cutters, the various societies of Pottery Workers, the London Society of Cigar Makers, the British Steel Smelters, the Tin and Sheet Millmen, the Chain Country Workers, the Sheffield Hand File Cutters, even the Cumberland Miners' Union* —either opened its doors to women or formed an allied women's society; whilst the " black-coated " unions and the general labour unions, which were formed about this time, included women members from the start. Between 1886 and 1896, the female membership of all trade unions increased from about 37,000 to nearly 118,000. The advance was afterwards less rapid; but the figure rose again to about 167,000 in 1906. Of this number, 143,000 women belonged to textile unions, and over 125,000 to cotton unions. Probably not more than 5,000 women were organized in all-women's societies.

The Women's Trade Union League not only welcomed the men's movement, but decided to co-operate. In 1889, a scheme was devised under which any *bonâ fide* trade union admitting women to membership was invited to affiliate to the League for the small fee of ½d. a year per female member, whilst the League offered in return the services of a woman organizer. The men's trade unions responded immediately, and the League now enjoyed for the first time a recognized status in the trade union world. The General Union of Textile Workers affiliated the same year, and some fifty to sixty societies, including thirty local associations of cotton operatives, followed suit in the 'nineties The requests for the services of a woman organizer were, indeed, so numerous that the League was obliged to hold rigidly to the terms of its bargain, and to refuse assistance to unaffiliated societies, unless the whole of the expenses were guaranteed About the same time, it was decided by the League to invite the more prominent officials of the men's trade unions to form a " Committee of Counsel " for the purpose of advising women on matters of trade union policy This committee counted among its earliest members Mr. Cross, secretary of the Northern

* The Union included a few female " screeners," employed at the pithead.

Counties Weavers' Association, Mr. Mullin, secretary of the Association of Card and Blowing Room Operatives, Mr. Mawdsley, secretary of the Cotton Spinners' Amalgamation, and Mr. Allan Gee, secretary of the General Union of Textile Workers. Miss Marsland, a member of the Mossley Association of Card and Blowing Room Operatives, was appointed one of the first organizers under the scheme.

"Please send an organizer at once, for our Amalgamated Society has decided that if the women of this town cannot be organized, they must be exterminated." This ultimatum, received by the League, and quoted by Miss Mary Macarthur, expressed a not uncommon point of view amongst men trade unionists; and their object in organizing women was not entirely disinterested. In the skilled trades, to which organized men mainly belonged, the problem of female labour was already acute. The progress of machinery, together with the new sub-divisions of labour, incidental to the growth of the "great industry," had increasingly the effect of adapting these trades to semi-skilled classes of workers, and underpaid women were more than usually dangerous competitors. The men's object was not so much to exclude women entirely from employment—an aim generally viewed as impracticable—as to confine them to certain branches of the trade, or to certain districts. Under the circumstances, some degree of sex antagonism was almost inevitable, and did not tend to make organization easier. The feeling was especially bitter on the part of the men, who directly attributed to women's competition their own apparently increasing liability to unemployment. According to Mr. Gavin, secretary of the Scottish Operative Tailors, women in certain districts had almost completely displaced men in tailoring.

"There has been a gradual displacement of men by women in the tailoring trade in Scotland," he stated, "for more than twenty years It has become more general and been more acutely felt within the last decade, and especially within the last few years They were first employed by the introduction of the sewing machine, then by and by they began to make vests and trousers ; and have been gradually introduced into the making up of the lighter kinds of work, until they are now employed making nearly all kinds of garments They have at times directly displaced the men—many such cases having occurred within the last few years The men either have been dismissed, or their work so lessened as to practically starve them out of the trade altogether This is evidenced by many of them, after going idle for a time, requiring to betake themselves to other occupations to earn a living The reason for this preferment, in my opinion, is because they are cheaper—the employer getting them (with few exceptions) at his own price It is computed there are between three hundred and four hundred women employed in Edinburgh, and a larger number in Glasgow—this in customer trades—many of them being engaged in the very best shops making ladies' and gentlemen's garments In Aberdeen and Dunfermline, within the last two or three months, women have been engaged, either displacing the men or lessening the work for them The men, with few exceptions, are paid by the piece, while the women are generally paid weekly wages Where piece prices are paid to the women, they rarely get the same prices as the men, being generally paid much less for the same work. Several firms from time to time have locked out their men, filling their places principally with women We have had cases of this kind in Edinburgh, Glasgow, Greenock, and elsewhere. We had also direct displacement through the employment of women in Kilmarnock This displacement is not confined to the large towns, but also applies to the smaller ones For example, there used to be between thirty and forty tailors in Forfar, but now there are only a few—women largely taking their place Airdrie, Coatbridge, Dumbarton, Dundee, Falkirk, Inverness, Kincardine, Motherwell, Perth, and many other towns have women employed, which has had the effect of generally lessening the work for the men In the slack seasons the women are often preferred , the men either doing very little, or being suspended until trade improves."

The Society was opened to women, but only about a dozen joined. Tailoresses were suspicious of tailors, not only as jealous trade competitors, but as exploiters to some extent of female labour. The old rule of the Amalgamated Society of Tailors, by which one member was forbidden to accept employment from another, was not enforced in the case of women, who were hard to convince of men's good motives in assisting them. Women, on the other side, had to face the bitter hostility of employers, who saw in each attempt to organize them a threat to their vested interest in " cheap and docile " female labour. " Opposition," wrote Mr. Flynn, secretary of the men's society, " fierce intolerant opposition has been exhibited by the employers. Over 100 women in Plymouth have been out for two months because their employers wished them to sign away their right to organize."

Similar obstacles had to be overcome in the printing trades At the important International Conference of Typographical Societies of 1886, it was resolved that, " while strongly of opinion that women are not physically capable of performing the duties of a compositor, this Conference recommends their admission to membership of the various Typographical unions upon the same conditions as journeymen, provided always the females are paid strictly in accordance with the scale." One woman compositor, who succeeded in fulfilling the terms of the resolution, was admitted to the London Society of Compositors in 1892, and remained a member for some years; but the resolution generally was a dead letter The men had, indeed, no other object in view than to exclude women from employment by offering them apparently impossible terms They further protected themselves against women's competition by refusing to teach girl apprentices, whilst prohibiting the employment of any except apprenticed tradesmen. In the provinces, where women compositors were already employed to some extent, the Typographical Association made no attempt to organize them Members were only prepared to recognize women as "layers-on" or assistants. Boys did and girls did not "constitute a danger to society" by seeking promotion without apprenticeship! The policy was afterwards severely censured by the National Union of Printers' Assistants. The problem was most acute in Edinburgh, where women compositors had been introduced by Miss Emily Faithfull in the 'sixties. The experiment of a "women's printing society" it is true was a failure; but the hint was taken by employers, who brought in women as strike-breakers during the great Edinburgh strike of 1872-3. Women were similarly employed by one firm in Perth. "The women put in a bill at the end of each week," wrote the secretary of the Perth Typographical Society, "worked out on the men's scale of rates, and the cashier then divides the total by two and pays the women accordingly." Female labour was, however, successfully prohibited in Glasgow. According to representatives of the Master Printers' Association, who gave evidence during the important Glasgow arbitration case of 1904, women employed by a first-class Edinburgh firm were paid $3\frac{1}{2}$d. an hour and men $7\frac{1}{4}$d. for corresponding work, whilst the rate was $8\frac{1}{4}$d. in Glasgow. Edinburgh firms had the additional advantage of piece-work, which was prohibited in Glasgow, women being paid 4d. or $4\frac{1}{2}$d., and men $7\frac{1}{2}$d. per thousand ens. "Even if it should be held that a woman does not accomplish as much work in an hour as a man does," the employers stated, "it is without question that the extra cost to the Glasgow employer owing to the exclusion of female labour is very great." Valuable printing contracts were declared to be passing from Glasgow to Edinburgh, and more than one important Glasgow house was said to have opened a branch in Edinburgh for the purpose of utilizing women in the "book" and simple "jobbing" trade. The depressed conditions of employment in Edinburgh similarly were remarked by representatives of the Scottish Typographical Association "There are 1,300 compositors in Edinburgh," they stated, "of whom 1,000 work on piece-work, and taking the outside figure receive 30/- a week. Then of 1,500 men in Glasgow, at least 1,400 receive not less than 34/-." The hours of work were, moreover, $52\frac{1}{2}$ in Edinburgh and 52 in Glasgow. The two parties to the arbitration came, nevertheless, to entirely opposite conclusions. According to employers, the employment of women in Glasgow would be no disadvantage, but rather an advantage to men. "It seems to be taken for granted by the men's society in Glasgow that every woman who is employed at type-setting means the displacement of one of their members there. That is not the opinion of the masters. They feel, on the other hand, that were it not for the limitations enforced by the men's society the volume of work done in Glasgow might be much greater, and with more suitable conditions there might be greater prosperity to the trade." In view, however, of the depressed conditions of employment in Edinburgh, the workers were not prepared to follow its example. Nor were they convinced by the Edinburgh experience that women's employment would lead to increased men's employment. "The presence of females," wrote the secretary of the Edinburgh Typographical Society, "it cannot be disputed, seriously affects the employment of the male compositors who are engaged on the piece system. While work is plentiful no harm is felt; but when slackness sets in, the females get the preference—the line-men having to go idle. Summing up, the general opinion entertained in Edinburgh is that females may pay the employers, but that the employers use them as an effective deterrent against the journeymen making a similar movement to that attempted in 1872-3" The workers, however, lost their case. "The Masters will only be enabled to pay higher wages to their men," the arbitrator declared, "if they are in a position, by the employment of female compositors, to extend their business and increase their profits. . . In short, but for the lower wages, the longer hours and the employment of female labour in Edinburgh, I should have been prepared to allow a rise of 1/- a week. . . . It may be the fact that, owing to the shorter training to which they have any sufficient motive to submit, women cannot deal with the more difficult work so rapidly and so skilfully as men But it is admitted that they have proved their fitness in Edinburgh and elsewhere for ordinary book printing and jobbing work. I have heard neither fact nor argument justifying the exclusion of Glasgow women from the work done elsewhere with satisfaction and profit to first-class houses and without injury to the men's interests. I am satisfied that the employment of female compositors in Glasgow, while it would increase the total volume of work done there, and admit of the natural development of the Glasgow book trade, would not injure the position of the Glasgow men printers." The Scottish Typographical Association, meanwhile, decided that "females in the case-room shall not be recognized by the union, but that each branch must work out its own salvation in districts where the women are already introduced"; and the Edinburgh Typographical Society, in order to recover its lost position, immediately started a campaign for the limitation of women apprentices. "The total abolition of females," men trade unionists were obliged to admit, "or to insist that they should be paid the same wages as men, would be absurd." Employers were, however, not prepared to give up any part of their advantage. "The employment of female labour was largely introduced owing to the existence of many extras in the scale unknown in places competing with Edinburgh. . . . It might be

different if the Typographical Society was prepared to consent
to a revision of the scales which would remove any of these
harassing extras which handicap competition with other printing
centres." The matter came to a head in 1910. "The Edinburgh
members set themselves no small task when they decided to
eliminate cheap female labour from the case-room. The sufferings
of the line-room during the past few years has created strong
feeling."* Exasperated at last by the procrastination of employers, members served in their notices, which action gained "the
enthusiastic support of the females in every office." The Masters'
Association came at once to terms, and, before the notices had
expired, the two parties concluded the famous Edinburgh Agreement, laying down that "no female apprentice compositors shall
be taken on until June 30th, 1916." Success was frankly acknowledged by the Society to be in large measure due to "the
hearty support of the ladies themselves," and "the obligation
was then undertaken that should the help asked by the men be
forthcoming, the Association would in the near future see to it
that the girls would participate in the benefits accruing from joint
action. . . . The elimination of female compositors on account of
sex is not and never was the policy of trade unionists; but to
allow their labour to be exploited because it can be purchased at a
lower price must be prevented at all costs. . . . To accurately
represent the value of the services of females as compared with
male journeymen compositors working on stab (time) may present certain difficulties; but these difficulties, especially when
piece-work obtains, are not insuperable." The National Union
of Printers' Warehousemen and Cutters came forward and
organized an "Edinburgh Branch of Women Compositors",
and this branch of some 200 members was transferred by friendly
agreement to the Edinburgh Typographical Society in 1912.

The London Society of Journeymen Bookbinders pursued a
similar campaign of prohibition against women who trespassed
in the skilled branches of bookbinding. Women were not admitted to the Union; and in 1892, an agreement was concluded
with the London Chamber of Commerce (Bookbinding Section),
by which all skilled operations (including such apparently feminine
work as "cutting cloth and lining," "colouring edges of books
when done indoors," or merely "pasting down") should be
reserved to journeymen and apprentices, provided that "the
representatives of the journeymen agree that they will not make it
a grievance if female or unskilled labour is placed upon :

The rolling, pressing before sewing, or papering of outboard
    work

---

* *Annual Report of the Scottish Typographical Association, 1906.*

The laying-on, washing up or cleaning-off of cloth work.

The varnishing of cloth or Bible work.

The taking work out of the press after pasting-down and opening-up.

The carrying of loads about the workshop."

The National Union of Printers' Warehousemen and Cutters was not vexed by female labour to the same extent   A fixed rate of wages had so far not been secured by men members, and the policy of the union for both sexes alike was to organize first, and to build up a standard afterwards.   The Union had, moreover, no means of excluding women from employment.   Organization was begun in 1889, when the men assisted some women in forming a Women Bookfolders' Union. The experiment was not a successful one. A popular employer got herself elected as secretary, and members presently drew up a programme which included, not only a minimum wage of 15s. a week, but exemption from the night-work prohibition clauses of the Factory and Workshops Act   The men, some of whom were employed at night on women's machines at about double women's wages, became not unnaturally alarmed   They withdrew their support from the women's society, which apparently did not have a strong hold even on its own members.   The employer-secretary retired, the "young person who kept the minutes" married, and the Union broke up insolvent   A second experiment was made in 1894, and this time with better success.   The Printing and Kindred Trades Federation, "anxious to mark the members' appreciation of the courage and loyalty with which the women had supported the men in a recent strike," invited the League to co-operate in forming the National Union of Women Bookfolders.   Women members were, however, placed under proper masculine guidance. A joint-committee of men trade unionists and members of the League drew up the constitution, whilst Mr Jones, a member of the men's trade union, was appointed secretary. The society took root and flourished; and ten years later, at its own request, was admitted to the men's organization.

The story repeated itself in the pottery trades.   Mr. William Owen, who represented the trade unions in the general arbitration case of 1891, gave the following graphic description of the serious results to men from women's competition in the flat-pressing department:

"Before I leave the flat-pressing branch altogether," he said, " let me say that cheapened production in this department is not limited to the decreased prices (consequent upon the use of machinery) that I have quoted   Through the introduction of this awfully mis-named apparatus called the "jolly," women now make, at some manufactories, the smaller-size plates   I could, but I will not, dwell upon the unwomanly character of this work—it is neither good for the living female nor the future offspring—but will merely point out that the cost of producing plates is on the average still further reduced through the cheap labour of the women   All this women-labour in this department has been introduced since 1872."

The fact that men were being ousted by women from employment was not denied by employers; but, on the contrary, it was held as a threat over the heads of men trade unionists, who claimed advances of wages.

" With regard to cup-makers," Mr Boddam stated, on behalf of employers, " they are gradually being driven out of the market by women labour, and if they don't care to take our terms we can supply their places with women and apprentices   We do not wish to do so.   We think, if the workman will put himself to the collar, he can make so much with the assistance of the labour-saving appliances, with a 10 per cent. reduction, that he will be able to continue to earn an average wage.   We believe, if they choose to work a little harder, they can make wages almost exactly the same as they obtain to-day   If, however, they prefer the luxury of ease to added industry, well, of course, we say they must take the consequences, because we are not in a position to give them any luxurious prices at the present time "

The Printers' and Transferers' Union and the United Ovenmen, Kilnmen and Saggers' Union, decided, however, to organize the women; and, with the assistance of the League, women's branches were formed at Hanley and Burslem.   Progress was slow and uncertain.   Speaking at a trade union meeting in 1894, Lady Dilke reproached both men and women for their failure.   " When I come to such a meeting as this, as a rule, I find I have to reproach the women for not taking hold of the vigorous help offered by the men; but when organization, as here, is not on a satisfactory basis amongst the men, I do not see how we can reproach the women. Why are you so slack? Think of the wages some of you earn.   Are there not many at 5/- a week?   Compare even the best with the earnings of capital.   Are you satisfied? You who get the best, are you ever sure that you are going to maintain your present rate?   I am not.   Do you want to know what is going to happen?   The next thing will be that you women will displace you men, either at a lesser wage, or, if the wage remains nominally the same, is there not a trick called an allowance to the employer, by which the female worker pays toll to him for being allowed to do the man's job. . . . What is this other thing, too, of which I have been told of women here?   Two years ago, 1,300 in unions, and now but 500; that spells 800 traitors to the cause.   Forgive me, if I seem to think it is easy for you to pay out of the wage—the whole of which is sorely needed in the home—the weekly contribution to the union.   In many cases, I know it is cruelly hard, but it is worth it.   Only by loyal support to your union, only by constant support will you do what our Lancashire men and women are doing—protect not only themselves, but the future of your children "

The League assisted the potters' unions in promoting the Factory and Workshops Act of 1891—known as the Potters' Charter of Health—by which power was given to the Home Secretary for the first time to investigate dangerous trades, and to lay down " special rules " for the protection of the workers.   The agitation was continued in support of the Home Office recommendations, which prohibited women and young persons from working in lead.   The League criticized severely " the action of some well-meaning ladies in bringing to London the wealthiest workers they could find in order to protest against interference."

Organization began under similar circumstances amongst cigar makers.   " I have seen in a great Liverpool cigar factory," declared Lady Dilke, " every room filled with women, where once every room was filled with men "   In London, where the best work was reserved to men, the League assisted the Mutual Association of Cigar Makers in 1890 to form a London Society of Female Cigar Makers, which a few years later joined the men's organization.   The Nottingham Society of Female Cigar Makers, established in 1887 in order to resist reductions of wages, preferred, on the other hand, to retain its independence.   Members were especially fortunate in the person of their secretary, Mrs. Bryant.   In the record year of 1889, the membership rose to 1,200 women, and branches were formed in five neighbouring towns.   This society, which was one of the few successful women's societies, remained always in close touch with the men's organization, but did not amalgamate until recent years.

Trade unionism was most backward amongst women metal and wood-workers.   The problem of female labour was so far not an acute one except in the Birmingham and Black Country small metal trades.   Men brass workers had been vexed by women's competition almost from the beginning of the century, but the National Union of Brass Workers and Metal Mechanics persisted in its refusal to recognize female labour   The Black Country chain and nail-makers, who were faced by a similar problem, as we have seen, decided to organize women, but the joint campaigns of the League and the Midland Trades Federation, had hardly begun to bear fruit.   The shockingly low rates of women's wages were apparently an insuperable obstacle to organization.   The Amalgamated Society of Engineers followed the example of the Birmingham Brass Workers' Union, and refused to recognize women.   Since 1886, the Society had been compelled by circumstances to relax its rules and admit to membership unapprenticed tradesmen provided that they earned the full trade union rate of wages; but this condition was equally unattainable by women.   In Manchester, under the auspices of the Manchester Women's Trade Union League, a little Society of Female Machinists and Electrical Workers was established in 1889, but its members counted barely 100, and could not win recognition from the men's societies. The engineering unions were, however, not seriously affected by female competition until the end of the century, when the introduction of automatic machinery led to a fresh influx of women According to trade union witnesses before the Poor Law Commission of 1905-9, men's unemployment was largely due to this cause. "The women are ousting the men in most trades, including the iron trades. . . . Women in the ironworks were unknown a few years ago, but there are hundreds of thousands of them now. . . . There are many machine shops where the work is principally done by women and girls. They are, of course, got at a much lower rate of pay." In 1904, the Sheet Metal Workers and Braziers' Union passed a resolution for the first time prohibiting women from soldering. " On principle we object to it, and also to the fact that there is a tendency to reduce wages. It is to evade the paying of proper rates to individuals."

The " black-coated " unions, which had only begun to establish their position in the 'nineties; were not faced with quite the same problem The woman clerk and shop assistant had always had the free entry of her trade. Men were almost as backward as women in organization, and there were no barriers to keep up or to break down, except those of trade or social tradition. The National Union of Shop Assistants adopted the new form of " industrial " unionism, and admitted to membership, irrespective of " craft " or sex, all workers employed in the industry of distribution.

The general labour unions similarly made no distinction of sex. Members were composed of semi-skilled and unskilled workers who belonged to every variety of trade and industry. They had mostly no standard of wages to maintain, and no interests to protect in one trade more than in another. There was, moreover, little or no competition between men and women labourers, to which class men members mainly belonged. Men had a natural monopoly of muscular strength, and competition between the sexes was practically confined to women and boys. The National Union of Gas Workers and General Labourers, established in 1889, opened a women's branch at Singleton in the same year, and other societies followed suit.

Apart, however, from any problem of " unfair female competition " the task of organizing women appears to have been by no means a light one. " It is not true," declared Mr. Skipton, secretary of the London Trades Council, at the annual meeting of the Women's Trade Union League in 1897, " that the men have been out of sympathy with the women during the last twenty-five years, but the women won't help themselves " The National Union of Journeymen Felt Hatters, which had established an allied women's society in 1886, seems actually to have experienced a deliberate opposition to trade unionism The disastrous Warwickshire strike of 1892, which ended in women ousting men from certain processes in the felting department, had effectually checked organization in this district; but in the well-organized Denton area, where women were successfully confined to their own branches of hat-making, they were invited to join the women's society. They, however, " didn't believe in paying their hard-earned pence to keep people walking about in their coats." The irritation on both sides came to a head in 1906, when some women " trimmers," employed by a good " union " firm, flatly declined to join the union. The men, who acted as officers to the women's society, made three separate proclamations. In the first one, the women were asked " to attend a meeting to consider the question of becoming members on the most lenient terms possible at present." In the second one, they were told that " they would be allowed to join the union free of entrance fees, but if they failed to take advantage of this opportunity they would afterwards be dealt with by the committee." In the third one, they were threatened that " if all the trimmers working in this shop are not members of the Felt Hat Trimmers Society by Thursday evening week, we, the members, will tender seven days' notice, and cease to work with ' non-union ' trimmers." The case was taken to arbitration, and Miss Henshall, representing seventy-two " non-union " women, put forward a carefully prepared defence. " We think," she declared, " that by joining the union we shall lose our individuality. We shall become part of an organization over which we shall have no control, and it will be of no benefit to us whatever, so far as we know, therefore we resent the action taken by the unionists in refusing to work with us until they have coerced us into their union. . . . We fail to see what right they have, legally or morally, to dictate terms to us when they don't employ us. Their idea is to force us in, to use us as a lever to force other girls in out of other works in the town who prefer to be free, even at the risk of being subject to shouts, jeers and insults from their fellow-workers who have joined the union either through threats or a desire to receive union pay in the event of a strike. There has been talk about our being too mean to pay the contribution; but as the money would come out of our wage, and not out of our pocket-money, there is nothing in that We are quite satisfied as we are, and prefer the settlements of any disputes with the masters themselves without the intervention of the union It appears that we are not fit to work with them, not holding the same views.

They tell us we are receiving benefits for which they pay. This is untrue. What the men receive for their work, and what we receive for our work, is a different matter. They never help us when we ask for an increase, nor should we think of appealing to them." The men tried to gain their point by persuasion. " If the women could see their way to join us—perhaps against their will at present—I am sure they will see the advantages. Like children who object to go to school, although it is for their good, and afterwards bless their parents who had to force them to go, many trimmers are in their infancy as far as trade organization is concerned." The firm, apparently, did its best for conciliation. It was finally decided that the journeymen felt hatters and the " union " trimmers should return to work, whilst the " non-union " trimmers should " agree to discuss all matters in dispute with the representatives of the union, a representative of the Board of Trade being present." The rebels eventually joined the women's society and became some of its staunchest members.

Women's apathy, or indifference, was a common subject of complaint. An inquiry into the difficulties of organizing women, undertaken by the League in 1900, brought a whole volume of lamentations from trade union officials. On the whole, women officers were the least pessimistic. " Of course, in common with everyone who has had much experience in the struggle of organizing women on trade union lines," wrote Miss I. O. Ford, honorary secretary of the Leeds Society of Workwomen, " I consider the struggle a most disheartening and painful one   But I hold very strongly that the fault does not lie with the women themselves. Those women, who really grasp the aim of trade unionism, grasp it, I think, more firmly than men, because more religiously. Trade unionism means rebellion, and the orthodox teaching for women is submission. The political world preaches to women submission, so long as it refuses them the Parliamentary franchise, and therefore ignores them as human beings. Society encourages selfish indifference amongst women, in that it considers a woman's home must make her sacrifice to it everyone else's home and all public honour." Miss Margaret Bondfield, the young assistant general secretary of the National Union of Shop Assistants, was equally alive to the present limitations but great potentialities of her sex. " A woman wage-earner who is a convinced trade unionist overtakes her brother man   She throws herself into the work of the union with a loyalty and singleness of purpose which greatly benefits the branch to which she is attached. . . But I have only referred to convinced trade unionists, and they, alas, are painfully few compared with the vast army of women wage-earners." Amongst men officials, Mr (afterwards Sir) David Shackleton, secretary of the Northern Counties Weavers'

Association, was able to boast the extraordinary success of the Lancashire cotton weavers. " Organization was an accomplished fact in Lancashire, and women were reliable, although not active trade unionists." ‾ But this case was exceptional. Mr. Gee, secretary of the General Union of Textile Workers, emphasized chiefly the need for education. " When the idea has permeated their minds thoroughly, and they have given in their names to join a union, women have been as loyal as men . . . One reason which, I think, tends to keep women out of the union is the lack of training which women have had in managing such an organization as a trade union. It is quite true that men-folk have been to blame in not educating their sisters and daughters; but, there it is, a stumbling-block. When they have been educated sufficiently to do the work of negotiating with employers, and also in keeping the accounts, I think that women will be far better organized than they are to-day; for, after all, it must be admitted that women can understand women's grievances better than men can " Mr. Jones, secretary of the National Union of Female Bookfolders, looked in the same way to education. " I find it very hard," he said, " to get women to join, and when you have persuaded them you have all your work to keep them. . . In conclusion, I must say the weaker sex has certainly proved weak trade unionists, but still things are improving, and I hope before long women workers will be able to show the lead to men." Mr. Will Thorne, secretary of the Gasworkers' and General Labourers' Union, remarked similar shortcomings in women, but he also found some excuse " Taking women collectively, they do not seem to grasp the real need of trade unions. Then again, I find that women as a body do not attend to the branch business as well as the men (and they are bad enough in many places) . . When a man has done his day's work he becomes free, and that is not so with women." Other officials wrote in desperation. " Women are kittle-cattle," declared Mr Hendry, organizer of the Scottish Mill and Factory Workers, " and if anyone has lingering doubts on that point, which he desires to dispel, let him spend a few weeks in organizing work amongst women, and his cure will be complete. Broadly, from the trade union point of view, women are bad subjects " Mr. Keegan, secretary of the Birmingham Pen Makers, was driven to actual despair. Men-folk disliked the " go-to-meetings " woman, and feminine weakness bowed to masculine dictums Indeed, the folly of woman was infinite " There are yet other and greater difficulties in organizing women which are fundamental and apparently ineradicable. First I would place their impatience We have had hundreds of instances where after having paid 2d. a week for a month or two, they have torn up their contribution cards in disgust, saying that nothing was done for them. They are unstable to a degree. . . . We have had an inspiring and enthusiastic meeting one week, and the next the self-same women will be scandalizing the union. We have had nearly 2,000 names on our books, and we have only an effective membership of about 350. But their uncharitableness to each other is probably the most biting and disintegrating force which works against their solidity. . . . The evil is far-reaching, and I fear endemic." The Editor of the *Women's Trade Union Journal,* in summing up the results of the inquiry, wittily compared the man trade unionist to the writer of the *Pilgrim's Scrip.* Asked for an example of his ideas on sex, he said, " I expect women will be the last thing civilized by man."

CHAPTER IV.

THE NATIONAL FEDERATION OF WOMEN WORKERS AND THE
MODERN WOMEN'S TRADE UNION MOVEMENT.

1906—1914.

Thirty years of continuous effort in organizing women had so
far done little to check the pitiless exploitation of " cheap and
docile " female labour   The only exception was in the cotton
industry, where men and women weavers did the same work and
received the same rates of wages.   According to the Board of
Trade Report on Earnings and Hours for 1906, the average earnings of an adult woman in a full working week were 18/8 in the
cotton industry, compared with 15/5 in all textile trades (including cotton), 13/6 in the clothing trades, 12/2 in the printing
trades, 12/8 in the metal trades, 11/10 in the pottery and chemical
trades, or 11/3 in the food and tobacco trades.   About one-third
of the whole body of working-women earned less than 12s a
week.   Mr. Sidney Webb estimated from the Board of Trade
figures that the average net earnings of an adult woman throughout the year were 10/10½,* compared with 25/9 for an adult man.
Conditions were equally depressed for women clerks and shop
assistants, who accepted wages of less than 10/- a week for the
sake of genteel employment.   Home-workers, such as needle-
women, cardboard boxmakers, artificial flower makers, or brushmakers, whose wretched working conditions were revealed by the
Daily News Sweated Industries Exhibition of 1906, earned about
1d an hour.   Government uniforms, farmed out in the home,
would be paid at the rate of 6¾d. for a pair of trousers, 5¾d. for a
waistcoat, or 1/6 for a coat.   Employers who introduced women on
men's work had no scruples at all in cutting rates by one-half.
Some interesting examples were given by trade union witnesses
before the Fair Wages Committee of 1907   In the hosiery trade,
where men knitters were employed at Leicester and women in Scotland, men received 1/9½ for the same dozen articles for which
women received 10½d.   In the wholesale clothing trade, where
women had recently been introduced in the warehouse, they were
paid 4/- and 5/- a week   In the leather trades, where men and

* The estimate allowed for an average of five weeks' lost time in the year
through sickness, unemployment, etc

44

women were employed in harness-making, the men's rate was 8d
an hour and the women's 3d. an hour.   In brush-making, where
both sexes were employed on " piece " work, the women's rate
was invariably reduced by one-half.   In the printing trades, where
the men's time-rate was from 32/- to 36/- a week, women and girl
machine operatives earned from 8/- to 15/- a week on piece-work.
Nor were these wholesale reductions of wages viewed by the
Government as a breach of the " fair wages clause " in Government contracts.   In an official note sent to the Printing and Kindred Trades Federation, it was expressly laid down that women
employed on men's work should receive only *women's* rates of
wages.   As a matter of fact, the Government set the worst example
in its own workshops.   In March, 1906, Mr. Robertson, Parliamentary Secretary to the Admiralty, was able to boast that he had
effected a saving of £235 a year on the wages of six women
polishers, and a further saving of £300 on the wages of six upholstresses recently introduced into the Devonport dockyards.

Miss Mary Macarthur became secretary of the Women's Trade
Union League in 1903, and the National Federation of Women
Workers was founded by the League in 1906   Miss Macarthur
referred the instability of women in trade unions to two principal
causes.   " There is," she said, " no inherent sex incapacity to
recognize the necessity for corporate action.   The probability of
marriage is not the insurmountable obstacle we are often led to
believe it is   One recognizes, of course, that lack of permanence
in women's employments militates against organization, because
it discourages technical instruction and lowers the standard of
work.   The lack of permanence, however, from other causes
affects men in the same ways.   First, the low standard of living
may be stated to be at once the cause and consequence of women's
lack of organization   This sounds paradoxical, but it is nevertheless true that, while women are badly paid because of their unorganized condition, they may be unorganized mainly because they
are badly paid.   The low rate of wages constitutes the most serious
difficulty in the way of women's trade union organization. . . .
This brings me to my second difficulty, which is found chiefly
among the higher grades.   It is a narrow class prejudice which
causes the semi-professional class of workers to look askance upon
anything in the nature of trade unionism."   Small and struggling
local trade unions were not in a position " to do anything practical
in the way of improving working conditions.   A national organization with local branches was more likely to win in any en-
counter with the employer."   The Federation was formed on the
model of a general labour union, membership being open to all
women belonging to unorganized trades, or not admitted to their
appropriate trade union.   The rules provided for the election of
D

three members of the League as advisory members of the executive committee of the Federation, and a close connection continued between the older and the newer body. Miss Macarthur was first president of the Federation, but exchanged this post for that of general secretary in 1908, when Miss Gertrude Tuckwell took her place as president The Federation was in other respects an ordinary trade union, and as such was affiliated to the Trades Union Congress and to the General Federation of Trade Unions. By the end of a year, it included over 2,000 members, and seventeen branches in England and Scotland. The London group of women's societies and a women's branch of the Cradley Heath Hammered Chain Makers were absorbed within the new organization.

The wave of industrial unrest, which swept over the country in 1910, spread as before to women. In the East End and in the South of London, the jam and pickle workers, biscuit makers, bottle washers, tin box makers, cocoa makers, distillery workers, rag pickers, " sweated " and unorganized women and girls, earning from 5/- to 10/- a week, emulated the action of the London transport workers, and came out on strike. The League seized its opportunity, and sent out its organizers. "A strike of unorganized workers," Miss Macarthur declared, " should always be utilized to form a trade union amongst them. In such cases one is frequently able to point out that had an organization existed the strike in all probability would not have occurred, because the employer would not so confidently have ventured to assail the rights of trade union workers. It is quite a mistaken idea that strikes are caused by trade unions " The strikers joined the Federation, and secured advances of wages from 1/- to 4/- a week In Bermondsey alone, the sum amounted to no less than £7,000 in one year, covering 1,500 women and a score of firms.

The " Millwall " strike was a typical one. Some fifty women employed in a food-preserving factory, indignant at the action of the firm in introducing young girls at low rates on to adult women's machines, had come out on strike. They were followed by the whole body of 1,200 workers—men, women, girls and boys. The Federation, and the National Union of Gasworkers' and General Labourers' Union, flew to the rescue, and between them enrolled the strikers, about 960 women joining the women's union. The League appealed for funds, and raised a sum of £400. Three public meetings were held in Poplar Town Hall, and a great demonstration took place in Trafalgar Square, when Mr. Will Crooks, M P., Mr R C. Phillimore, L.C C., Mr. John Scurr, Miss Lena Ashwell, Miss Mary Moore, and other public personages, came forward in support of the strikers " Both men and women fought pluckily, and with perfect loyalty to their trade unions and one another. . . . No one who was present could ever forget the splendid enthusiasm of the three meetings in the Poplar Town Hall. The struggle ended in a complete victory for the strikers, and the women secured not only the object for which they struck, but advances of wages from 1/- to 2/- a week on time-rates and from 10 to 25 per cent on piece-rates. The secretary of the Millwall Branch reported at the end of the year that "our members have only to complain and things are put straight."

The next event was the revolt of the London County Council charwomen Miss Susan Lawrence, L.C C , had struggled for many months to improve the conditions of employment in elementary schools, but apparently without effect. In desperation, she advised the women to organize, and they formed a branch of the Federation. The effect was almost instantaneous. With the union behind them, they had no difficulty in securing practically the whole of their demands, including a minimum wage of 14/- a week, full pay during holidays, and direct employment by the Council. Miss Susan Lawrence now joined the League, and became one of its most distinguished members.

The movement was not confined to London "Girls are joining the Federation," wrote a Scotch correspondent, describing a strike of unorganized net-workers at Kilburnie, "who used to sneer at the members. . . . The enthusiasm and courage of these girls is magnificent When the strike had lasted some twenty weeks, five of the six employers issued post-cards inviting the girls to resume work at the old rates. This caused so much indignation that people came from far and near to wait for black-legs. As a result, there was a skirmish with the police, batons being drawn, one policeman, one girl and a man all being carried home with their heads split open. It will be noticed that the disturbance was caused by the general public, not by the strikers, who, during the whole of the dispute, displayed the greatest self-restraint." The League and the Scottish Trades Union Congress raised a strike fund of £1,300. The strike lasted twenty-two weeks, and ended in a complete victory for the workers.

The achievement was even more remarkable in the Black Country. Under the Trade Boards Act of 1909, a minimum wage of 2½d. an hour had just been fixed for the Cradley Heath chain-makers.

"The workers' representative agreed to the minimum, low as it is, because it was felt that it would give a basis upon which improvement in the future could be built Absolute chaos had previously reigned in the trade, and any ordered system of payment was felt to be welcome The three months' probationary period for giving notice of objections expired on August 17 No sooner were the legal rates definitely notified than a number of employers in the trade issued agreements which they asked the women to sign, contracting out of the minimum wage for a further period of six months, as is allowed by the Act It was felt that, apart altogether from disappointment at the delay, there was very grave danger that during this additional period of six months still greater stocks of chains might be accumulated, and when the rates became definitely binding a lengthy period of unemployment might result   It was therefore decided to recommend those women who had signed the agreements to cancel their signatures, and those who had refused to sign to maintain their attitude.   Some 500 or 600 women were members, and about an equal number were non-unionists A meeting was arranged with the Manufacturers' Association, at which an agreement, perhaps unique in the annals of trade unionism, were submitted by the employers, and finally signed by both parties to the dispute   The Manufacturers' Association undertook to recommend its members to pay the minimum rate so long as the workers fulfilled an undertaking to support financially all women who refused to work for less than the rates   This practically amounted to a request from the employers that the Workers' Trade Union should protect them against the non-associated employers   It was only after long consideration that the workers decided to agree to the proposal   The non-unionists seemed a serious difficulty in the way, but the public response to the appeal for funds issued by the Women's Trade Union League was so generous, nearly £4,000 being collected, that we were able to fight to a finish ; and after thirteen weeks' struggle the women returned to work victorious, every employer in the district having signed the White List ''

'' Naturally the result of the dispute has been a tremendous influx of members, and we have now on our lists about 1,700 ''

'' Though the branch is not as strong as it was immediately after the chain strike,'' two years later wrote Mr Sitch, Secretary of the Chainmakers' and Strikers' Association, and also acting for the women, '' it has maintained a very good membership.   Our members state that without the Federation the benefit of the minimum wage would be lost in many cases.   Recently the minimum has been increased from 2½d   an hour, or 11/3 for a 54 hours' week, to 2¾d , or 12s 4½d. for a 54-hours' week   When one remembers that before the Federation came to the district the prevailing wage was 5s or 6s a week, one can only sum up the change as a marvellous transformation ''*

The revolt of the Cradley Heath hollow-ware workers, encouraged by the success of the chain-makers, followed immediately afterwards.   The women formed a branch of the Federation and, '' as the result of conferences between twenty employers of the district and the women's union, it was agreed to establish a minimum wage of 10/- a week of 54 hours in the summer of 1912. ''

'' This agreement was entered into, not because we considered the amount adequate, but because we considered it would give our members a starting-point from which they could advance in the future, and because, miserable as the amount was, it represented an increase for a very large number of women The best employers conceded the rate at once, but several still refused to adopt it   In October 840 men engaged in the trade handed in their notices for a 10 per cent increase on their wages, and a 54-hour week.   Twelve of the forty-five firms conceded their terms at once, leaving 600 men on strike   As a result, many women workers were asked to do men's work, and there seemed a likelihood that the employers would try to use women's labour to defeat the men We decided, therefore, that we should call the women out to demand the 10s minimum for a 54-hour week, and at the same time support the men in their demands   All the women called out received strike benefit

* *Annual Reports of the National Federation of Women Workers*, 1912-1914

" There was, however, another body of women and girls, those whose work automatically came to an end because of the strike of the other workers, and these were not entitled to any benefit in the usual way An appeal on behalf of these workers was made by the *Daily Citizen*. The paper also gave splendid help by sending their special correspondent to the district, and giving publicity to the conditions under which the women worked The Women's Trade Union League also issued an appeal which met with a most generous response "*

In 1914, this branch included a membership of nearly 1,000 members. " Though rates of wages have been established by law for this industry," the secretary of the Cradley Heath branch wrote, " it is always the Federation that has to see that the agreements signed by the employers were carried out. The minimum wage was paid at once in all cases taken up by the Federation." The Federation was further able to check such abuses as " deferring the payment of the minimum wage to workers after they had reached the age of 18," or " putting women on men's work at tremendously reduced prices."

The Federation followed the example of the League in co-operating so far as possible with the skilled men's societies, and its members gave active support to the policy of the joint-organization for men and women employed in the same trade or industry. More than once a branch of the Federation was transferred to a men's society, which had decided to open its doors to women. Thus, when the Amalgamated Society of Bleachers, Dyers and Finishers began to organize women, the Federation agreed that " the time had now come when the interests of trade unionism could best be served if all the women engaged in the bleaching and dyeing industry in Scotland were enrolled in the same unions as the men;* and, early in 1914, " by arrangement with the Amalgamated Society of Dyers, Bleachers and Kindred Trades, which very generously made a grant of £250, several hundreds of women, who had been organized as members of the National Federation, were transferred to their organization." In the same year, a London branch of upholstresses was transferred from the Federation to the Amalgamated Union of Upholsterers, which had recently decided to organize women. " It is hoped that now that men and women are organized in one union," the Federation reported, " good progress may be made, and a successful and powerful organization built up throughout the trade."*

" They are like a lot of sheep," declared an employer in condemning the women's trade union movement. " Women much above them in class organize them, and then hand them over to pay their subscriptions into the treasury of the men's union, and I doubt very much whether they know what they are doing, or get very much out of it." The unusual degree of hostility shown by employers to the Federation was, perhaps, the best testimony to

* *Annual Report of the National Federation of Women Workers, 1914*

the success of its policy. " It has frequently been experienced," declared Miss Macarthur, " that women who form a union, or may be leading it, are victimized by an employer, who would not do so in the case of a man." In a typical example, " while the masters' association, recognizing the men's union, voluntarily sat around an arbitration table to discuss grievances and agreed to minimum rates of wages and other important questions, they absolutely declined to admit representatives from the women workers, also organized, despite the fact that the men themselves tried to get the employers to recognize that women should be included in the agreements." Women were, however, not prevented from joining the Federation " An encouraging feature of the present movement," Miss Macarthur wrote in 1914, " is that where workers now are organized their impulse is to organize all the other unorganized women in their district." Some of the greatest difficulties to be overcome were those in the traditional women's trades. Not only were there no men who set the example, but other circumstances were especially unfavourable to organization. Amongst domestic workers, the personal relationship to the employer, together with the living-in system, made this class of worker almost impossible to approach. Nor did the domestic servant, whose employer was in most cases at least as anxious to keep her as she was to stay, feel the usual need for combination. At the outbreak of war, the Federation included between seventy and eighty branches and over 10,000 paying members, whilst almost equal strides had been made by other general labour unions.

The women's movement of 1910 was, however, not confined to unorganized trades The female membership of all trade unions which had only risen from 166,000 to 183,000 between 1906 and 1910, nearly doubled in the next four years. The cotton unions alone increased their membership in four years by over 50,000 women. The campaigns of that period against " non-union " labour were chiefly directed against women, and men struck work failing other means of persuasion Men members were enjoined to persuade, or to compel, their women-folk to join the union; and some local associations went so far as to lay down that " no person shall be eligible for any official position, whose wife and children, if working, are not members of the union." The comparative weakness in organization amongst warpers and winders was directly attributed to the fact that men were not employed in these trades. Similar campaigns were pursued with equal vigour by non-textile unions, which were building up for the first time a substantial female membership The most successful of these societies were the National Union of Boot and Shoe Operatives, with a female membership of 9,000 in 1914, the National Union of Printing and Paper Workers (formerly the Printers' Warehousemen and Cutters), which now counted some 6,800 women, and the two important distributive unions, the National Union of Shop Assistants and the Amalgamated Union of Co-operative Employees, each with some 8,000 women members.

Until about 1910, a women's standard of wages—or regulation of any kind—was mostly conspicuous by its absence, and practically confined to one or two textile trades The piece-work " list " of the Blackburn Cotton Weavers' Association dated from 1853, and the weavers' uniform " list " from 1892. In these " lists," no distinction was made of sex or age, and women weavers employed on 4-loom machines earned as much as men, or from about 22/- to 32/- a week. The earnings of men and women cotton weavers were said by some critics to represent a women's and not a men's standard, and women were accused of having retarded men's progress. In so far as they were more backward than men in organization, the charge was not entirely unfounded; but the achievement of the cotton weavers during the nineteenth century was none the less remarkable. From being one of the worst-paid classes of workers, they had pushed up wages until in the beginning of the present century they enjoyed earnings at least as large as the men's average in all trades, and more than twice as high as the women's average in all trades. The full measure of the trade union achievement may, perhaps, be most clearly shown by a comparison between the organized Lancashire and the unorganized Bristol district, where cotton weavers still belonged to the class of " sweated " workers. In 1914, weavers' earnings in Bristol were as low as 10/- a week, and men weavers had been driven from employment. Weavers' earnings were, in fact, below the minimum rates fixed about that time for " sweated " workers under the Trade Boards Act.

The piece-work scales of the Huddersfield woollen weavers dated from 1881, but applied only to this district. There were two scales, one for men and another for women, with a difference of about 10 per cent between the rates for identical items of work. For this reason, although the terms were in operation, the agreement was never actually signed by representatives of the General Union of Textile Workers. The piece-work price lists of the Leicester Hosiery Workers' Amalgamation similarly dated from the latter part of last century, but men and women were mostly employed on different work, and the women's rates were fixed so as to work out at about one-half the men's standard. Until 1910, women's achievement in most industries was confined to casual advances of wages, which in the absence of a minimum wage, or basic rate, were practically impossible to enforce beyond the immediate period of agitation. These advances, moreover, seldom applied to more than one or two firms. Even in the cotton industry, amongst comparatively well-organized card and blowing-room operatives, there was no uniform "list" for women until after 1910

A women's wages movement now became general, extending to non-textile as well as to textile workers. As a result of arbitration, the National Union of Boot and Shoe Operatives secured its first scale of minimum rates for women in 1912. This scale applied only to the Nottingham district, but its terms were soon extended elsewhere; and, in 1914, it was embodied with certain advances in a national agreement. The rates varied according as the women were employed on first-class or second-class operations, ranging from 14/- to 18/- a week, or 14/- to 17/- a week for women from 18 to 21 years of age. The figures roughly represented about two-thirds of the men's standard, but men had the advantage of piece-work statements, which were not drawn up for women who were similarly employed on piece-work. The Union took the opportunity to confine women more strictly than before to their own departments, and a clause of the national agreement laid down that " it is undesirable that females should be employed amongst male operatives in the Clicking, Press, Lasting and Finishing departments of the trade, in which male labour is now almost exclusively employed; and the Conference therefore recommends that where females are now so employed, such conditions shall gradually cease by effluxion of time, and that in future no fresh female labour shall be employed in the aforesaid departments."

The movement was less successful in the printing trades. The London Society of Compositors rigidly enforced its rule that women should be paid " strictly in accordance with scale," but it counted only two or three women members. Elsewhere, and for other groups of women, wages were practically unregulated. A beginning towards standardization was, however, made in London and Edinburgh. In the summer of 1914, the London branch of the National Union of Printers' Warehousemen and Cutters drew up a scale fixing a rate of 17/- a week of 51 hours for bookfolders and sewers, 18/- for vellum sewers, 20/- to 30/- for forewomen, whilst a corresponding piece-work statement was drawn up for piece-workers. The terms were not formally agreed to by employers, but in practice they were enforced by the Union for its own members. In the provinces, rates varied indefinitely below the London standard. In 1913, a *maximum* wage of 13/6 a week, after five years of experience, had actually been discussed by the Printing and Kindred Trades Federation for the Derby district, but the terms were indignantly repudiated by the Warehousemen and Cutters' Union on the ground that its members had not been consulted. The condition of a five years' experience was especially criticized by members as " an impossible learnership period for women." The same year, 1914, the Edinburgh Typographical Association concluded an agreement with the local Master Printers' Association, fixing a minimum wage of 17/- a week for women compositors. This rate represented rather more than one-half of the men's standard.

The Society of Male and Female Pottery Workers was as yet in too weak a position to enforce a standard for female, or even for male members, and women's wages were shockingly low. Neither the practice of " allowances " to employers (women employed on men's work returned about one-third of the piece-rate, or, in the case of young girls, two-thirds), nor the old " butty " system, by which women were employed by men as assistants, made it easy to standardize wages. Amongst smaller unions, the Mutual Association of Cigar Makers was successful in enforcing a piece-work statement for female as well as for male members, but there was a difference of about 20 per cent. between the men's and the women's rate for identical brands of cigars.

Similar campaigns with the object of fixing rates of wages were opened by the " black-coated " unions. The postal unions had the least difficult task, scales of wages being laid down by the Post Office ranging from 16/- to 56/- a week for men, and from 14/- to 36/- for women employed on corresponding work. The National Union of Clerks stood boldly for " equal pay " and claimed a minimum of 35/- a week for men and women clerks, but had no means of enforcing its claim even in trade union and socialist offices. The National Union of Shop Assistants adopted the opposite policy of a double standard, but the decision was not arrived at without serious discussion. The movement began at the annual general meeting of 1908, when a minimum wage committee (to which two women were later co-opted) was appointed to report on the following matters :—

(a) Should a minimum wage be fixed for each trade?
(b) Should there be a district minimum for women?
(c) Should it be fixed for each district?
(d) Should the wage be calculated weekly on the basis of a 60 hour week?
(e) Should the number of apprentices or juniors be regulated?

The committee issued a confidential circular, asking members for detailed information on all matters of wages, commissions, premiums, " living-in " and similar allowances The returns showed an average of earnings which ranged from 5d. to 9¾d. per hour for men and 3¾d to 5½d for women. These earnings, however, represented comparatively well-paid classes of workers.

Large numbers of women were known to earn wages as low as from 5/- to 10/- for a week of 70 to 80 hours. The committee, which reported in 1910, therefore, decided to fix two separate scales on the basis of a three-quarter standard for women, and gave its reasons as follows :—

" On this question of women's rates we regret we have been unable to come to a final agreement

" In the case of women their general economic position complicates the question greatly   The circle of the commercial system is vicious, and the whole question of women's labour is not so much a single proposition as a series of problems.   If it were possible to insist on the ideal—equal payment for equal work—we agree that even more might be driven on to the surplus labour market than at present.   For the rank and file we are unanimous in recommending lower rates   In this case the test is output, and the question of physique comes in.   Women are not equal to men in physical strength, and accordingly when this governs value, they are not worth so much as men to an employer of labour.   In addition to this the field of women's labour is handicapped by the greater supply, including the pin-money women, and the result is that the prevailing wage rate of the average woman does not bear even the men's ratio in intrinsic value   For the sake of a practical figure, therefore, your committee have unanimously assessed these women's wages on a three-fourths basis   Even if this cannot be obtained a great improvement will have been achieved

" With regard to manageresses, however, the Committee is divided   The majority feel that the ideal must in this case be insisted upon , and commercial worth compelled, if possible, to follow intrinsic value   In many cases, especially where correct training has been acquired, and the question is merely one of ability, women's capabilities are quite equal to men's   In such cases, as in the management of a business, the value is the same, and the moral right should be maintained   The majority on the Committee, therefore, urge manageresses to demand men's rates   On the other hand, for the same reason that the majority recommend a three-fourths basis for the rank and file women, i.e., ' for the sake of a practical figure,' the minority are in favour of this three-fourths figure being applied to manageresses also.   They consider that they need only bring to your notice the fact that 100 per cent. of the manageresses, from whom the Committee had returns, are below the suggested scale, to demonstrate the strength of their position   On this point the Committee leave the Conference to decide

" In the mantle trade we find that for several reasons the rates of pay rule higher than in other departments where women are employed, and we feel justified in recommending a scale which approximates more closely to men's rates

"To prevent, if possible, the employment of women at lower rates in what are at present exclusively considered men's departments, we recommend the adoption of the principle in operation in Victoria, Australia, i e., that when women are employed in such departments as the dresses, silks, ' Manchester ' and linens, they shall be paid at the same rate as men.   We fear that if this is not done there would be a gradual displacement of men by women workers, with the sole object on the employer's part of reducing wage-cost."

The minimum rates laid down by the committee were 18/- a week for women, and 24/- for men, with higher rates for special classes of workers   In London, these rates should be supplemented by a sum of 5/- a week, the effect of which would be to raise the women's minimum from a three-quarters to a four-fifths standard. In the case of "living-in" workers, deductions from wages should be allowed for board and lodging amounting to 13/- a week for men (15/- in London), and 10/- for women (12/- in London). Other provisions laid down that the number of apprentices should be limited to one junior per ten seniors in departmental stores or drapery establishments, and one junior per three seniors in small shops. Further, apprenticeship "should not be permitted to be entered upon after the seventeenth birthday." The committee was reappointed in order to carry out the recommendations of its report; whilst district committees were set up with powers (subject to approval by the national committee) to fix local rates not lower than the national minimum.

Even a three-fourths standard was, however, almost impossible to enforce for women members. This failure was attributed by men at least partly to women's indifference. "The ultimate future of the average woman is marriage," an experienced member declared, "an event which terminates (or should do so) any further idea of employment. The idea being well rooted in the average girl's mind, she naturally recognizes her position and acts accordingly, and just jogs along, not endeavouring in any way to specialize or become fitted for a position. The 'flapper' brigade are hopeless to themselves, an insult to their sex and becoming a menace to their men-folk by reason of their incompetence and consequent cheapness."* The suggestion made by the Chairman of the Minimum Wage Committee that women had not taken their part in the minimum wage campaign was, however, indignantly repudiated by Mrs. Bessie Ward, the leader of the feminist party. "I want to say," she declared, "that in connection with your disputes, the same effort is not made to bring the women into line on the basis of the trade union standard as has been put forth with respect to the men The difficulties are greater with regard to the women, and it is because the difficulties are greater, and because of the continual influx of women who have to be educated, that the task of organizing women is so extremely hard. In one or two districts lately, women organizers have not been drafted into the districts. There has been a fear on the part of the men, that if they included the women they would lose the day, and they have been inclined to go for their own reforms and to leave the women in the background. It is four times as hard to organize women than it is to organize men, and we should therefore receive a proportionate amount of help." Miss Talbot, one of the two women members of the Minimum Wage Committee, was inclined to blame the women, but urged that women organizers should be appointed. "Reviewing the work of the Minimum Wage Committee, the apathy of the

* Article by Mr. Bolton in *The Shop Assistant* (March, 1915)

women has been a matter of sincere regret.   As an illustration, I have in mind the negotiations which took place with one large firm.   Good conditions were won for the men, but in spite of the efforts that were made on behalf of the women, we were unable to induce them to formulate any demands or to secure any advances for them.   This is only typical of what has been taking place in many districts, as our organizers could testify.   Women accept a lower standard of comfort or are partially dependent on parents and do not know the value of their work.   Every local Minimum Wage Committee should have, if possible, a fair proportion of women members, and if women are involved, the services of women as well as men organizers should be concentrated on the work."*

More important, however, in its practical results was the joint campaign of the Amalgamated Union of Co-operative Employees and the Women's Co-operative Guild, whose members now claimed a minimum wage for all women co-operative workers. The movement began in 1896, when a claim was put forward by the Union for a minimum rate of 24/- a week; but the rate was not enforced for men, and did not even apply to women, many of whom earned as little as 7/- or 8/- a week.   The women's movement was not started until 1906, when the representatives of the Women's Co-operative Guild at the Ipswich Co-operative Congress succeeded in carrying a resolution in favour of a minimum wage for all women co-operative workers.   This resolution was reaffirmed at each successive Congress up to 1912, at which meeting a committee was appointed, composed of representatives of the United Co-operative Board, the Women's Co-operative Guild and the Amalgamated Union of Co-operative Employees, and the famous co-operative scale was drawn up, fixing minimum rates of wages for men and women employees.   These rates ranged from 6/- to 24/- a week for men from the age of 14 to 21, and from 5/- to 17/- a week for women from the age of 14 to 20.   Before the outbreak of war, the standard had been adopted by no fewer than 240 co-operative societies, including the Co-operative Wholesale Society, and covered over 12,000 women.   "This quarterly meeting," declared a delegate when the scale was adopted by the C.W.S. in 1912, "will go down to history as having given a living wage to all the female workers of the C.W S , and a message of hope to all outside."   The expression was not too strong, and a standard was laid down for the first time which could be applied to all classes of women workers

In the large body of unorganized trades, however, the general labour unions had little or no prospect of enforcing a

* Article in *The Shop Assistant,* 1915.

reasonable standard of wages. The Workers' Union and certain other societies concluded an agreement with the Midlands Engineering Employers' Federation in 1913, fixing rates of 23/- a week for men and 12/- for women. The terms set the standard for metal workers in the Midlands district, but this agreement covered an exceptionally wide field. For the most part, agreements related only to one or two firms, and the terms were sometimes grossly inadequate. Rates of wages as low as 8/- a week were agreed by general labour unions in 1914. Women were badly-paid because they were unorganized, and unorganized because they were badly-paid Escape from this vicious circle seemed to be almost impossible. For this reason, the Federation was amongst the earliest advocates of a legal minimum wage, and took a leading part in promoting the Trade Boards Act of 1909. Miss Macarthur, accompanied by other members of the Federation, was one of the principal witnesses before the Select Committee on Home Work of 1907-1908. " My experience," she stated, " is that in the unskilled women's trades there is no standard by which wages are computed, that there is very seldom any uniformity whatsoever in home-work or in factory work." In illustration of her statement, Miss Macarthur gave a number of instances In the case of two clothing factories, there was a difference of 100 per cent. in the rates paid by a " union " and a " non-union " firm. In the case of two cartridge factories, the first firm paid 100 per cent more than the second firm for the same work in one department, but 40 to 50 per cent. less than the second firm in another department. In a tin factory at Hull, where the employer arbitrarily passed from piece-work to time-work, he gave as his reason that " the workers took advantage of the piece-work rates to earn too much, and that some of them had earned 16/- or 17/- a week." The women's time-rate was 6/- a week. In a bottle-filling factory, where the piece-work earnings of the women were from 10/- to 12/- a week, the employer gave notice one morning " that the piece-rates would be reduced by one-half," as he had come to the conclusion that " the bottles could be filled with blacking by girls under 18." He, therefore, intended " to dismiss all the women, and in future only to employ girls under 18 " On a threat of publicity, however, the employer changed his mind. The women joined the Federation, and were at once taken back at their old rates of wages. Even the good employer could not rise above the level of unscrupulous competitors. " We will pay equal rates to what is being paid by other firms," more than one employer had stated, " if you will prove it to us." Employers were, moreover, discovering that the worst-paid workers were not necessarily the most economical " The badly-equipped employer, who paid the worst wages, made the smallest profit " A model employer declared that " the conditions I give my workers are not philanthropy—there is 5 per cent. in it." Miss Macarthur advocated a legal minimum wage, not only for its own sake, but as a starting-point for organization in " sweated " trades. " If we raised their wages even a very little, we would be able to organize them and so improve their general conditions." The Trade Boards Bill became law in 1909, and the Federation turned its attention to the administration of the Act " Not only was there need," declared its leaders, " for the sweated workers to unite and strive to secure the passing of this Trade Boards Bill which was to assist them so materially, but also there is now just as great, and indeed even a greater, need for them to unite and strive to secure its proper administration."* Chain-making, machine lace-making, paper box making, and wholesale and bespoke tailoring were immediately scheduled as " sweated " trades, food preserving, sugar confectionery, shirt making and hollow-ware making being added to the list in 1913 † Mr. J. J. Mallon, secretary of the Anti-Sweating League, also an advisory member of the executive committee of the Federation, acted on most trade boards as secretary to the workers' side; and to his untiring devotion the real success in raising wages was very largely due. He estimated that in three years the average weekly earnings were raised from 5/- to 11/3½ in chain making, from 7/- or 8/- to 11/11 in lace making, from 8/5 to 13/- in paper box making, and from 8/- to 14/1 in wholesale and bespoke tailoring. Nor was the Act disappointing in its effect on organization. The female membership of the tailors' unions, which up to this time had numbered only a few hundreds, suddenly grew to thousands The same effect, as we have seen, followed in the Black Country, where after twenty years of fruitless effort, women chain-makers at last succeeded in establishing a sound and stable organization.

The campaign for amending the Truck Acts was only second in importance. The National Union of Shop Assistants, whose members were chiefly concerned, now took the lead, and Miss Margaret Bondfield, assistant general secretary of the union, was appointed a witness before the Truck Committee of 1907. Her evidence was based on her own experience. Fines, she told the Committee, would amount to as much as 5/- out of wages of 10/- a week. " For being late," the fine would be 6d., or for each five minutes 2d " For addressing a customer as *miss* instead of *madam*," " not using paper or string with economy," " wrongly

* *Annual Report of National Federation of Women Workers,* 1911
† The Provisional Order Bill of 1913 included calendering and machine ironing in laundries, but the latter trade was withdrawn from the list by the Select Committee of the House of Commons

adding up bills," "wrongly addressing parcels," it would be 3d.
" For answering the shop walker impolitely," it would be 1/-,
" for losing a billhead," 5/-. Miss Bondfield criticized the whole
system of fines as unjust to the worker, and ineffective or unnecessary for discipline. " In my experience of business life,
the mistakes which occur are mistakes mainly due to either
nervousness or overwork, for which fines are absolutely no remedy
whatsoever. . . . One employer had publicly stated that his
reason for abolishing fines was that it was no incentive to discipline
whatever, but that the assistants felt themselves to be quits, they
had discharged their obligation for whatever they had done
amiss . . . If assistants wilfully or deliberately disobey orders
they are liable to dismissal, and that is infinitely better for the
discipline of the staff than these petty fines." The " living-in "
system, affecting some 400,000 out of 750,000 shop assistants,
was equally condemned. " I was put into a room with a woman
of mature age who led a life of a most undesirable kind. That
was my first experience of a ' living-in ' house. There was
another girl in the same room who was suffering from consumption. I was in that house for three years and could have been
out any night during those three years without the firm knowing
anything about it. Not only are the assistants inadequately
catered for, but in order to maintain health they have to spend
considerable part of their small money wage in the purchase of
nourishing food. In a number of West End houses, this need
is exploited by the employer as another source of profit making.
In the worst houses the hardships of the assistants are indescrib-
able. Frankly, from my point of view, actual immorality would
not be so poisonous and injurious to all that is pure and best in
life as the kind of atmosphere which so many young girls are
brought into in these living-in barracks. . . . The environment
creates an over-sexed condition of mind and body from which the
ordinary work girl with her rompings in the street and her very
much rougher life, perhaps is entirely free." Miss Bondfield,
therefore, proposed " to extend to shop workers the provisions
of the Truck Act, by which their wages shall be paid *in full* in
current coin of the realm and not partly in kind, i.e., in board
and lodging." This proposal for abolishing the " living-in "
system was adopted by a minority of the Truck Committee, but
the recommendation came to nothing. The shop assistants,
therefore, continued their agitation right down to the outbreak
of war. At a great demonstration organized by the League in
1914, and attended by workers of every kind, it was unanimously
resolved that " all fines and deductions from wages and the living-
in system shall be abolished by law."

The Shop Assistants' Union, on the other hand, was success-

ful in promoting the Shop Hours Act of 1910, by which shop
workers became entitled, for the first time, to one half-holiday
a week and to stated meal times.   The original Bill, as introduced by Sir Charles Dilke, included a further clause limiting
hours of work to sixty a week.   Hours of work in shops were
exceptionally long, amounting to seventy and eighty a week, but
the opposition of employers was too strong, and this clause was
withdrawn by the Government.   The Shop Hours Act, 1913,
which allowed an alternative scheme, limiting hours of work to
sixty-five a week, applied only to restaurant workers.   The
" early closing " campaign of the shopkeepers received little or
no support from shop assistants, who maintained that the provisions afforded no real protection to the workers, who might or
might not be detained after the shop was closed.   The National
Union of Shop Assistants was one of the first unions to claim
legal protection for its members, without regard to sex.

The amendment of the Factory and Workshops Act was another
matter of interest to industrial women's organizations.   The
Federation programme included such measures as further protection against accidents, a break during, or the shortening of,
the " five-hour spell," and the abolition of overtime.   There was
a similar and most successful agitation to amend the National
Health Insurance Act of 1911.   The Federation had been
registered as an Approved Society under the Act, count-
ing in 1914 as many as 20,000 " insured " members.
A large number of these were married women, upon
whom the defects of the Act pressed with unusual severity
By an oversight of the Government, which apparently
had seen no reason to take women's advice, the " incapacity "
due to pregnancy or to the after-effects of confinement, had been
ignored in the estimates for sickness.   The result was a false
actuarial basis, which threatened with early insolvency all societies
composed of married women   At a conference of trade union
approved societies, summoned by the League, it was claimed that
" such financial rearrangements should be made as will enable
societies to meet without fear of deficit all just claims from women
members, and that adequate provision from national funds should
be made for women during pregnancy and when incapacitated as
the result of complications arising out of confinement."   Miss
Macarthur represented the Federation on the Departmental Committee which was subsequently appointed to inquire into and
report upon " the alleged excessive claims in respect of sickness
benefit "   As a result of the campaign a large part of the women's
demands were embodied in the new Act of 1912

Women had, meanwhile, begun to find their feet within the
joint organizations.   The old criticism by Mrs Paterson that

they " took no part in management " still substantially held good.
It was not a question of sex disabilities Women were necessarily admitted to membership on a reduced scale of contributions
and benefits—commonly about one half of men's—and for this
reason it was provided by some societies that they should rank
only as half members at delegate meetings or be disqualified for
certain offices; but these cases were comparatively rare, and the
tendency was to remove old disabilities. In some tailors' unions,
indeed, where badly-paid men as well as women were admitted
as low-scale contributors, it was not unknown for men to rank
as *half* members and women as *full* members, because they " were
less likely than men to take advantage of their opportunities."

The failure of women to play an effective part in management
was becoming, nevertheless, more and more conspicuous by
reason of their growing numbers. The Northern Counties
Weavers' Amalgamation, of whose 200,000 members women
counted two-thirds, was entirely controlled by men.' In one or
two districts, such as Oldham, Wigan or Manchester, where
men formed less than 10 per cent. of members, women were
elected to district committees. The Oldham Weavers' Association
could boast a woman president in the 'nineties, but her case was
almost unique. The " textile hall," which had replaced the old-
fashioned public-house as the place of meeting, still preserved
in many districts something of its sanctity as a men's club, and
it needed not a little courage on the part of women even to stand
for election. The nomination of a woman candidate at Heywood
in 1913 appealed to men members on the score of its novelty,
and she was returned at the top of the poll; but a first woman
to be elected the same year at Bury caused the " boos " of men
members to be heard all over the town. Women members had,
however, themselves at least partly to blame. The secretary of
an important local association told an American visitor in 1908
that women would come freely to report grievances and collect
benefits, but " although the division of membership was the same
as it was in the trade, or about nine women to one man, and
the women had gained an increase of 50 per cent. in wages since
the union was started twenty years ago, they were too indifferent
to the success of the union to come out to meetings. And that
year they put in such a poor appearance at the annual meeting
. that the woman who had represented them for fourteen years at
their trades council was defeated and a man sent in her place."*
Generally speaking, the attitude of women was one of indifference,
" or at least of complete confidence in the ability and integrity
of their men officials."

A feminist movement was, indeed, so little apparent amongst

* *American Bulletin of Labour,* July, 1919 Page 10.

E

women cotton operatives, that it is worth while to record the slight skirmish which took place between the great Northern Counties Weavers' Amalgamation and the little Manchester and Salford Power Loom Weavers' Association.   This all-women's society, established under the auspices of the local Women's Trade Union Council in 1903, had for several years been the only local association of weavers.   Its members, therefore, approached the Northern Counties Weavers' Amalgamation with a request for affiliation   This request was refused apparently on grounds of finance.   The women's contribution was only 2d. a week, and 3d. was the minimum advocated by the Amalgamation.   Their benefits further included "sick pay"—a luxury almost unheard of amongst cotton operatives.   In spite of its reckless finance, the little society prospered exceedingly, so that in 1908 it had 1,200 members.   The Northern Counties Amalgamation, reconsidering its decision, now approached the women and reopened the question of affiliation.   By this time, however, women had grown ambitious.   They claimed, not only the usual degree of local autonomy, but the right to appoint a woman secretary and a woman representative on the Northern Counties Executive Committee   Men officials were seriously alarmed.   They once more drew back, and started a rival association in Manchester, even persuading members to leave the women's society.   The result was most unfortunate, and for many years the female membership of the two associations was actually less than that of the women's society at the time of the dissension.

Outside the textile trades, where trade unionism was a comparatively recent growth, old traditions were not so hard to break down.   Both sides were dissatisfied with the women's position, and it became common about this time for special machinery to be devised with the deliberate object of encouraging women to come forward.   A separate *female section* or all-women's branch, with a women's committee and a woman secretary, was a usual device of this kind.   Amongst societies who made this experiment one of the first was the National Union of Boot and Shoe Operatives   Its Leicester women's branch had every appearance of success   It included over 1,000 members—active and reliable trade unionists—when unfortunately a difference of opinion on the question of piece-work arose between the national executive and the women's committee.   Members of either sex were pieceworkers.   Both were protected by a guaranteed minimum wage, but men members further enjoyed the protection of certain piecework statements drawn up by the Union for men's departments. A similar advantage was now claimed by women, but the national executive apparently saw no need to move.   It would even seem that men members disapproved, or at least were not inclined to encourage, women's employment on piece-work. The consequent speeding-up was believed to be bad for their health, and high wages none too good for their morals—tempting them to leave home for industry. The quarrel was no doubt aggravated by personal animosities. It ended in the women's branch leaving the union in a body, and setting up as the Independent National Union of Women Boot and Shoe Workers, whilst another women's branch was opened by the union at Leicester. Branches composed entirely of women, however, suffered as a rule from too little and not too much vitality. For one reason or another, such experiments were mostly given up; and men and women deliberately preferred to mix together in the branches. Without this close association, they believed that women's interests were liable to be overlooked, or their point of view to be misunderstood by men. The London women members of the Printers' Warehousemen and Cutters' Union formed one of the few successful examples of an all-women's branch.

Another device of the same kind adopted about this time was that of reserving places to women on committees of management. The Dundee Jute and Flax Workers' Union, formed with the assistance of the League in 1906, modelled its constitution on that of the cotton unions, but members were determined that women should not neglect their duties. A number of places on the executive committee was, therefore, apportioned to each sex in exact proportion to its membership The rule succeeded on the whole in its object, but had to be modified afterwards because women did not come forward for election in due proportion. The reservation of places to women on committees of management was more often adopted in the case of an amalgamation between a women's society and a men's trade union. The object was to give women every chance of holding their own with men, but such provisions had commonly a fixed time-limit. Women clerks and shop assistants, amongst whom a feminist movement was most marked, were definitely opposed " to any woman being appointed to any position (other than woman organizer) simply and solely because of sex."

Women shop assistants now started a vigorous campaign of their own. Miss Macarthur, who had served her apprenticeship in the National Union of Shop Assistants, was elected a member of the executive committee in 1904, but her example was not easy to follow. Mr. James Macpherson, then general secretary of the union, criticized severely the men's attitude toward the women's movement, calling it at best negative. " They say that they are sympathetic until they are put to the test, and then impediments are put in the women's way, and because of this it requires three times as much power behind the woman before her ability is

recognized." A small group of women members, however, deter-
cined to prove their capacity for management   " There had
always been some active women in the union, but speaking
generally the average woman member did not take much interest
in her trade union.   She would attend meetings, but being usually
in a minority, she rarely expressed her views or took much interest
in the business, except to pay contributions."   On the initiative
of Mrs. Bessie Ward, a *women's council* or advisory committee, composed of women representatives of local branches,
was formed for the Manchester district in 1909.   The movement
gained ground at once. " The object of these councils," explained
Miss Talbot (afterwards president of the Union), " was simply the
educating of women members, and encouraging them to take an
active interest in their branches and district councils, the annual
conferences and the national administrative work, hoping in this
way to secure representation of women on all bodies.   We felt
that in working along these lines, rather than demanding that the
rules be altered to include proportional representation of women
on all committees, we were taking the better course.   Not making
for special treatment for women, but in allowing every opportunity for their firm development along the same lines as men."
In the space of five years, no less than twelve women's councils
were formed on this plan, whilst a women's advisory committee
was appointed in connection with the national executive.   Owing
to differences of opinion between the national executive and the
women's councils on the subject of finance, the movement met
with a set-back afterwards   It was even suggested by men members that it had already served its purpose, and that women were
in danger of becoming aggressive.   The women's advisory committee was disbanded, whilst local activities were brought to a
standstill by want of funds   The London women's council, which
later took the name of the women's advisory committee, was
alone able to carry on, and it continued to play an influential part
in the union.   " Whilst in 1909," according to Miss Talbot, " it
was found impossible to call together a meeting of twelve women,
in 1912 we organized a meeting at which we had 500—a record
unknown in the history of the movement."   Not only did the
number of women who took an active interest in the branches
increase year by year, but they succeeded in electing one, two,
and at one time three women on to the national executive committee.

Women members of the Shop Assistants' Union had always
been keen advocates for the appointment of women organizers.
Miss Bondfield held this post for a few months in 1898, but later
appointments proved to be more or less of failures, partly
because of breakdowns in health, until Miss Tynan was

appointed as national organizer in 1911. She was afterwards reappointed as one of two responsible organizers for
the London district, and filled this office successfully for five years.
Women members were, however, by no means content with a
single representative of their sex, and carried on a perpetual
agitation for further appointments. " I consider it very unfair,"
declared Mrs. Bessie Ward at the Annual Delegate Meeting of
1915, " that London and the Home Counties should have a woman
organizer, while the rest of the country is left without one. . . .
Over the last twenty-five years our male organizers have failed
to bring the women into the union in satisfactory numbers,
although we have had as many as seventy male organizers. The
men have been fairly well organized, but the great bulk of the
women workers are still outside our organization. I believe that
if you appoint the right kind of woman—one who is familiar with
shop life—you will have more success in the enrolling of women
members. The union has never appointed a woman who under-
stands the conditions of shop life, and yet you turn round and say
the women cannot do organizing work." No one disputed the
merits of a good woman organizer, but the difficulty apparently
lay in finding the right type of woman. The hesitation to appoint
women organizers was due partly at least to their heavy claims
on " sick leave," and the consequent extra cost to the union.

The new vitality now appearing in the women's movement was
reflected at meetings of the Trades Union Congress. Since the
days of Mrs. Paterson there had been practically no discussion of
women's questions. The cotton unions sent their first woman
delegate in the 'nineties, but women seldom counted more than
four or five out of as many hundred delegates, and mostly represented small and unimportant women's societies. Miss Whyte,
secretary of the London Society of Women Employed in Printing
and Bookbinding, was almost alone in raising women's questions.
In 1894, faithful to the early policy of the League, she condemned
the clause of the new Factory Act, " by which power was given
to the Home Secretary to stop women from working in unhealthy
trades "; but her motion did not find a seconder even amongst
women delegates. On another occasion, she criticized the policy
of " equal pay," on the ground that, without " equal work," the
effect might be to drive women printers from employment; but
her argument fell again on deaf ears. Small local women's societies were too unimportant for their delegates to carry weight with
the Congress, whilst the great joint-organizations were almost
entirely represented by men.

With the advent of the National Federation of Women
Workers, however, women delegates came once more to the fore.
Miss Macarthur now took her place as leader, and she spoke with

the authority of some thousands of organized women behind her. At the Nottingham Congress of 1908, a resolution was before the delegates urging that "the strongest regulations should be made in all cases where women are employed in unhealthy trades, and that women should not be permitted to work at metal polishing, turning or screwing." The final clause had been inserted on the instigation of the National Union of Brass Workers and Metal Mechanics, whose members had always refused to recognize female labour, so that the many hundreds of women who were already employed in these trades had in no way been consulted. Miss Macarthur at once challenged men's right to drive women arbitrarily from employment, to which they had grown accustomed, and she tabled an amendment to delete the objectionable final clause. The women's amendment—presumably a matter of small account—failed, however, to find its place on the agenda. Miss Macarthur rose to a point of order. "Surely that amendment is in order?" The president ruled in her favour, that "no grouping committee had the right to take out an amendment" Mr Clarke, representing the Scientific Instrument Makers, then moved the amendment, and Miss Macarthur, in supporting it, criticized severely the motion of the brass workers.

"She was amazed, she declared, that any suggestion of the kind should be made Perhaps she should not be surprised that it had emanated from the brassworkers, because there was something peculiarly appropriate in the brassworkers being identified with so impudent proposal. If the competition of women was to be got rid of in that way, why did they not go further and propose the entire abolition of women altogether? The problem of female competition was not to be solved by a resolution of this kind The only way was for the men to assist them in organizing the women as the cotton operatives had done. They should receive the same money as the men for the same class of work. They had lately been trying to get the women in effective organizations, and they had not received the assistance from the men which they had a right to expect."[*]

The amendment was carried by a large majority of delegates; but the discussion was reopened next year, when Mr. Davis, on behalf of the Birmingham Brass Workers' Union, moved "to obtain an amendment of the Factory and Workshops Act to prevent the employment of female workers in metal polishing, turning and screwing." Miss Macarthur thereupon proposed the following amendment :—

"That this Congress, deploring the growing tendency of employers in all trades to substitute underpaid women's labour for men's labour, reaffirms its belief in the principle of equal wage for equal work, and calls upon the women wage-earners in all trades to organize in Trade Unions in order to put a stop to a competition which is as unfair as it is detrimental to the interests of men and women alike
"Further, it instructs the Parliamentary Committee—
        (a) To endeavour to secure the legal prohibition of employment of young

* Report of Trades Union Congress, 1908

persons under 18 years of age of both sexes in all trades at present scheduled as dangerous or unhealthy

(b) To impress upon the Government the necessity for further safeguarding the health of the men and women employed in such trades

(c) To request that every possible precaution for the protection of such workers should be made obligatory upon employers, and that wherever possible the use of poisonous ingredients and materials be prohibited."

" She said ' Last year we voted against the resolution, and I regret to say that there has been a good deal of misunderstanding, some misconception, and a good deal of misrepresentation upon this matter. Leaflets have been circulated which tell me that we think that women are admirably fitted to be beasts of burden. I do not attempt to reply to that accusation, if the work of the Women's League during the past twenty-five years is not sufficient refutation of it I am asked if it be true that we want to get women back into the mines again We have helped to get women out of the mines, and out of the white lead works. Where there is special danger to women, where there is proof of the injurious effects to children, we are prepared to advocate that women should not be allowed to work until such time as the trade can be made a healthy one. Nor are we concerned for the interests of women alone. Take the china trade in the Potteries, it will not satisfy us to protect the women , we want to protect the men as well For my part I would rather drink tea out of a wooden cup than have a man go blind through working in the glazery. The same may be said as to the phosphorous works. The question is not, " Shall women be allowed to work in this particular trade or not?" It is, " Shall this Congress take a sane and scientific view of the problem?" Are you going to handicap women? If you pass this resolution you will not abolish the women ; but you will put a weapon in the hands of those who are fighting us in our attempts to improve the women's conditions.' "*

Mr. Davis withdrew his motion, and the amendment was carried by a show of hands.

* *Report of Trades Union Congress,* 1909

CHAPTER V.

THE CRISIS OF THE GREAT WAR.

1914—1918.

The first effect of the war was to throw thousands of women out of employment. Not only had women, unlike men, no alternative of enlisting for service, but their trades were amongst those most affected by the general dislocation of industry. In September, 1914, the net contraction of employment in all trades, which was only 8.4 per cent. for men, was 14 per cent. for women. Dressmakers, milliners, shop assistants, confectionery workers, and cotton operatives, were at first especially unfortunate. Employment was already slack in the cotton industry and the contraction now amounted to nearly 15 per cent. Men further had the advantage of the sudden expansion of the munition and army clothing trades. The figure of female unemployment remained substantially above the normal until the spring of 1915.

About this time, however, there was a rapid recovery. With the growing shortage of male labour and the enormous expansion of the munition trades, unemployment practically disappeared. Married women—especially soldiers' wives and widows—returned to industry, whilst young girls left school or home prematurely and were promoted to women's work. Even middle-class women who had no previous industrial experience were impelled by patriotism, or by economic necessity, to pass into industry, mostly entering Government offices or munition factories, or undertaking some form of land work. A considerable transfer of workers took place at the same time from one industry to another, women leaving the slack textile or clothing trades, or unpopular domestic service, to take up some form of Government or men's work. It is worth recording that, of the women employed in other trades than their own, one-third were drawn from paid or unpaid household work, and about one-quarter were domestic servants Skilled domestic servants, dressmakers and milliners, clerks and shop assistants, as well as educated women of the middle-classes were in high demand in munition factories because of their adaptable qualities In the more skilled branches of engineering, women of secondary education were definitely preferred by employers and thousands of these underwent considerable periods of special training. On ordinary munition work, however, the necessary period of probation was seldom more than about three weeks, and

68

sometimes less than three days. Between July 1914 and July 1918, it is estimated that the number of women employed in all industry had risen by a million-and-a-quarter, and of this great new army of industrial women, about 99 per cent. were employed, directly or indirectly, in place of men.*

The men's trade unions became naturally alarmed at the abnormal state of affairs. The problem was most acute in the engineering trades,† to which belonged the large body of munition workers. Not only was the influx of women to these trades overwhelming from its mere numbers, reaching to half-a-million in 1918,‡ but the feeling between employers and men trade unionists was already embittered by recent attempts to introduce women on men's work at cut-throat rates of wages. Trade union rules, as we have seen, strictly prohibited women's employment in engineering shops. They were only tolerated on automatic or boys' machines in certain "non-union" districts, or in the Birmingham small metal trades. In general engineering shops they were practically unknown. The powerful Amalgamated Society of Engineers now saw, for the first time, its members directly threatened by unfair female competition In the autumn of 1914, there was already a shortage of male labour in shell and fuse factories, whilst the adoption of modern methods of "mass" production, following the huge expansion of these trades, offered exceptional opportunities for the employment of semi-skilled and female workers. The first serious dispute took place at Crayford, where a great armament firm, without consulting the trade unions, had introduced women into shell-making at about one-half men's rates of wages In one or two districts, women had for some years been employed in *fuse*-making, but not in *shell*-making. All recent attempts, indeed, on the part of great armament firms to employ women in this way had been successfully defeated by the Amalgamated Society of Engineers. The dispute was patched up for the moment. Under a local agreement between the Engineering Employers' Federation and the Amalgamated Society of Engineers, women's employment was allowed "on purely automatic machines used for the production of repetition work," but no attempt was made to face the real issue of wages. The agreement had, moreover, a purely local application. In December, 1914, the Engineering Employers' Federation formally approached the five principal engineering unions—the Amalgamated

---

* According to the Board of Trade's estimates, the increase of women in all industry was 1,650,000. This figure was, however, exclusive of domestic service and small dressmakers' establishments, in which group the displacement was estimated at 400,000.

† The following account of "dilution" in the engineering trade is largely taken from *Women in Engineering,* by the present writer

‡ Including both private factories and Government establishments

Society of Engineers, the Amalgamated Toolmakers' Society, the Steam Engine Makers, the United Machine Workers' Association and the Scientific Instrument Makers—and proposed the terms of a national agreement   The trade. unions were asked to give a general undertaking to relax their rules and regulations for the period of the war, whilst employers on their part gave a general promise to observe standard rates of wages and to return afterwards to pre-war conditions.   Trade unionists were, however, by no means content with a mere general assurance from the Engineering Employers' Federation, which did not even represent the whole body of employers   Certain counter proposals were made by the trade unions, but these were in turn rejected by employers   A final agreement was not reached until March, 1915, when the two parties, under pressure from the Government, concluded the important " shells and fuses " agreement.   This agreement, which applied to all shell and fuse factories, provided for women's employment " on operations on which skilled men are employed at present, but which by reason of their character can be performed by semi-skilled or female labour," whilst the trade unions received in return certain definite guarantees of restoration and wages.   " Substituted " women were to be " the first affected by any necessary discharges either before or after the war period," and to receive, when employed in the place of skilled tradesmen, " the usual rates of the district for the operations performed "   The terms apparently gave satisfaction to the workers, but unfortunately nothing was said as to women employed in the place of *semi-skilled* or *unskilled* men, whose interests were only very partially represented by the Amalgamated Society of Engineers   The oversight was serious, for not only did semi-skilled men form the majority of workers in shell and fuse factories, but there was no clear line of demarcation between skilled and semi-skilled work, which might be done by either class of worker.   It is, however, extremely doubtful how far such good terms could, under any circumstances, have been secured by workers who were comparatively unorganized   The Engineering Employers' Federation immediately issued a note to its affiliated firms to the effect that " female labour undertaking the work of semi-skilled and unskilled men should be paid the recognized rates of the district for female labour or *youths* on the operations in question."   To this note, the Amalgamated Society of Engineers replied that " female labour undertaking the work of *semi-skilled* or *unskilled* men must receive the rates paid to *the men they displace* ", but, unfortunately, the protest came too late.

With a view to preventing further disputes, the Government now decided to give an official character to undertakings entered into between employers and trade unions; and, in March, 1915, Mr. Lloyd George, then Chancellor of the Exchequer, summoned an important conference of thirty-three leading trade unions, all concerned in the output of munitions or equipments of war, the outcome of which was the Treasury agreement. This famous agreement, which became afterwards the basis of the Munitions of War Act, was divided into two parts. In the first part, stoppages of work were made illegal, and arbitration was substituted for strikes and lock-outs. In the second part, the trade unions agreed " to give a favourable consideration to such changes in working conditions or trade customs as may be necessary with a view to accelerating the output of war munitions or equipments," whilst the Government undertook in return to impose certain conditions on employers, of which the following related to semi-skilled and female labour:

" The relaxation of existing demarcation restrictions and admission of semi-skilled or female labour shall not affect adversely the rate customarily paid for the job."

The Amalgamated Society of Engineers further secured a pledge that " the Government will undertake to use its influence to secure the restoration of previous conditions in every case after the war."

Trade union claims appeared at last to be satisfied. To women suffragists, indeed, the terms seemed too good to be true; and Miss Sylvia Pankhurst, secretary of the East London Women's Suffrage Federation, wrote to Mr. Lloyd George asking for an exact interpretation of the words " shall not adversely affect the rate customarily paid for the job " Mr. Lloyd George replied to her letter as follows: " The words which you quote would guarantee that women undertaking the work of men would get the same piece-rate as men were receiving before the date of the agreement. That, of course, means that if the women turn out the same quantity of work as men they will receive exactly the same pay." In other words, women were entitled to men's *piece*-rates but not to men's *time*-rates The interpretation was all the more bewildering in that semi-skilled and unskilled men, who came apparently under the same terms, were entitled to both time-rates and piece-rates of the skilled men whom they replaced.*

---

* It was afterwards argued by official representatives that the terms in question were never intended to cover the time-rate as well as the piece-rate; and that the semi-skilled and unskilled men owed their privileged position to a previous clause of the Agreement, which laid down that " where the custom of a shop is changed during the war by the introduction of semi-skilled men to perform work hitherto performed by a class of workmen of higher skill, the rates paid shall be the usual rates of the district for that class of work " If this contention is correct the Government must still be blamed for using terms which were studiously ambiguous

The result was to leave employers practically a free hand in fixing women's rates of wages, and so far as these were concerned to knock the bottom out of the Treasury agreement.

For, in munition factories, not only were many thousands of women munition workers necessarily employed on time-work, but in the general readjustment of processes men's piece-rates had practically disappeared. Even in normal times, engineering workers rely mainly on a guaranteed day-rate, or time-rate, in order to safeguard the standard on piece-work as well as on time-work. They are otherwise at the mercy of unscrupulous employers, whose object is to extract from employees a piece-work effort at a time-work wage, and who therefore reduce the piece-rate on one pretext or another at each effort made by the worker to raise his earnings above the time-work level. " What can one do, when a girl is earning as much as 15/- per week, but lower the piece-rate?"* This exclamation by a works manager was unusually frank, but it expressed none the less the mind of a far from uncommon type of employer. As a matter of fact, the great armament firms mostly preferred to adopt the *premium* bonus system, which seemed to combine the advantages of both time and piece-work.

This system may take various forms   Under that commonly adopted in munition factories a certain number of hours or *basic time* was allowed for the job. The worker was guaranteed a fixed time-rate on a *basic* rate ; but if he could finish the job in less than the basis time, he might receive, above and beyond the basic rate, a bonus on output equivalent to one-half, or other fixed proportion, of the time so saved   The method differs from the ordinary piece-work system in that the worker is paid for only a *portion* instead of the *whole* of the time he saves by his additional effort ; and, for this reason amongst others, it has always been opposed by trade unionists, who now discovered an even worse objection   The same employer who might hesitate to cut the piece-rate and thereby break the letter of the law (as interpreted by Mr Lloyd George) had no compunction whatever in cutting the time-rate. In the case of women employed on men's work, the usual number of hours was allowed for the job, the usual proportion was fixed between the bonus and the time-rate, but the time-rate was reduced by one-third or one-half, and women might equal or even excel men in output and yet only receive about two-thirds or one-half of men's wages.

Comparisons are proverbially odious, but those now made by employers between men and women munition workers were cer-

* Statement by a manager in defending a breach of the " particulars " clause under the Factory Acts   (*Annual Report of the Chief Lady Inspector of Factories and Workshops*, 1915)

tainly not to the disadvantage of the latter. The extravagant praise lavished on women in the press was, indeed, as distasteful to themselves as it was unfair to the men, who had overcome old prejudices in order to teach them their trade. It would, however, seem that on light, or moderately light, " repetition " work of the type upon which women were mainly employed, their output compared not unfavourably with that of men. " On piece-work," declared the manager of a great national shell factory, " a woman will always beat a man. . . . On mass production she will come first every time. . . . We have never been able on this particular class of work to get the men to cope with it; they would not stand it. Men will not stand the monotony of a fast repetition job like women; they will not stand by a machine pressing all their lives, but a woman will."* This aptitude for certain branches of men's work, which now revealed itself in women, however, did not convince employers that women should receive men's wages. It convinced them instead that women's wages should have been paid to men " The fact of the matter," to quote from the official organ of the Engineering Employers' Federation,† " is really not that the women are paid too little—or much too little— but that the men are paid too much for work which can be done without previous training. High wages are paid on the false assumption now almost obscured by trade union regulations, that it takes long to learn the craft. Everyone knows now, as all managers knew long ago, that no long period of training is necessary, and the whole argument of high wages based on long training falls to the ground." It is not surprising that a circular issued by the Government in August, 1915, urging employers to use women in skilled engineering and tool-making work, roused such hostility amongst trade unionists that it had to be withdrawn.

The National Federation of Women Workers was not a party to the Treasury agreement; its members were not even invited to attend the conference, but it now came forward on behalf of the women munition workers. The small ammunition trades—fuse and cartridge making—in which women were employed to some extent before the war, belonged notoriously to " sweated " industry. A rate of $2\frac{1}{2}$d or $2\frac{3}{4}$d. an hour was a common wage for an adult woman, and these deplorable conditions of female labour, aggravated by the rise in the cost of living, now threatened to extend to all men's trades to which women were introduced. The relaxation of legal restrictions on overtime and night work at the same time paved the way for fresh abuses. Certain special regulations had been issued by the Home Office For example, overtime should be limited to $7\frac{1}{2}$ hours a week, and

* *Report of the War Cabinet Committee on Women in Industry* Page 83.
† *The Engineer.* October, 1915

hours of work (including meal-time) to fourteen a day. Sunday work must be confined to night-shift, and night-work prohibited to young girls under the age of 16. Considerable latitude was, however, allowed to the great armament firms. Official permits were given to employ women on Sunday work, and children on night-work. In the early years of the war, a week of $73\frac{1}{2}$ hours was in some cases sanctioned by the Home Office. Employers seem, in fact, to have generally gained the impression that the Factory Acts were in total abeyance, and they acted accordingly

Women's agitation began in March, 1915, when the Board of Trade, notwithstanding the fact that in London alone over 30,000 industrial women were unemployed, invited women of all classes to register for national service. The War Emergency Workers' National Committee, of which Miss Macarthur was a member, thereupon summoned a conference of important trade unions and women's societies. This meeting, with Miss Macarthur as chairman, unanimously resolved that " no Emergency Act should be allowed unnecessarily to depress the standard of living of the workers or the standard of living of the working conditions," and women were advised to join their appropriate trade unions It was urged that " equal pay for equal work " should be strictly enforced, and further that *all* women, whether employed on *men's* or on *women's* work, should receive an adequate living wage. Proper facilities should be provided for training, security should be given against unemployment after the war, whilst women representatives should be appointed on the newly-constituted Labour Advisory Committee, and on courts of arbitration.

Under the direction of the Women's Trade Union League, a vigorous campaign was started at the same time amongst women munition workers. The National Federation of Women Workers already included one or two small branches of these workers, and new branches were now opened in nearly all important munition centres Women joined the union in thousands; and, in one factory after another, advances of wages were secured amounting to $\frac{1}{2}$d. or 1d. an hour on time-work, and to as much as 5/- a week on piece-work, together with a shorter working day, and various improvements in working conditions The women's union even gained the recognition of Mr. Lloyd George, who invited its representative to attend a further conference which was summoned in order to accept the provisions of the Munitions of War Act.

More significant, however, was the alliance entered into during this summer between the Federation and the Amalgamated Society of Engineers. Since 1886, the latter society had opened its doors to less and less skilled classes of workers until finally, in 1912,* it included unskilled labourers and assistants. The further question arose of admitting women to membership, and the matter was discussed at its triennial delegate meeting ; but the old prejudice against female labour was too strong. The motion was rejected by an overwhelming majority of members, who were not prepared to recognize women beyond the period of the war, and foresaw an obvious inconvenience in admitting them to membership, and in excluding afterwards their own fellow-members from employment. The leaders on each side were, however, fully alive to the urgent necessity for organizing women, and to the advantage to be gained by mutual support. Men trade unionists unofficially had already done yeoman service in helping inexperienced women, and in June, 1915, the two societies signed a formal agreement, under which local joint committees should be set up for the purpose of fixing rates of wages and other conditions of female labour,† whilst both sides should join in enforcing these decisions on employers. The two societies further arranged a deputation to the Minister of Munitions, and put forward an immediate claim for £1 a week for all women over the age of eighteen employed in engineering and ship-building establishments, except on such work as " prior to the war has been recognized as women's work by the Amalgamated Society of Engineers and the Allied Trades in the district or districts concerned " The terms only applied to " substituted " women and erred, if anything, on the side of moderation; but they had at least the essential quality of explicitness and could not afterwards be whittled away by employers. Payment would have to be made in good coin, a fact which was evidently realized by the Minister of Munitions. Dr. Addison, who received the deputation on the Minister's behalf, expressed every sympathy with its objects Women, he agreed, ought not to be underpaid, and the danger of depressing men's wages ought to be guarded against, but, unfortunately, the Minister of Munitions had no power to enforce rates of wages except in national establishments !

The harsh operation of the Munitions of War Act served meanwhile to aggravate the sense of injustice amongst the workers. The provisions of the Act, which prohibited strikes and lock-outs and substituted arbitration, told inevitably in favour of employers, and against the workers. At the time of a boom in trade, no employer, it was obvious, would desire a lock-out, whilst such conditions were especially favourable for a strike. Arbitra-

* This latter decision was subsequently reversed, but only in order to avoid friction with the general labour unions, which already included large numbers of unskilled workers

† The later national awards and statutory orders made the work of these local committees largely unnecessary, and few in fact were set up.

tion was, moreover, slow and uncertain in its effects. Women's comparative weakness in organization caused them, as usual, to come off worse than men. Awards were often delayed for months and months, and then not made retrospective Rates actually awarded were sometimes as low as 2¾d. an hour   The Act further laid down that a person should not "give employment to a workman who, within the previous six weeks, had been employed in or in connection with munition work," unless he had a discharge certificate from his employer, or one from the munitions tribunal, stating that consent to his discharge had been unreasonably withheld.   The ostensible object of the clause was to check employers from bidding one against the other for each other's work people, and so forcing up the price of labour—as that of other commodities—to a famine level.   "Profiteering" must be forbidden to the workers at all costs, but the result was also to interfere seriously with their personal liberty in moving from one factory to another in order legitimately to improve their position.   The chain pressed with almost intolerable severity on women who were tied to " sweated " conditions of employment   In one great munition centre, six months after the passing of the Act, when a woman ventured at last to bring an appeal against the refusal of her employer to grant a discharge certificate. her case was summarily dismissed.   Her wages were given by the firm as 8/5, 10/1, and 10/6 respectively, for the three previous weeks, and she had found a new job at 17/- a week. Her ambition did not seem to be unreasonable, but in the opinion of the tribunal " poaching " on the part of employers was a more serious offence than " sweating," and her claim was accordingly refused.   Such cases were not uncommon at one time.   Inexperienced women were naturally loath to appear in court at all, whilst employers found a new weapon of tyranny in the threat to drag them up before the tribunal.

The Government could, however, no longer ignore the growing discontent of the workers.   In September, 1915, the Minister of Munitions appointed a new Labour Supply Committee, amongst whose members was Miss Macarthur.   This Committee set to work and drew up a comprehensive scheme for the " dilution of skilled labour."   It was laid down that " no skilled man shall be employed on work which can be done by semi-skilled or unskilled labour," and certain " notes " or rules were drawn up for the guidance of employers.   These included a list of occupations " within the limits of a woman's physical capacity," and generally " being work of suitable dimensions and a repetition character," upon which women should be employed.   Employers further were advised that any proposal to introduce women in the highly-skilled branches of the engineering trades should be referred by them first of all to the Minister of Munitions; that young girls under eighteen years of age should not be employed on shells over six-pounders; that forewomen should be appointed in order to supervise female labour and act as intermediaries between the women and the manager or foreman; and that suitable lavatory and cloakroom attendants should be provided for the exclusive use of female workers, who should also be supplied with caps and overalls. The Committee finally drew up a memorandum fixing rates of wages for women employed in engineering and ship-building establishments on " work not recognized as women's work before the war "

Under this important memorandum—known afterwards as circular L2—a standard wage of £1 a week of normal hours was fixed for the first time for all " substituted " women over the age of eighteen, who should also receive men's overtime, Sunday, holiday and night-work allowances. The circular further laid down that " women employed on work customarily done by *fully-skilled tradesmen* . . . shall be paid the time-rates of the tradesmen whose work they undertake "—a direct concession to the power of the Amalgamated Society of Engineers, whose 200,000 members belonged almost entirely to the class of skilled tradesmen. Women employed in the place of semi-skilled and unskilled men, although their organizations were equally parties to the Treasury agreement, were not entitled to men's time-rates; but, " on systems of payment by results," it was laid down that " equal payments shall be made to women as to men for an equal amount done." Premium bonus, and piece-rates must, moreover, be fixed on the basis of the *men's* time-rate, and must not be reduced without a definite change in the process of manufacture. By these elaborate means, the worst abuses of piece-work were checked to some extent. The circular fulfilled by no means the whole of the trade union demands, but it laid at least a foundation for future advances. Unfortunately, however, it had one fundamental defect—*the provisions were optional and not compulsory on employers,* so that its practical effects to all intents and purposes were nil. Except in national establishments immediately under the control of the Minister of Munitions, employers—even the Admiralty—snapped their fingers in the face of Mr. Lloyd George, and openly proclaimed their refusal to pay women £1 a week.

The Amalgamated Society of Engineers was, however, in no mood to be put off with promises, nor to enter further agreements by which the workers were bound, whilst employers were left . free. A deputation of its members waited at once on the Labour Supply Committee and claimed that, " as the price of their cooperation in the Government scheme for the dilution of skilled

F

labour," the terms of the two circulars L2 and L3—the latter relating to " substituted " men—" should be made incumbent on the employers." An assurance to this effect was received from Mr. Lloyd George, but the Government was apparently powerless to enforce its orders. During the autumn of 1915, thousands of " substituted " women were still receiving rates substantially below £1 a week. The Workers' Union concluded an agreement with the Midland Engineering Employers' Federation in November, which fixed a scale of 16/- a week for women over the age of twenty-one, and no distinction was drawn between " substituted " women and others. The terms were severely criticized by the Amalgamated Society of Engineers and the Federation, on the ground that they prejudiced the position of " substituted " women; but these represented none the less a substantial advance of wages for large numbers of women munition workers. About this time it became the practice of munitions tribunals not to refuse a discharge certificate when the wages of the applicant fell below the standard of the Workers' Union.

In November 1915, however, a Bill was introduced by the Government for the amendment of the Munitions of War Act. Power was given to the Minister of Munitions to fix rates of wages and other conditions of female labour, but certain grave defects of the Act were left unremedied An attempt was made by the Government to hurry the Bill through Parliament without discussion, but this plan was defeated by the Amalgamated Society of Engineers, whose executive committee took the important step of summoning a national conference of trade unions in support of its amendments to the Bill. The Society's energetic action, together with ominous signs of rebellion apparent on the North East Coast and on the Clyde, caused the Government to consider amendments to the Bill. Amongst those proposed by trade unionists and finally accepted by the Government were power to fix rates of wages for " substituted " men, the reconstitution of munitions tribunals, assuring additional representation to labour and the appointment of women assessors, new safeguards against imprisonment under the Act, and improved machinery for the notification of workshop changes by employers to trade unions. It had been proposed by trade unionists that no worker should be retained by his employer against his will for a period longer than six weeks, but this amendment was refused, and the objectionable clause of the original Act remained in force until August, 1917, when it was finally repealed.* The Government similarly refused to embody in the Bill the terms of the two circulars L2 and L3, but Mr. Asquith, the then Prime Minister, gave his own word that these should be made " legal and mandatory " on employers.

* In the case of women, the repeal was unconditional.

From the point of view of women, however, the chief interest attached to the clause which gave power to the Minister of Munitions to fix rates of wages and other conditions of female labour This provision, which had been inspired by the National Federation of Women Workers, applied not only to "substituted" women, but to *all* women coming under Clause 7 of the original Act, by which they were restricted in moving from one factory to another. The basis was somewhat broader than that of the corresponding clause which related to semi-skilled and unskilled men and whose terms were inspired by the Amalgamated Society of Engineers. These latter applied almost exclusively to semi-skilled and unskilled men employed in the place of skilled tradesmen. The distinction was not without significance. Under the same Act, the Minister of Munitions took power to appoint a Special Tribunal or Tribunals (whose members should include at least one *woman* in all cases relating to women) which should advise the Minister on matters of wages and other conditions of labour, and also settle disputes which might be referred to it by the Board of Trade. The new Act came into force in January, 1916, and the two famous circulars were made "legal and mandatory" in the following February. The Special Tribunal for women, of which Miss Susan Lawrence was a member, began work in the same month.

The Act bore fruit at once. In a typical shell factory, which employed many thousand women, basic rates were raised straight away from 15/- to 23/- a week, the earnings on premium bonus being increased by at least 10/-. The promised minimum of £1 a week was now an actual fact; but, in spite of the elaborate provisions of circular L2, little else was really assured. On one pretext or another, piece-rates were based on a *women's* standard, or at least on a standard appreciably lower than the men's. "If we paid the women the men's rates," the representative of a great armament firm told Miss Macarthur, "their earnings would be £12 a week."* The terms of circular L2, moreover, did not apply to young girls, although these were equally employed on men's work. Nor was this defect made good by the decision of the Minister of Munitions, who laid down a scale of time-rates ranging from 14/- to 18/- a week, according to age; whilst deductions were allowed from the piece-rate amounting to 30 per cent. !

* In this case there was no doubt some speeding up due to improved working conditions "A woman is doing it better," to quote the evidence of an employer before the War Cabinet Committee on Women in Industry, "not because she has got very much greater speed, but she has got very much better methods laid out to enable her to do it. She has the quantity, she has the continuity of production." There was nevertheless no doubt in the minds of men trade unionists that women's rates represented a standard substantially below their own.

The important question of demarcation was another matter to be decided by the Minister of Munitions, which led to similar heart-burning. *Shell-making* was pronounced a *semi-skilled* trade, although skilled tradesmen were not uncommonly employed, and the trade at Sheffield was entirely reserved to their class. *Fuse* and *cartridge-making* were declared to be *women's* trades, although in several important munition centres all the workers were men and boys The chief indignation of the Amalgamated Society of Engineers was, however, directed against the pronouncement of the Minister of Munitions that, " where a woman is introduced to perform a part only of the work previously done by a skilled man, she is not in the opinion of the Minister entitled by the terms of circular L2 to receive the full district rate customarily payable to that skilled man, inasmuch as 'she is not performing in its entirety the work customarily done by the skilled man."   The interpretation struck at the root of the special clause in circular L2 which related to skilled workers, and for which the Society has chiefly fought its battle.   The feeling was most embittered on the Clyde, where thousands of women had already been introduced under cover of the circular into general engineering shops—the last sanctum of the skilled tradesman.   The Clyde Dilution Commission, which was appointed by the Government in the early part of 1916, did its best to arrange a compromise.   It recommended that " where a woman is put on any portion of a job customarily performed by a fully-skilled tradesman," the starting-rate should be £1 a week, whilst after the fourth week the rate should be raised each week until the men's full rate was reached at the end of the thirteenth week.   This compromise was accepted by the Amalgamated Society of Engineers, whose members over-came their objection to a probationary rate for adult workers, but it was rejected by the great armament firms. Of the 13,000 women employed during this year in the Clyde engineering shops, only a small minority received more than the women's minimum of £1 a week, as against the men's standard of 50/- or 55/-. Nowhere did the patriotism of the workers stand a severer test than on the Clyde.   On the Tyne, employers were less obstinate in their resistance. Local agreements were reached on the lines proposed by the Clyde Commission, so that at the end of 1916 between 500 and 600 " substituted " women were receiving approximately men's rates of wages.   The ceaseless agitation of the Amalgamated Society of Engineers and the Federation had meanwhile its effect; and, in February, 1917, the Minister of Munitions issued a new general order (49), which practically embodied the terms of the Clyde Commission's recommendation. Not only women employed on the whole of the job of a fully-skilled tradesman—an obviously insignificant minority—but women employed on *part of the job of a fully-skilled tradesman* must receive men's full rates of wages after three months of probation. A deduction from these rates amounting to 10 per cent. was, however, allowed on account of extra supervision or assistance in setting the tools—a deduction which employers never failed to make in full, although women might be actually employed as supervisors! In the same general order, the women's standard was raised from 20/- to 24/- a week, and in April, 1917, the normal week was reduced to 48 hours. Further, it was provided that women employed on specially laborious or responsible work might appeal to arbitration and secure special rates. By this means, the Federation was able to obtain rates as high as 8d. and 10d. an hour for large numbers of its members, but appeals to arbitration were necessarily reserved to well-organized workers. In March, 1917, a new question arose as to men's war advances, and it was now officially discovered that women were less affected than men by the extraordinary rise in the cost of living! Those advances to which women were already entitled could not at present be withdrawn from them, but in future they must no longer receive men's full allowances. For some reason best known to the Special Tribunal for Women, an exception was made in favour of women crane drivers, and of women labourers employed in the South Wales steel works, but the number of such women did not exceed a few hundreds. At the time of the armistice, generally speaking, the women's war bonus was 11/- a week, as against 16/6 a week plus 12½ per cent. on earnings received by men. Thus, the cup of " equal pay " was once more dashed from the lips of the workers.

These statutory orders covered, or were supposed to cover, all women munition workers employed in engineering and shipbuilding establishments on work " not recognized as women's work before the war." The special clause of L2 relating to skilled workers was not extended to aircraft woodworkers, nor to sheet-metal workers. The Amalgamated Union of Carpenters and Cabinet Makers, whose members had relaxed their rule prohibiting women in the skilled branches of woodworking, now claimed that the protection of L2 should be extended to aircraft wood workers, and appealed to arbitration. The claim was vigorously opposed by employers, who maintained that, owing to the new methods of " mass " production, women were employed, not on *men's* work, but on *new* work. The workers lost their case, but they indignantly denounced the ruling as unjust, and the agitation continued. A national instruction was at once sent out to all societies affiliated to the National Woodworkers' Aircraft Committee, urging their members no longer " to teach any operations to women and girls which were previously performed by skilled

men,'' unless an agreement were immediately arrived at by which
'' women and girls shall receive the same rate as received by the
skilled woodworkers whose work they perform.'' The women
were organized by the Federation, whose members were loud in
their protests '' against the cynical discrimination in the case of
workers \engaged in aircraft and woodwork. The dispute was,
however, cut short by the armistice, and the subsequent discharge
of women aircraft workers.

The little Society of Women Welders, established under the
auspices of the London Women's Suffrage Society in 1916, made
a similar unsuccessful attempt to establish the claim of its members to be technically classed as skilled workers. The process
of oxyacetylene welding, which is largely used in aircraft manufacture, was a comparatively new one; but, until women were
employed, its claim to rank as a skilled trade was not disputed
by anyone During the war, it is true, the rapid growth of aircraft manufacture had led to new sub-divisions of labour, but
this fact did not alter the essentially skilled character of the work.
The condition by which each worker necessarily worked on his
own, or on her own, was a sufficient reason in itself to place it
in the category of skilled trades. As a matter of fact, although
the trade could be learned in six or eight weeks, it could not be
learned at all except by intelligent workers, and those selected
for employment belonged to a class at least as well-educated as
that of fully-qualified tradesmen. The work seemed, moreover,
to be especially adapted to women, who admittedly compared well
with men in output. The dispute began when women were asked
to accept about one-half men's wages, or 5d and 6d. instead of
10d. and 1/- an hour. The Society of Women Welders was able
to secure for its members a starting rate of 7d an hour, soon
raised to 8d , but employers refused point blank to grant further
advances A group of London firms, with the object of establishing a permanent rate of 8d. an hour, actually tried to persuade
women to sign away their right to claim further advances for
the whole period of the war ! The women fortunately refused,
and the agitation continued. With the full support of the Amalgamated Society of Engineers, the Society appealed to arbitration, and after a delay of six months a first award was granted
in February, 1919. The terms, which followed broadly the lines
of the statutory orders, fixed a starting rate at 8d. an hour for
women employed on *fully-skilled* work, rising to the men's full
rate (less the usual deduction of 10 per cent.) at the end of three
months, and a starting rate of 5d an hour for women employed
on *semi-skilled* work, rising to 8d at the end of three months;
but the crucial point as to which work was *fully-skilled*, and which
was *semi-skilled,* still remained undecided, and women received

meanwhile only semi-skilled rates. The matter was referred to a sub-committee, and thereafter at intervals of a few months, women were picked out by name for promotion to skilled rank in batches of twos and threes. At the time of the armistice, the number of these fortunate women had risen to about a score, but on what principle the selection was made they were never able to discover. In May, 1918, the Society appealed once more to arbitration, but the result was only to emphasize the previous failure. They were now told that their work was " generally sufficiently paid after six months at 8d. an hour, but work which involves the use of several blowpipes, or requires ability to work in several metals, or which includes a fairly wide range of operations, would merit a higher rate, and in proper circumstances would be entitled to skilled rate." As the Society pointed out in an admirable report, in the first place, steel was almost the only metal at that time used in aircraft, secondly, practically all aircraft work could be done with two sizes of blowpipe; and thirdly, the distribution of the work could be arranged so as to prevent any welder performing a variety of jobs. The actual effect of the ruling was " to make it impossible for women welders to secure the skilled rate except in very unusual circumstances "* Individual members were sometimes able to obtain for themselves substantially better terms than the award, and the Society entered into conversations with the Government. The new claim was for a national minimum rate of 10d an hour, and this rate was apparently secured when negotiations were cut short by the armistice " The purpose of L2," observed a high official of the Ministry of Munitions to a deputation of the Society, " is to preserve the continuity of rates in settled trades and not to establish the principle that women should receive equal pay for equal work," to which cryptic utterance he added the significant remark that, " the Government and the employers have a common interest in keeping down wages." The support given by the Government to employers in defeating the little Society of Women Welders in its claim for " equal pay " may not unrightly be described as the meanest episode in the sordid story of the " dilution of skilled labour " in munition factories.

Outside munition factories, which covered the greater part of engineering and a large part of wood working and chemical manufacture, " substitution " followed a similar course, but the problem was comparatively unimportant In the textile and clothing trades, and in the printing trades, where women were already employed in large numbers, there was an actual decrease in the figure of female employment during the war. Some of these trades were slack and women were attracted elsewhere; whilst,

* *Second Annual Report of the Society of Women Welders,* 1919.

in others, where women had been employed for several generations, men's employment was practically confined to one or two
exhausting or dangerous operations, to labouring work or to posts
as overlookers, and there was little or no place for further " substitution." The Bradford men woolcombers complained bitterly
that women's competition had already doomed many of their sex
to almost perpetual night-work. Conditions varied, however,
from one trade to another. Of the 30,000 " substituted " women
employed in the cotton industry, two-thirds were weavers, who
had as much right as men to the trade. Amongst wool and worsted
operatives, the most conspicuous feature was women's promotion
to night-work " Substitution " was more important in textile
dyeing and bleaching, where in well-organized Yorkshire and
Lancashire districts women were employed for the first time outside the warehouse. It was common for three or four women
to take the place of two men, so that, generally speaking, their
labour was uneconomical, and employers were not inclined to
keep them except at excessively low rates of wages. Similar
phenomena were remarked in clothing factories, where women had
been employed for many years in all suitable branches. " Substitution " to the extent of many thousand women took place amongst
army clothing workers, but the experiments were not entirely
successful By means of new subdivisions of labour, women were
relieved from men's arduous duties, but with the result of throw-
ing an undue share of these on men, who complained of fresh
hardships. Women seem, indeed, to have achieved their greatest
success in " passing " or overlooking, where they were able to
do the whole of men's work. "Substitution" was extensive in boot
and shoe factories, but related chiefly to boys' work. The printing
trades were generally slack, and the problem of " substitution "
was in any case no new one. Nor was it a new one in the pottery
trades, or in the tobacco trades In some food trades, such as
bread making, grain milling, brewing and malting, large numbers of women were employed for the first time, but here again
the laborious character of the work made it evident that their
employment would not continue permanently.

The threat of " substitution " caused, however, nowhere so
great a commotion amongst men trade unionists as in those trades
with a long history of female labour. The spinners' unions were
up in arms at once. In the spring of 1915, members passed
repeated resolutions, condemning the Home Office proposals to
introduce women in mule-spinning, and advocating instead the
employment of Belgian boys They even made common cause
with the Master Spinners' Association, and approached the Government with a proposal to lower the age of school attendance from
fourteen to thirteen years, and the age at which youths should

cease to be classed as " young persons " from eighteen to seventeen years—a request which was fortunately refused. " A stoppage of mills," wrote a spinner in the *Cotton Factory Times,* " would be preferable to going back to the days of fifty years ago, when women's labour was not at all uncommon in the spinning rooms." The women themselves, apparently, were not consulted. At a small meeting of women " joiner minders " and " piecers," belonging to one or two " non-union " mills, it would seem that they were " very resentful that their work should be considered harmful, probably from fear of losing their employment."* Men's opinion was, however, unanimous. " I do not know one single spinner," wrote another correspondent in the *Cotton Factory Times,* " who would let his own girl do the work. Apart from the moral standpoint (which is sure to be complicated where men and girls disrobe together), have the advocates of girl labour foreseen the consequences? We shall have the employers saying that there is nothing in spinning if a girl can learn it, and will pay according." The Cotton Spinners' Amalgamation afterwards decided that " it would not oppose the introduction of female labour if terms could be arranged between the local associations and the employers," and in several districts, following the Bolton example, women were admitted as "piecers" or assistants, but the agreements expressly stipulated that " no females shall be employed as minders or joint-minders." The agreements varied to some extent in detail, but it was commonly provided that women " piecers " who were mostly paid by men spinners should receive the usual rates of wages after a period of four weeks' probation, during which the remuneration was to be " and in no case shall it exceed 7/- a week." This sum was subsequently raised to about 14/-.

There was the same outcry from members of the old-established printers' unions, who immediately pledged themselves " to continue their opposition to female labour in the skilled branches of the printing trades." " In the abstract," wrote the secretary of the London Society of Compositors, " women are entitled to all the rights conferred upon men; but that is not to say that they should be allowed to exercise them regardless of consequences Rightly or wrongly certain trades in industry have become recognized as giving employment only to men, just as there are others giving employment only to girls. Certain favourable conditions have been built up by the trade unions and their maintenance is largely dependent on the power of the unions to control the labour supply within the limits of the requirements of the trade . . . The natural fear that the proposal to introduce female labour is intended to afford the employers an opportunity of pav-

* *The Girl in Industry.* D J. Collier, 1917

ing the men's bonus out of the saving effected on wages does not help to convince the men that the change would be for their benefit. They cannot forget their duty to the boys at the front. Relaxation of rules ought to be and must be conceded at the proper time and place, but as to being hitched to cheap female labour—No thank you, John."* The Scottish societies afterwards agreed to relax their rules, and in some districts outside Edinburgh a few women were introduced as compositors; but members were determined that the Edinburgh experience of "cheap female labour" should not repeat itself, and in most cases they stood out successfully until women secured men's full rates of wages. The situation was not made easier by the attitude of the Government towards women employed on men's work under Government contracts. Mr. Montagu, then financial secretary to the Treasury, in receiving a deputation of the Printing and Kindred Trades Federation in October, 1914, made this attitude plain "If you can show me," he said, "that in a particular firm and at a particular place, women are being paid a rate of wages *which is unfair for women,* then I think you have a grievance and that is an infringement of the Fair Wages Clause; but I am not in agreement with you that it is our business in interpreting the Fair Wages Clause to insist that women should obtain the same wages as men If we did so, it would lead to women losing a considerable amount of employment . . It may be that in certain branches of your trade there is a growing tendency, as female labour comes more and more into the market, for work which used to be men's work to be done now by women That is a phenomenon which is going on in other trades and which it would be very unfair to use the Fair Wages Clause to put an end to "

In so far, however, as a shortage of male labour was proved, in one trade after another the men's trade unions relaxed their restrictions on female labour, and women were admitted on men's work under certain conditions of restoration and wages Outside the munition trades these conditions were mainly regulated by means of private agreements or arbitration. The Committee on Production was the principal authority in disputes affecting the whole or a large part of an industry while individual cases were determined by single arbitrators The agreements, or awards, broadly followed the same lines as those of the Treasury agreement and the subsequent statutory orders In all cases relaxation of the rule prohibiting female labour was strictly confined to the period of the war, whilst other provisions were added with the object of protecting men against immediate or future unemployment The important agreement for the wool and worsted indus-

* *The London Typographical Journal* February and May, 1917

try, subscribed to by nineteen trade unions and almost as many employers' associations, laid down that "female operatives shall only be engaged in substitution of male labour where and so long as it is not found possible to obtain male operatives, . . . and shall be the first to be discharged in the event of any shortage of work, either during or after the war." These terms were typical, and in some cases the provision as to restoration was strengthened by a definite time-limit. Thus, a local hosiery agreement provided that "female labour shall be withdrawn at the expiration of three months after the declaration of peace " The textile warehousemen's unions* claimed similar protection against unemployment for " substituted " women, who " shall be guaranteed their late positions on the termination of the war or when not employed on work previously done by males," but this considerate provision was by no means usual. The general agreements mostly included a schedule of suitable occupations, to which " substituted " women should be confined The object was partly to protect some inner sanctum of men trade unionists, but also to restrict women to work " within their physical capacity." These clauses related to such various matters as excessive cold or heat, fumes, the carrying of heavy weights, proper meal-rooms, heating and cooking facilities, washing accommodation and seats, the appointment of women supervisors on night-shifts, the prohibition of night-work to women with young children, and " the desirability, where possible, of separate working conditions " for men and women. The object of other provisions was to protect men from an undue share of disagreeable or exhausting work For example, the Yeovil men glovers secured a clause, that " all classes of work shall be equally divided between males and females," and the Basford hosiery trimmers one providing that " no member of the trimmers' society shall be expected to work all night to make room or to give preference to females to work during the day." The agreement of the London bookbinders limited the number of " substituted " women to 10 per cent. of the workers, but this clause was unusual, and its effect was said by employers to have made the agreement inoperative

The clauses relating to wages had a more contentious character. Trade unionists were practically unanimous in claiming that "substituted " women should receive men's full rates of wages, time-rates as well as the piece-rates, war advances not less than basic-rates. This claim was as invariably resisted by employers, who revived all the old arguments Men's rates of wages were intended to meet the needs of the family man and not those of the single woman. The unaccustomed rise would lead to idleness,

* Societies (1) and (2) of Makers Up and the Female Workers in the Shipping Industry.

cause discontent amongst other women, or jealousy amongst men
" who would not work for women's wages." Upon " cheap and
docile " female labour, indeed, the British export trade depended
in order to keep its place in the world's market   That women
could equal men in output was a supposition so manifestly absurd
that mere facts could not prove it.   Women lacked, moreover,
men's proper qualifications, or they did not do the whole of men's
work.   Or, if so, the work was not " essentially men's," but
women had already been employed at some other time or place.
Or the trade did not belong any longer to men, but had been
transformed into a new one   The cotton weavers reaped as usual
the advantage of a long tradition of " equal pay."   Not only
did women receive men's piece-rates and earn as much as men,
but employers apparently were unable to discover any defects in
female labour, and did not even complain of bad time-keeping.
" I think the employers would be inclined," their representative told the War Cabinet Committee on Women in Industry,
" if there was sufficient female labour to give the females the
preference, although it is a system which has gone on for such a
large number of years that the employers have no feeling in the
matter at all "*   Few trades enjoyed, however, this simple and
happy state of affairs.   Most agreements provided that women
should receive men's *piece*-rates; but, in the wholesale changes
of process—the effect of which might be actually to increase the
output per worker—men's piece-rates had mostly disappeared,
and new ones had been fixed on more or less a woman's standard.
Women were not entitled to men's *time*-rates except " for an
equivalent amount of work done"—an equivalence which was soon
found by the workers to be quite impossible to prove.   In some
textile agreements, a clause was added to the effect that, " if a
larger number of women took the place of a smaller number of men
' the aggregate wage should not be reduced ' "   This provision
gave real security against a general reduction of wages, but did
not always work out fairly towards women, who received an
unduly low share of the common wage   The injustice was not
necessarily the fault of employers, who in the pottery trades
actually made it a matter of grievance that women were unfairly
treated by men   The most satisfactory agreements were those
by which women were entitled to a minimum wage, such as that
of the wool and worsted workers, which was fixed at not less than
four-fifths of the men's standard   The question of war advance was
another matter of chronic dispute.   Percentage advances were
generally the same for either sex; but in the case of flat advances,
women seldom received more than from one-half to two-thirds of
the men's bonus.   Some examples of " equal pay " did no doubt

* *Report of War Cabinet Committee on Women in Industry*   Page 89

exist.   Such were women machine woolcombers who were
employed on men's night-work, and various small groups of textile workers.   Such again were women compositors who belonged
to London or to certain Scottish districts, or London women
cigar makers, who even succeeded in abolishing the pre-war
difference of 20 per cent. on piece-rates.   But these instances,
all told, represented only a small minority of " substituted "
women.   Generally speaking, it is true to say that " substituted "
women received wages which worked out at about half-way between the men's standard and that of other women belonging to
the same industry.   The fact, however, that women were already
largely employed in textile, clothing and similar industries, so that
further "substitution" frequently resulted in unsuitable employment, makes it probable that these groups of " substituted "
women had a lower relative productive value than that of " substituted " women in many branches of engineering and wood-
working.

In industries or trades not of the factory type, the comparatively unorganized " black-coated " workers were more or less
at the mercy of employers.   By reason of mere numbers, the
problem of " substituted " women was an important one for
clerks.   The Government alone accounted for over 150,000 temporary women clerks, mainly employed in place of men, whilst
twice that number of women (including shop assistants) were
introduced by commercial firms.   Owing to the absence of any
fixed standard of wages, or of definite lines of sex demarcation,
the trade union position was a more than usually weak one.
The National Union of Shop Assistants was, however, not unsuccessful in its campaign.   In the case of "substituted " women,
it claimed a four-fifths instead of a three-quarter standard, and
this claim was enforced for a large number of members.   The
new standard represented a genuine improvement on the old one,
but all women were not satisfied.   At annual delegate meetings,
Mrs. Bessie Ward repeatedly moved resolutions in favour of
" equal pay."   " There has been a good deal said in the past,"
she declared in reference to women grocers' assistants, " about
the necessity of fixing the women's minimum below the standard
for men because the women are less efficient.   That statement
is absurd upon the face of it, but it is made more absurd from the
facts which can be obtained from the places where the women are
working as substitutes for the men who have been withdrawn for
the purposes of the war.   In the North of England, in the Manchester district, out of twenty-five shops, there is not one where
the staff has been increased during the past six months; and yet
the majority of the staff are women.   In the London area, the
same remark applies.   The women are inexperienced at first,

and that naturally causes a temporary increase in the staff. The same thing would happen if inexperienced men were taken on. But the strange thing is that it takes a very short time to train the women in the grocery trade. I have been told that in London it takes six weeks to train them. Well, at all events, I have seen the work they accomplish for myself. I have enquired at the provision and grocery shops, and I find that they soon get a wonderful grip of their duties." But members as a whole were not prepared to support a policy which they did not believe at that time to be possible to carry out.

In co-operative stores, the Amalgamated Union of Co-operative Employees was not handicapped to the same extent as societies of ordinary commercial workers by depressed conditions of female labour, but before "equal pay" could be secured members had to face no less than seventy strikes. The co-operative agreement laid down that women "should be intimated of the temporary nature of their service" and men reinstated on their return, but the official note of explanation frankly declared that "the statement that substituted female labour is only a temporary expedient is not likely to be borne out by facts." The problem of shop assistants was, however, small compared with that of clerks. The National Union of Clerks fought gallantly for "equal pay," and, in order to avoid the usual abuses, claimed this for "similar duties"; but the union was unable to secure a general agreement. For the most part, little or no difference was made by employers between "substituted" women and others In the case of Government departments, where men and women clerks had at least the advantage of fixed rates of wages, the Government was frankly opposed to "equal pay." In November, 1915, whilst the Minister of Munitions was enjoining on private employers to observe at least "equal payment by results," Mr. Herbert Samuel, the then Postmaster-General, had nothing better to offer a deputation of Post Office employees than the following homily. "Equal pay for equal work. That," he said, "is a phrase in itself very plausible, but it is one which I have always regarded as quite unsound. . . . The right phrase, I think, in this connection is 'equal standard of comfort for people doing equal work.' If you pay a single woman the same wage as you pay a family man, you are giving her a much higher standard of comfort than you are giving him. . . . I could elaborate it a good deal, because I have thought very often on this subject. .   . I would point out that the Parliamentary Committees which have examined the question of Post Office wages have never accepted the doctrine that the wages should be the same for men and women in the Post Office. In the recent arbitration the principle of differentiation was confirmed and the Woodhouse award gave a different war bonus to women.''

In transport and similar out-door trades, where women were not employed in normal times, trade unionists had a comparatively easy problem to face. There was at least no bad tradition of female labour to be lived down. Reversing the tendency of previous years, between 30,000 and 40,000 women replaced men on the land. Some thousands of women even reappeared at the pithead, being introduced into saw milling at about one-half men's wages. Miners' societies, although women's employment about mines was definitely opposed, had always been open to women in certain districts, and was now joined by them in considerable numbers A similar movement to organize women was made by agricultural unions, but in spite of their efforts and those of the general labour unions, these workers remained mostly unorganized, or they only joined such bodies as the Women's Land Army. Wages were regulated by the Agricultural Wages Board, but women's rates were fixed at a level appreciably below the men's standard From the trade union point of view, the chief interest attached to women transport workers. On railways and tramways alone, there was an influx of over 80,000 women. The experiment was on the whole successful, although women employed on long shifts tended to lose more time than men through sickness, or need for rest. On tramways, shifts were known to extend to fifteen or sixteen hours a day, and the strain was especially trying to women. The usual assurances were required as to restoration, and the transport unions further tried to confine women's employment within the limits of certain '' suitable '' occupations. Women should not be used in ''manipulating traffic ''—on the whole a wise provision of the National Union of Railwaymen Neither should they be employed as tram or 'bus drivers, nor as taxi-drivers—an iron rule of the Societies of Vehicle Workers. Men's working conditions should, moreover, be strictly observed, and women's employment not encouraged by means of short shifts. The great transport unions threw their doors wide open, and invited, or even compelled, women to join the union. The railway companies agreed with a comparatively good grace that women should receive men's minimum time-rates in each grade, but men's war advances were flatly refused The point was a not unimportant one, the men's war bonus being 35/-, and the women's 20/6 at the end of 1918. In the case of vehicle workers, conditions varied considerably. Commercial and private motor-drivers, who so far as women were concerned represented the skilled section of transport workers, were unfortunately in the main unorganized. Neither the efforts of men trade unionists, nor those of the London Society for Women's Suffrage, which tried to form a Society of Women Motor Drivers, succeeded in reaching more than a fraction of these women, whose wages were often as low as 30/- or 35/- a week. The large numbers of women motor drivers employed by the Government similarly remained unorganized. Effective organization was confined to women tram and 'bus conductors, who had been practically compelled by men members to join the union. The companies and municipal authorities agreed without difficulty that women should be paid men's full rates of wages, but disputes began on the usual question of war advances. Under an important national award of January, 1918, men transport workers were entitled to an aggregate war advance of 20/- a week, whilst a clause laid down that, " where agreements or awards already exist providing for the same rates to be paid to women as men, such agreements or awards are to hold good, and an increase to be paid accordingly." In the absence of such agreements, women transport workers were only to receive an advance of 4/- a week on current rates. Outside London, the women's claim had been prejudiced for the most part by the terms of previous awards, by which they received not more than about two-thirds of men's war advances. In London, however, their claim was undeniable, and here they secured the full sum of 20/-, bringing up their earnings to 63/- a week In the following July, a fresh appeal was made to arbitration, and men were granted a further advance of 5/- a week, but this time the women were left out The award met with an unexpected storm of indignation. London women 'bus conductors were not accustomed to such treatment; they had, moreover, begun to taste power. A protest meeting was held at once, when they announced their intention of " taking drastic action " unless their claim received attention. It did not receive attention. It was, apparently, not even communicated by their union to the company. In August, therefore, the women struck work without further notice, and the men came out after them The public was surprised and not a little incommoded, but its sympathies were in the main on the side of the women. Even the *Times* admitted the strength of the women's case, which " lay precisely in this that their work was as well done as any man could do it and that everyone could see that it was." The Committee on Production, by which body the award had been given, was obliged to yield to the storm and to reconsider its decision, and the women won their case. The Committee stated in explanation that since the previous award was given the claim of women munition workers to the men's bonus of $12\frac{1}{2}$ per cent. on earnings had been settled by a bonus of 5/- a week. In view of the otherwise wide disparities of wages between men and women munition workers, the reference was—to say the least of it—a rash one Miss Macarthur seized her opportunity, and appealed to public opinion through the Press, urging that all women should be placed on a par with the London women 'bus conductors. She declared the award to be " the absolute vindication of the principle for which we are contending."* The Committee was already aware that the award " involved the determination of a general principle applicable, if adopted and established, not only to women employed on tramways and motor 'buses, but to women employed in many other trades." Finally, it recommended that " the whole question of women's wages and advances should be made the subject of a special enquiry," which recommendation led directly to the appointment of the important War Cabinet Committee on Women in Industry. The victory of the London women 'bus conductors forms one of the landmarks in the history of industrial women.

The comparatively high rates of wages enjoyed by " substituted " women now caused a general rise of women's wages. A large part of the employers' objection to " equal pay " was due to the unrest which was expected to follow in women's trades, where conditions were not dissimilar from those of "substituted " women. The Minister of Munitions, as we have seen, had power to fix rates of wages, not only for " substituted " workers, but for all women restricted under the Munitions of War Act in moving from one factory to another. Progress was slow at first—so slow that Miss Macarthur was soon impelled to make a vigorous attack in the Press on the Minister of Munitions.† She complained that the standard of 4½d. an hour, laid down by the statutory orders for other than " substituted " women, was not only miserably low, but that it was not enforced. " I unhesitatingly assert," she wrote in the *Times,* " that there are thousands of women to whom no protection has yet been accorded by statutory orders fixing wages. There are to-day women actually working on munitions of war for 2¾d. and 3d. an hour. One case I have in mind has been before the Ministry for nearly nine months; another case is at present the subject of arbitration, and no award has yet been given. It is true that a special Arbitration Tribunal exists before which their grievances theoretically may come, but in many other cases we have had months of negotiation before reaching the Tribunal, and after our case has been heard we have had to wait months for the award. In one case concerning women entirely engaged on Government work of a very heavy and disagreeable character, the women applied for an increase of wages last June. The award was only issued just before Christmas, and was not retrospective. The rates fixed for women on women's work, if valued according to the Board

* *The Daily News,* August 23rd, 1918   † January 5th, 1917

G

of Trade statistics of the rise in the cost of living, are worth less in real wages to-day than rates fixed legally for some sweated trades under the Trade Boards Act before the war." An elaborate apology was issued in reply by the Minister of Munitions. "It is comparatively easy to deal with direct munitions. Shells and fuses have no use except in war, and no purchaser but the Government. But the progress of the war has led to the control of thousands of establishments of the most diverse character, from great firms making patent foods for babes. It has brought within the definition of munitions of war thousands of articles of ordinary commercial uses, many of which have long been made by women   The trades involved have their own customs, their own rates of pay, their own systems of apprenticeships, all framed under the stress of national and international competition.   To interfere rashly with them would be like sticking a knife into the works of a watch, and in this field the Minister of Munitions has had to proceed with caution.   The Special Tribunal has been engaged, however, on this task for many weeks.   It has examined hundreds of cases, and if the new orders which result from its labours leave any trades uncovered, it can, as the need arises, deal with these by arbitration"   It was officially estimated that at least 100,000 women employed in munitions factories were still uncovered by statutory orders, and these women who belonged to the most helpless class of unorganized workers were now invited by the Minister of Munitions to fight it out with their employers.   The Federation and other general labour unions took up the challenge, and formed a "joint committee on women's wages and working conditions"   In one factory after another women were organized, whilst hundreds of appeals were carried to arbitration   The Federation was unusually fortunate, and won over 90 per cent. of its cases—an amazing record of success   At the end of 1918, the women's standard had been raised to 5½d an hour (½d. less than that of the "substituted" women) with a war bonus of 11/- a week.   On the pre-war standard of 2½d. or 2¾d. an hour, this roughly represented a gross advance of 200 per cent. during the war, or taking into account the rise in the cost of living, a *net* advance of 50 per cent.

The success of women munition workers encouraged women in other industries to claim similar advances of wages, but these seldom represented more, and often less, than the rise in the cost of living   In the cotton industry, war advances amounted in four years to 110 per cent., but of this sum only 5 per cent. was received before July, 1917.   Amongst wool and worsted workers, corresponding advances amounted to 104¾ per cent. on time-work, and 89 per cent. on piece-work   Women's advances on piece-work were actually higher than men's. The object of the arbitrator had been to grant such advances in each case as would work out at about the same on piece-work as on time-work, and the difference was due to the interesting fact that normal time-work and piece-work earnings approximated more nearly in the case of women than men. In the general absence of any pre-war standards, however, these advances were by no means easy to enforce. " The entire absence of pre-war standards for the women textile workers," wrote a trade union correspondent in the *Bradford Pioneer* (June, 1917), " makes the position thoroughly unhappy and unsatisfactory. . . Of all the thousands of men involved, there is not a single man who has not a minimum trade union standard, upon which his claims can be based. Of all the thousands of weavers, spinners and burlers, there is not a single woman who enjoys a minimum standard upon which her claim can be based." It was not until February, 1919, that the unions succeeded in securing a national minimum wage. In other industries, war advances varied considerably, but seldom amounted to more than 100 per cent Women pottery workers were amongst those who secured the least increase, or about 60 per cent. In "sweated" trades under the Trade Boards Act, war advances ranged from about 70 per cent. to about 90 per cent. The United Garment Workers' Union was successful in securing for its female members an advance of 1d. an hour (afterwards raised to 3d.) beyond the legal minimum of 5d.—the first achievement of its kind. There was no common standard for clerks, awards mostly relating to individual firms. The extraordinary demand for clerical labour of every kind had undoubtedly some effect in raising wages Women civil service clerks received a war bonus of 15/- as against one of 23/- received by men; whilst typists and other badly-paid grades secured in addition a small advance on salaries. Amongst commercial clerks, under certain awards of the Committee on Production, the war bonus received by women was more than that granted to boys, but less than that granted to youths between the ages of 18 and 21. The women's war bonus was estimated by the National Union of Clerks at anything between 2/6 and 25/- a week Large numbers of women shop assistants similarly remained at wages substantially less than 25/- a week. Dressmakers and milliners were the worst paid of all. Even after the armistice, reputable London firms were not ashamed to pay wages of 14/- a week to women with long years of experience, whilst deductions from wages were made for cotton, needles, oil, etc , reducing this sum to 12/-. At Edinburgh, in 1917, as the result of an important strike involving 1,200 dressmakers, and about a score of firms, the National Union of Shop Assistants succeeded in fixing a minimum wage of 21/- a week of 52 hours (living out) for adult women after seven years of service—the first minimum wage to be fixed for dress-makers; but, in Aberdeen and other Scotch towns, it was impossible to secure a minimum higher than 12/- a week (living out) for women with five years' experience, or 14/- for a responsible woman " working on her own." Domestic servants, owing to the large excess of demand over supply, were practically able to dictate their own terms, but many women did not know or care to use their advantage   Inefficient girls, moving from one place to another at the end of every month, might secure an advance each time, whilst old and trusted servants received literally no rise at all.   Laundry workers, who began to organize towards the end of the war, obtained local minimum rates for the first time about the date of the armistice, but these sums did not exceed from 18/- to 23/- for a week of 54 to 60 hours.   The trade union campaign in the traditional women's trades had, indeed, hardly begun in 1918.   The movement amongst dressmakers was typical.   " Here was a class hitherto wretchedly paid, viewed as helpless and hope-less, yet having once awakened they had shown an amazing determination. Beginning with Aberdeen in the far North, led by an exceedingly capable woman organizer, where they ceased work to obtain their charter—and obtained it—the movement rapidly spread.   Edinburgh followed suit, and the Union was engaged in the biggest dispute yet fought   After a stubborn contest, 1,000 women gained nearly £14,000.   Southwards the wave came, and London saw organizing meetings which for attendance and enthusiasm were unsurpassed   Right on to Land's End the move-ment had spread, and only the other day increases were obtained in Cornwall.   It has been truly a remarkable revolution, setting a glorious example to other wage-earners "*

" Our conclusion is," reported the Standing Joint Committee of Industrial Women's Organizations in December, 1916, " that, in trades *where the organizations concerned have been sufficiently strong*, war conditions have produced a marked rise in the wages of women, whether engaged on women's work, or in substitution for men; that some small rise in wages has been paid in many other trades, but that, as far as the evidence goes, the bulk of the depressed women's industries have not obtained a rise in wages anything like equivalent to the increased cost of living, nor is there any evidence to lead us to believe that women engaged in substitution for men have, unless under exceptional cases, obtained the men's full rate "   Broadly speaking, this conclusion held good throughout the period of the war, and advances of wages followed no principle except that of a strong trade union organization

For the first time in history, women outside the cotton industry

* *Annual Report of National Amalgamated Union of Shop Assistants, 1917-8*

were learning the power of trade unionism. The impulse to organize was most remarkable amongst "substituted" women, whose comparatively high rates of wages could be directly traced to trade union action. "Curiously enough," declared Miss Ellen Wilkinson, organizer of the Amalgamated Union of Co-operative Employees, "it is the dependence of these substituted females on union action and their recognition that their wage rates have been fixed by the union and not by tradition that has at last aroused many of the girls in the drapery and other departments to take a belated interest in their unions' work—an interest they could not be persuaded to take in pre-war times." In the four years of the war, the female membership of all trade unions rose from less than 400,000 to well over 1,000,000. The movement followed as usual that of semi-skilled and unskilled men, and was most conspicuous amongst general labour unions, of which the female membership rose from about 24,000 in 1914 to about 216,000 in 1918. The National Federation of Women Workers had a membership of about 80,000 at the time of the armistice, whilst the female membership of the Workers' Union numbered about the same, and that of the National Union of General Workers about 60,000. This great expansion of general labour unions was partly due to the policy of skilled men's societies. The Amalgamated Society of Engineers, as we have seen, refused to relax its rule and admit women to membership, and entered into an alliance with the National Federation of Women Workers. A similar policy was adopted by other engineering unions, whilst the two important Societies of Carpenters, Cabinet Makers and Joiners, whose members were affected by the large influx of women into aircraft wood-working, likewise refused to open their doors to women. The great body of women munition workers, reaching to three-quarters of a million in 1918, fell, therefore, to the share of general labour unions. The Federation was, in fact, almost transformed for the time being into a women's engineering union. Under the auspices of the London Society for Women's Suffrage and other middle-class women's organizations, an attempt was made to form little craft societies for skilled women employed in engineering. The most successful of these was the Society of Women Welders, whose plucky adventure has already been described. Its membership rose to about 700 women, but it succumbed in the end, gallantly fighting the Government and the employers, on the one side, for " equal pay," and, on the other side, the skilled men's societies for the free entry to their trade. Generally speaking, however, skilled women mechanics threw in their lot with other women, and joined general labour unions   In the absence of a definite apprenticeship, indeed, a line of demarcation between skilled and semi-skilled workers was exceedingly difficult to draw. It is probable that at the time of the armistice, the National Federation of Women Workers included, in addition to skilled " fitters " and " turners," at least as many " welders " as all the members of the little craft society. But it was to its alliance with the Amalgamated Society of Engineers that the Federation chiefly owed its position as the leading women's engineering union No similar alliance with any skilled men's society was entered into by other general labour unions, some of whose members were at one time actually opposed to the policy of the Federation. For this reason, it would seem, as well as for that of its constitution as an all-women's society, the women's union was refused affiliation to the National Federation of General Workers.

Almost as remarkable as the rapid growth of general labour unions was the increase in the female membership of the great transport societies. The figure rose in four years from a few hundreds to between 50,000 and 60,000 (excluding clerks), new members being mainly "substituted" women. These unions, as we have seen, adopted a directly opposite policy to that of engineering unions, and even compelled women to join the union. In the absence of any previous problem of female labour, the feeling of men members had not become embittered. It was, moreover, assumed that the same reasons which had prevented women's employment before the war, would prevent it again afterwards The movement was less conspicuous amongst well-organized cotton operatives, but many important societies of textile workers, clothing workers, printing workers, pottery workers, shop assistants and clerks increased their female membership four-fold and five-fold; so that, from being a small minority, women counted in some cases an actual majority of members. Societies, which already admitted women to membership, made no difference as a rule between "substituted" workers and others. Some textile and printing unions went so far as to insist that " substituted " women should be drawn so far as possible from within their own membership. The civil service unions, however, refused to admit temporary workers, either men or women, who formed separate associations, two of which were postal unions. The Postmen's Federation was an important exception and included some 10,000 women at the time of the armistice. This policy of duplicating societies could no doubt be traced to the difference in status between permanent and temporary civil servants, but it did not assist organization Societies were further multiplied by the policy of Government departments which encouraged small departmental organizations. The large body of temporary women clerks remained for the most part untouched by trade unionism until the end of the war.

The absence of men members on war service, meanwhile, compelled women to come forward and take a more active part in trade union affairs. The National Union of Shop Assistants could actually boast at one time a woman president. Typical of this period was the breakdown of old traditions in some old-established textile unions. The Chorley Association of Cotton Weavers, which dated from 1853 and included 80 per cent. of women members, elected a first woman to its executive committee in 1916, but the next year the number rose to six, and women were appointed as auditors. Even the Kidderminster Carpet Weavers' Union—whose members had at last decided, after forty years of delay, to admit women to membership, but did not accord more than one vote to twenty-five female members— now elected four women to its executive committee. The position of the female section was improved in other societies by a rise in its rate of contribution, so that this approximated more nearly to the men's. It was resolved by the Scottish Typographical Association to place at least the *trade* contribution on the same basis for either sex. Women's sphere in trade union management was definitely enlarged, but their duties were still confined for the most part to the branches or districts. The general management of the joint-organizations remained substantially in the hands of men. In spite of the enormous increase in female membership, women were not represented on the executive committee of a single important general labour union. It is significant that, of twenty-eight women delegates to the Trades Union Congress of 1918, eight were members of the National Federation of Women Workers.

The Federation still represented the only important trade union whose policy was directly controlled by women, and its separate women's point of view was nowhere so conspicuous as at meetings of the Trades Union Congress. Without its initiative, indeed, it is probable that women's questions would have been entirely overlooked, or only raised because men's interests were involved. At the time of the agitation against women taxi-drivers, the Licensed Vehicle Workers' Societies carried a resolution urging that the licenses of women 'bus and tram conductors should automatically expire at the end of the war, and these women return to conditions '' not so harmful to their moral welfare.'' Similarly the Birmingham Brass Workers' Union reasserted its claim that, '' in order to sustain the physique of Great Britain and to prevent physical degeneration, women should not be employed in men's occupations in the brass trades, and revived its old dispute with the Federation It was not a question of newly '' substituted '' women, and the Federation protested vigorously. '' With regard to weights and that kind of thing,'' declared Miss Bondfield on behalf of the Federation, "why, bless my soul, a woman who carries a child carries a heavy weight," and she urged that the question should at least be tackled " in a more business-like way." With this object, the Federation advocated the appointment of an " inter-departmental committee," composed of women medical officers and women inspectors as well as men and women trade unionists, which should " consider what employment may be harmful to women and to make recommendations thereon." The resolution was carried Between men and women delegates, indeed, there was no fundamental difference of opinion, but they tended to move along different paths to the same goal. Whilst men were chiefly intent on preserving the old trade union barriers against " cheap female labour," women were trying to win their right to industrial freedom, and devoted most attention to enforcing " equal pay." The ambiguity of the phrase " equal pay for equal work " finally led the Federation to propose a new formula. " We have many friends to-day," declared Miss Symons, a delegate of the Federation, " who shout ' equal pay for equal work,' but many of them do not mean what we mean. Mere equal pay for equal work may mean anything or nothing. We want women on the same footing as the men. When a man is taken on, he is not asked to show if he can do as much as another man, but a woman has to go through the test, and wherever possible her wages are reduced " The terms now proposed by the Federation were " equal pay for the same job "—a formula adopted, not only by the Trades Union Congress, but afterwards by the International Labour Conference

The question of fixing wages remained the most important one with which industrial women were faced, and the Federation claimed that the protection of a legal minimum wage should be extended to all classes of badly-paid workers Its delegates advocated an immediate extension of the Trade Boards Act, so as " to cover all trades normally employing women at rates which do not give, with the prices obtaining, the possibility of maintaining a decent and healthy standard of life "; whilst, in other industries or trades, it was urged that " employment boards " should be set up, composed in equal proportions of representatives of employers and of men and women workers, in order " to decide upon the conditions under which women should be employed so as to secure economic equality between men and women workers," and further to discuss matters of training. The Federation was equally active in promoting the Trade Board (Amendment) Act of 1918. This useful measure gave power to the Minister of Labour to extend the provisions of the Act to any trade by special order—a great improvement on the old cumbersome and dilatory machinery of the provisional order which required in each case the express sanction of Parliament   Other improvements included a reduction in the waiting period before the legal wage became operative from nine to three months, with power to fix over-time rates and a guaranteed time-rate for piece-workers, and also to deal with apprentices   Not the least testimony to the improved machinery of the new Act was the angry outcry against it by the Employers' Parliamentary Council. Trade unionists were, however, unable to prevent the insertion of a clause by which six months must elapse between one decision and the next, a pro-vision which was afterwards to prove a serious hindrance to advances of wages.

Other important resolutions brought forward by the Federa-tion at the Trades Union Congress related to the matters of un-employment. The apparent indifference of the Government to the plight of women munition workers, who were repeatedly thrown out of work by men's disputes, and still more its irrespon-sible action in discharging large numbers of women at a week's notice after the Russian collapse of 1917, gave members a fore-taste of what might be expected to happen at the end of the war. The Federation therefore proposed (1) an inquiry as to which firms would require workers at the cessation of war work, this information to be distributed through the employment exchanges; (2) the recognition of employment insurance on a non-contributory basis; (3) free railway passes for workers drawn from their homes to distant localities; (4) reasonable notice or in lieu wages; (5) four weeks' holiday on full pay. It was not part of the Govern-ment's policy to act beforehand so as to prevent unemployment, but the influence of the women's agitation could be traced in the comparatively generous terms of relief which were provided later for discharged civilian workers. For six months from the date of the armistice, the scale of women's unemployment benefit was 25/- a week, although it was afterwards reduced to 12/-, and abruptly withdrawn at the end of the year

An almost equal importance was attached by women to matters of health. The Federation did not wait for the armistice to claim that the Factory Acts should be put " into unrestricted opera-tion." This and similar resolutions of the Trades Union Con-gress were followed up by a general agitation on behalf of women munition workers   " Conditions of work," reported the Health of Munition Workers Committee, at the end of 1915, " are ac-cepted without question and without complaint, which, imme-diately detrimental to output, would, if continued, be ultimately disastrous to health." A working day of twelve or fourteen hours, continuous night-work or Sunday work, a double shift of eighteen hours or longer, so that the workers fell asleep on their machines, inadequate sanitary or canteen arrangements, or even lack of proper precautions against the deadly T.N.T. and other forms of poisoning to which women munition workers were subject—such grave abuses were at one time far from uncommon; and it was this state of things that the Federation now set out to attack. By means of questions in Parliament, deputations to the Government, public demonstrations and agitation in the Press, members fought their campaign Repeatedly, and in spite of direct opposition from employers, they urged on the Government that the carefully considered recommendations of the Health of Munition Workers Committee should be brought at once into effect. To this tireless vigilance on the part of the Federation, the great improvement which took place in the health conditions of munition factories during the latter half of the war may be traced in no small part.   In some munition factories, not only were wages higher and hours of work shorter, but provision for the health and comfort of the workers was in every way superior to any hitherto known in industry.

The Federation was represented on a number of the new " Whitley " or joint-industrial councils, which were set up towards the end of the war. Members were, however, opposed to the setting up of joint workshop committees, representing employers and employed, in unorganized or semi-organized trades Nor, indeed, was this the intention of the " Whitley " Committee, of which Miss Susan Lawrence and Mr J. J. Mallon were members A crowd of unorganized workers was no match for employers in bargaining. It was a well-known fact that under cover of consulting the workers, women could be cajoled or bullied by their employers into signing agreements which might seriously hamper trade union action afterwards For similar reasons, trade unionists were gravely suspicious of the new movement of " welfare supervision," which had found much favour with up-to-date employers, and was now progressing with alarming rapidity in munition factories. The workers were by no means indifferent to " welfare," nor unappreciative of the new attention given by employers to their comfort; whilst the exceptional circumstances of the war, by which thousands of inexperienced women and young people found themselves employed away from their homes and ordinary avocations, called no doubt for special measures of supervision. Yet trade unionists were aware of a new danger.   The scope of welfare supervision, as then defined by its advocates, covered literally the whole life of the worker, waking or sleeping, playing or fighting, living or dying The true welfare of the worker being the truer welfare of the employer, and both the truest welfare of the State, the " welfare supervisor " naïvely professed that in serving one she served all three; but, unfortunately for her profession, it was not so easy to make the best of the two worlds of capital and labour. In the actual conflict of opposing parties, it was evident that the " welfare supervisor " could only truly serve that party which employed and paid her. There were, moreover, technical objections to an office which combined in one more or less inexpert officer a medley of expert duties properly belonging to such distinct functionaries as the " works manager " and the " shop steward," not to speak of the factory inspector and the medical officer. Under cover of " welfare supervision," women saw themselves threatened with a new form of " scientific management " carried by means of the " welfare supervisor " into their most private and personal affairs. A well-attended conference of women's societies, summoned by the Standing Joint Committee of Industrial Women's Organizations in May, 1917, unanimously condemned the system, and proposed the following resolutions :

" That this Conference declares its conviction that the establishment of a system of welfare workers in the service of the employers can never materially increase the well-being of the workers, and that, while it advocates the employment of women to supervise the work of women, it does not consider that such supervision should be regarded as having any other function than those of management.

" It protests against any extension of control over the private lives of the workers, and asserts that in every factory, the welfare—social and physical—of the workers is best looked after by the workers themselves.

" With this object in view, this Conference urges that in every workshop and factory there should be a Trade Union Committee, not only to look after wages and similar conditions, but to interest itself in all the concerns of the workers under their direction, and to make representations therefore, when necessary, to the management."

On similar grounds, women were opposed to the provision of canteens and hostels by employers. They did not want to see the employer acting as " universal provider," and advised that the local housing authority should provide the necessary refreshment rooms and hostels which should be jointly controlled by it and the trade unions. The Conference further advocated a large increase in the number of women factory inspectors. " One factory inspector was worth a hundred welfare supervisors."

Similarly, it was the Federation which represented women on Government Committees, its members being for the most part the only women to be appointed The multiplication and growing importance of statutory committees caused a new need to be felt amongst industrial women for some form of authoritative central

organization, which would make it its business to see that their
interests were properly represented on these bodies, both in their
capacity as trade unionists and as working-class wives and
mothers.   The setting up of the new Pensions Committees in 1916
brought the matter to a head.   It had for many years been the
custom of the Women's Trade Union League, the Federation, the
Women's Co-operative Guild (representing married women), the
Women's Labour League (afterwards the Women's Section of the
Labour Party), and the Railwaywomen's Guild (representing
wives of railwaymen), to appoint a joint-committee for the discussion of urgent public matters, and these now formed the Standing
Joint-Committee of Industrial Women's Organizations, of which
Miss Macarthur was appointed chairman.   This influential body,
whose constitution was afterwards enlarged so as to allow the
affiliation of any industrial organization having an important
female membership, became immediately recognized by the Labour
Party and also by the Government as the chief authority on industrial women's questions

Trade union women were meanwhile discovering a new interest in
political matters   The almost fanatical faith in women's suffrage,
which in the years immediately preceding the war led middle-class
suffragists to put their cause in the forefront of all other social
or political reforms, found comparatively few adherents amongst
industrial women, who mostly preferred to join with labour men
in the larger claim for adult suffrage.   Trade union women were,
however, none the less keen feminists.   At Labour Party Conferences, it was repeatedly urged by Miss Macarthur on behalf
of the Federation that " no reform bill could be acceptable to
the labour and socialist movement which did not include women "
In the early years of the war, the Federation drew the attention of
Parliament to the vital concern of its members in immediate political issues, and declared that " it is only through the franchise
that women can take part in choosing the national representatives who will settle these important questions."   The Representation of the People Act became law in 1918.   The Bill was supported by the Federation, but not without protest, and members
did their best to abolish the absurd age-limit by which the women's
vote was qualified.   The absurdity was all the more glaring because this age-limit of thirty years excluded from the franchise
the large majority of women war workers, to whose magnificent
achievement Cabinet Ministers actually professed to owe their
conversion to women's suffrage.   Members pledged themselves
not to rest content " until every woman was entitled to a vote
in virtue of her womanhood on exactly the same terms as every
man is now in virtue of his manhood."   The Emancipation Bill
of 1919, by which the Labour Party tried to remove the remaining

sex anomalies, found its most active supporters amongst industrial women. As soon as the vote was granted the Federation decided by an overwhelming majority of its members in favour of political action. At the general election of 1918, Miss Macarthur was accordingly put forward as candidate for the Stourbridge Division—the seat of her early successes in the Black Country. The personal enthusiasm aroused by the Prime Minister at the hour of victory—cleverly exploited by the " Northcliffe " Press in the interests of the Coalition—made her defeat a foregone conclusion, but few candidates of known pacifist sympathies fared better at the hands of the electors.

In the same year, Miss Margaret Bondfield, organizing secretary of the Federation since 1915, headed the list of unsuccessful candidates for the Parliamentary Committee of the Trades Union Congress; and, upon the resignation of Mr. Bramley, a few months later, she took his place on the Committee, and was the first woman to receive this honour. The new constitution of the Labour Party, by which four places on its executive committee are reserved to women, had meanwhile assured to labour women a direct share in political affairs. Miss Susan Lawrence was elected the first year, and was joined by Miss Macarthur the following year. The international labour movement found strong supporters from the beginning amongst trade union women. It was, perhaps, not entirely accidental that at the Trades Union Congress of 1888 the historic International Labour Conference of the following year was proposed by a woman delegate. At Labour Party Conferences in the years immediately preceding 1914, women delegates urged upon the Government again and again that it should check the mad race in armaments and renounce secret diplomacy, which they believed to be directly conducive to war. Miss Bondfield was appointed chairman of the Women's Council of Socialist and Labour Organizations, and represented industrial women on more than one foreign mission during the war. Later on labour women sent their full complement of representatives to the Berne International Labour Conference of 1918, and to the two important American conferences of the following year.

THE AFTERMATH.

Generally speaking, it may be said that the effects of the war were not to raise new problems of female labour, nor yet to solve old ones, but to bring matters to a head. These matters centred as usual round the question of wages. From one end of organized trades to the other, the old feud between employers and men trade unionists broke out afresh, the former maintaining their right to exploit for profit " cheap and docile " female labour, and the latter theirs to prohibit women's employment, or at least to

confine it within definite limits. Prompted by patriotism, or by
necessity, the two parties came to terms. Men trade
unionists agreed to withdraw their restrictions under certain conditions of restoration and wages, whilst employers promised
" equal pay." Concessions on both sides were, however, strictly
confined to the period of the war The chief anxiety of either
party, indeed, seems to have been to return so far as possible
to its old post of vantage. Employers had certainly no intention of extending their concession of " equal pay," or of such
approximate terms as had been agreed upon during the war, a
moment longer than the occasion required. In the light of war
experience, the offer of "equal payment by results," now made by
some enlightened employers, could hardly be taken seriously by
trade unionists Rightly or wrongly, the offer was suspected as mere
camouflage. It is not without significance that during the war
the few examples of " equal pay " were almost entirely confined
to trades for which women for one or other reason were not
particularly well-adapted, so that employers were not especially
desirous of keeping them. The hasty action of the London tram
and 'bus companies in discharging women conductors actually
led to strikes amongst their men colleagues who, in spite of
Congress resolutions, objected to see them turned out except
for foretime men employees. The United Vehicle Workers
deliberately championed its women members against attacks from
the Discharged Soldiers' and Sailors' Association Bitter opposition to " equal pay," on the other hand, came from employers
in such trades as engineering or aircraft wood-working, where
on light " process " work women admittedly equalled or
excelled men in output, and employers were notoriously anxious
to keep them Representatives of the Engineering Employers'
Federation told the War Cabinet Committee on Women in Industry that after the war they would actually prefer to employ
boys rather than to pay women more than 66 per cent. of men's
wages !

Under the circumstances, the men's trade unions were equally
disinclined to reverse their pre-war policy The old suspicion, that
women's employment was only desired by employers as " cheap
labour," was confirmed by recent experience, and men trade
unionists were determined to reimpose their restrictions on female
labour. Nor was this decision opposed by industrial women,
who were quick to acknowledge the common justice of the men's
claim that pledges given by the Government and the employers
must be redeemed in full This necessity seemed, indeed, so plain
to men and women trade unionists that the only matter for surprise
was that they should have had to insist upon it The Restoration
of the Pre-war Practices Act, which became law in July, 1918,

had the whole-hearted support of the National Federation of Women Workers as well as that of the great general labour unions representing "substituted" workers of either sex. The Act was only enforceable for one year, but the time was not too short to reinstate men in their own trades and to disperse women so effectually as to make their employment at least difficult in future. Possession is nine-tenths of the law; and powers were meanwhile given to the trade unions, whereby to compel employers to restore any customs which had been departed from during the war. The Act further laid down that, where new industries or new branches of an industry had grown up in an establishment during the war, or in new establishments, the employer should be under a similar obligation to introduce, or to permit to introduce, "such trade practices as obtained before the war in other establishments where that industry or branch was carried on under circumstances the most nearly analogous to those of the establishments in question." The trade unions were able to expel women by this means, not only from the old work places of their members, but from new factories or districts to which women had been introduced, or even from new industries, such as general aircraft or aircraft woodwork, which had largely grown up during the war. Such far-reaching powers of expulsion were severely criticized by middle-class feminists. To the latter, it seemed particularly unjust that "substituted" women should be expelled from certain new industries, which their own labour had done so much to build up. The fact, nevertheless, remained that women could not have been employed in these any more than in other men's trades except under cover of the Treasury agreement, and to have exempted them from the provisions of the present Act would have been an equally serious breach of good faith. By itself, however, the agitation of middle-class women's organization was obviously unavailing to upset the Act. It failed to gain support, not only from industrial women, but even from employers, who had their share in the framing of the Act.

Women's position at the end of the war can certainly not be described as enviable. As war work came to an end, or men returned to claim their old places, women were discharged wholesale. In the autumn of 1919, over three-quarters of a million less women were employed in industry than at the time of the armistice.* Of the huge army of "substituted" women, it is probable that not more than a few hundred thousands remained, and these were largely composed of clerks, men clerks having no "practices" to restore. Many women were not sorry, no doubt, to be relieved from the strain of men's work, and either to retire from industry or to return to previous occupations. In

* See Table III

order not to discharge them, some employers deliberately started new *women's* industries, whilst considerable efforts were made by the trade unions to replace women as well as men in their old positions. Thousands of women were, nevertheless, expelled from employment which they definitely preferred to any other known to them. The strongest pressure brought to bear by the Employment Exchanges, even to the extent of withdrawing unemployment benefit, failed to drive any large number of women back to domestic service and the uncongenial conditions of " living in." Large numbers of women drifted into unemployment At the end of 1919, when unemployment benefit was abruptly withdrawn by the Government, the number of unemployed women was estimated by the Federation at certainly not less than 100,000.*

But, if the position of industrial women after the war cannot be described as enviable, yet in all probability it was not so profoundly unenviable as at any time in past history. As the result of four years' experience in organized men's trades, thousands of women had learned a lesson which they did not intend to forget They had learned, in the first place, the power of organization and, in the second place, the value of their own labour One of the most remarkable and hopeful signs of the year following the armistice was the rapid recovery in the female membership of the general labour unions, which were largely composed of " substituted " women. As these women returned to their own trades, they not only rejoined the union, but they brought in new recruits with them. The impulse to organize, which had come from close contact with organized men, now spread from end to end of the traditional women's trades. Dressmakers and milliners, laundry workers, hotel and restaurant workers, even domestic servants began to form effective organizations. Within a year of the armistice, the general labour unions had practically recovered their female membership, whilst nearly all women's organizations were rapidly gaining in numbers, and learning to enforce their claims In comparatively well-organized industries, where women had hitherto been content with casual advances of wages, they now demanded a fixed standard. The question of a minimum time-rate, as a supplement to their piece-work " list," was even discussed by cotton operatives. In the wool and worsted trades, the dyeing and bleaching trades, the printing trades, the pottery trades, the tobacco trades, it was possible to fix national minimum rates for the first time, which at the end of 1919 ranged from rather less than 30/- in the pottery trades

* In January 1920, there were about 3,000 women being trained in *women's* trades under the Minister of Labour schemes The training, like that of local education authorities before the war, was mostly confined to domestic service, dressmaking and some wholesale tailoring

to rather more than 40/- in the dyeing and bleaching trades. The movement in standardizing wages was still more remarkable in the traditional women's trades. Dressmakers and women's light clothing workers, who had received practically no advances during the war, secured a national minimum wage of 28/- a week of forty-eight hours* in April, 1919, raised to 8½d. an hour in 1920. Organized women shop assistants were now able to enforce a four-fifths standard, whilst municipal clerks who were comparatively well-organized actually succeeded in securing "equal pay." Laundry workers, who at the time of the armistice had been content to receive a rate of from 18/- to 23/- for a week of fifty-four to sixty hours, secured under the Trade Boards Act a national minimum of 28/- (forty-eight hours) in November, 1919, raised afterwards to 35/- in London and 30/- in the provinces. Throughout the "sweated" food and clothing trades, there was a similar upward tendency of wages. No doubt this effect was partly due to improved machinery for regulating wages. Under the Wages (Temporary Regulation) Act, it was incumbent on employers to pay rates of wages "not less than the prescribed rate for the class of worker in question," or such other rates as should be determined by arbitration. This Act was operative for one year from the time of the armistice, and similar provisions were afterwards embodied in the Industrial Courts Act and prolonged to September 1920. This protection against an immediate fall of wages was especially to the advantage of weakly-organized classes of workers by whom it was most needed. Women's industries of all kinds, meanwhile, were being rapidly scheduled under the new Trade Boards Act, which was extended to such important groups of women as shop assistants, laundry and women's clothing workers, flax, and hemp workers. It is confidently expected that not less than a hundred separate industries will be scheduled under the Act by the end of 1920, covering some two and a half millions of workers. In other industries, joint industrial or "Whitley" councils were set up for the same purpose of regulating wages and working conditions. Finally, in adopting the report of the newly-appointed National Industrial Council, the principle of a national minimum wage and that of maximum hours of work were definitely accepted by the Government, which drew up both an Eight-Hour Bill† and a Minimum Wage Bill, "constituting a commission to enquire and report on minimum time-rates of wages" during the summer of 1919. The good or bad working of machinery depends, however,

* Fixed by special rates under the Wages (Temporary Regulation) Act of 1918

† The 8-hour Bill was reintroduced in 1920, as the Hours of Employment Bill, but the Minimum Wage Bill would seem to have been withdrawn.

H

primarily on the human will which controls it; and new machinery for regulating wages, unless effectually controlled by the workers, may be turned to their actual disadvantage. Trade unionists have still to rely in the main on their own exertions. It is through loyalty to their fellows in the workshop, through courage and devotion in serving a common cause—which may be said to be a just one in the measure that the equal claims of other units are respected—that men and women may best prepare themselves for citizenship of that greater community which constitutes the nation, or of that greatest community of all—the League of Nations Whilst trade union men are pressing forward towards the goal of economic freedom, trade union women—with infinite courage and patience, and free from bitterness against men because they are excluded from trades whose hard-won traditions they have been unable to uphold—have set themselves to the task of wiping out for ever from their name the time-long stain of " black-leg " labour.

PART II
SURVEY *of* WOMEN'S ORGANIZATIONS

CHAPTER I.
WOMEN'S UNIONS IN GENERAL.

AT the end of 1918, the female membership of all trade unions, excluding teachers' and artists' organizations,* was approximately 1,086,000, representing about 17 per cent. of the total number of organized workers.† The figure had risen by nearly 750,000 during the war, showing an increase of 160 per cent as compared with one of 45 per cent. in the case of men. There is, moreover, reason to suppose that this rapid advance was continued during 1919 Official figures are not available, but those given by industrial unions—notably by textile unions, tailors' unions, printing unions—point in this direction. The movement during the war was most remarkable amongst transport and general labour unions, whose membership was largely composed of " substituted " women From a female membership of a few hundred in 1914—mainly general workers belonging to the Dockers' Union —the transport unions in four years had enrolled 68,000 women, of whom 50,000‡ were employed on the railways. It is, however, probable that only a small fraction of this number remained at the end of 1919. The enormous increase in the general labour unions of from 24,000 to 216,000 women would seem, on the other hand, to have been well maintained, discharged munition workers rejoining the union as they transferred to other industries. The movement during the war was, however, by no means confined to " substituted " women, but was almost equally remarkable in women's trades The figure of female membership rose in four years from 253,000 to 423,000 in textile unions, from 26,000 to 119,000 in clothing unions, from 8,000 to 39,000 in printing unions, from 2,000 to 23,000 in pottery and chemical unions, from 34,000 to 145,000 amongst clerks (including post office workers) and shop

* The figure for women teachers is 160,000, but represents more than the actual number of women, many of whom belong to more than one organization.

† See Table I   ‡ Including 14,000 clerks

assistants The increase was relatively small in the case of women cotton operatives, who were already comparatively well-organized, being only from 210,000 to 260,000, but the cotton unions still represent the largest single group of organized women, or between one-quarter and one-fifth of the female membership of all trade unions.

It is not possible to estimate exactly the number of organized women in each industry In some cases the line of division between unions is an occupational rather than an industrial one, as in the case of clerks, whilst many thousands of women belonging to organized industries are included in general labour unions, which make no exact returns for industrial groups. The general labour unions include nearly one-fifth of the total number of trade union women, the proportion of these members who belong to organized trades being probably considerably higher in the case of women than men. The female membership of the metal unions, which was only 11,000 at the end of 1918, may be estimated at less than one-tenth of the organized women in these trades. This phenomenon is no doubt most remarkable in the engineering trades, where women are excluded from membership by the skilled men's societies, but it is also apparent amongst chemical workers, wood-workers, in food and tobacco, in some small clothing trades, and to some extent in textile trades, where the principal societies are local in character, and women are organized by general labour unions outside the main industrial centres. It is least conspicuous in the boot and shoe trade, amongst printing and paper workers, of whom practically none except paper-bag makers belong to general labour unions, and in such highly localized industries as the potteries Generally speaking, the female membership of each industrial group represents less than the actual number of organized workers; but, bearing this fact in mind, a comparison between different industries is not without significance Taking broad fields of industry, the proportion of organized women is comparatively high in the textile trades, or 52 per cent , being as high as 75 per cent. in the cotton industry, or 82 per cent. in textile dyeing, bleaching, etc. In the clothing trades, it is 54 per cent. amongst tailoresses and clothiers' operatives, but not more than 21 per cent. for all clothing workers. It was 66 per cent. amongst transport workers at the time of the armistice, but these women have since largely left the industry. It is 27 per cent amongst printing and paper workers, and 59 per cent. amongst pottery workers. Taking all manual workers (excluding domestic servants, who are practically unorganized, and black-coated workers) it is over 36 per cent. The proportion is comparatively small amongst commercial clerks and shop assistants, or less than 8 per cent , and not more than 25 per cent. amongst civil service clerks, organization being most advanced amongst post office workers, but it is as high as 56 per cent. amongst railway clerks. For all women workers (including clerks and shop assistants, but not teachers or artists) it is about 20 per cent., as compared with over 65 per cent. in the case of men.

Of the 383 trade unions which enrol women members, 347 are joint-organizations, and thirty-six are all-women's societies, the majority of the latter being small independent bodies, although some are controlled by allied men's societies. Apart from the National Federation of Women Workers, their aggregate female membership does not amount to more than a few thousands. The large majority of trade unions are affiliated to the Trades Union Congress. The rules make no distinction of sex, but the part played by women at its meetings is a comparatively small one and mainly confined to members of the National Federation of Women Workers. At recent congresses not more than about thirty women have attended amongst some 800 or 900 delegates; whilst Miss Margaret Bondfield, representing the Federation, is the only woman representative on the Parliamentary Committee. The Women's Trade Union League continues its good work in promoting trade unionism amongst women, and in watching their interests. Its constitution has not substantially changed since last century, and " sympathetic " persons are still included with trade unionists on its executive committee. For a fee of 2/6 per thousand members, any *bona fide* trade union may affiliate, in return for which sum the union is entitled to the services of a woman organizer for at least one week in the year. About a hundred societies are affiliated in this way, including many textile unions   The function of the Women's Trade Union League in summoning conferences and issuing reports on industrial women's questions tends, however, to be taken over at present by the Standing Joint-Committee of Industrial Women's Organizations, which represent such bodies as the Women's Co-operative Guild, as well as trade unions which are largely composed of women   This important body acts as official advisory committee to the Labour Party on women's questions   The Manchester and Salford Women's Trade Union Council, and its sister body the Manchester and Salford Women's Trades Council, after twenty-five years of promoting trade unionism amongst women, finally merged themselves in the Manchester Trades and Labour Council in 1919.

Chapter II.

Miners' Unions.

Miners' unions have not infrequently included women in the past, but the number was insignificant until the latter part of the war, when some fourteen or fifteen local societies had a female membership of about 10,000, representing 92 per cent. of women empoyed at the pit-head, "substituted" as well as regular workers. The Lanarkshire Miners' Union, whose female membership rose from a few score in 1914 to over 2,000 at the end of 1918, is a typical society. Women pay 4d. a week (raised from 2d. before the war) against 1/- paid by men, and receive strike pay in proportion, and the usual trade benefits. They are subject to no disqualifications, but, on the other hand, play no part in management. The policy of the union is to do away with women's employment at the pit-head, "owing to the conviction in members' minds that their employment about collieries is not suitable." The number of women employed, in fact, decreased considerably during 1919 Wages were mainly unregulated before the war, averaging from 1/9 to 3/- a shift, but since then rates have been fixed amounting to 6/3 a shift (including the war bonus of 3/- and the Sankey award of 2/-) for ordinary workers, 7/10 to 8/6 for coal pickers and 8/2 to 9/1 for drawers-off at the end of 1919 "Substituted" women employed in saw-milling received on an average 8/-, as against 15/6 paid to men.

CHAPTER III.

METAL UNIONS.

Women employed in engineering and the allied metal trades are almost entirely organized by general labour unions, not more than 11,000 being included in metal unions.* The skilled men's engineering societies, whose members prohibit female labour, are, without exception, closed to women. The National Union of Brass Workers and Metal Mechanics can record nearly half-a-century of unsuccessful opposition to women's employment in the Birmingham brass trades, and "females" were only recognized during the war "in order to help the country in its perilous condition"; but, in general engineering, women were not employed until recently, or were confined to "purely automatic operations" or boys' machines, so that the Amalgamated Society of Engineers was not directly affected. The important effects of "substitution" during the war have been sufficiently described in a previous chapter. Women were successfully introduced, not only in munition factories, but in general engineering and tool-making shops, aircraft and ship-building. Under the Treasury and other agreements, as we have seen, the engineering unions consented to withdraw their restrictions on female labour, subject to certain conditions of restoration and wages, but women were not admitted to membership. Their failure to secure men's wages could, indeed, have no other effect than to confirm men in their policy of prohibition, and members foresaw an obvious inconvenience in admitting women to membership and expelling them afterwards from employment. The Amalgamated Society of Engineers was, however, alive to the necessity of organizing "substituted" women, and with this object entered an alliance with the National Federation of Women Workers, to whose efforts its members gave active support during the war. The Electrical Trades Union opened its doors to women in 1915, but its female membership remained comparatively small. The Manchester and Salford Association of Women Machine and Electrical Workers, established by the Manchester Women's Trade Union Council in 1889, may be classed as a women's engineering union, but its members do not exceed 200, whilst the little Society of Women Welders did not survive the discharge of "substituted" women during 1919 The Women's Engineering Society, established by middle-

* Women's wages in engineering and allied metal trades are discussed under " general labour unions."

class women towards the end of the war, does not rank as a true union in the ordinary sense.

In the *tin-plate* trade (South Wales), the Iron and Steel Trades Confederation (incorporating the British Steel Smelters), has included a few hundred women since about 1906. They pay for the most part a boy's contribution of 3d. a week, but are subject to no disqualification, taking part in local affairs and acting in some cases as branch secretaries. Female labour is prohibited in the actual processes of smelting, but women are recognized with boys in cold-rolling, and to some extent in pickling and in opening plates—a comparatively heavy operation. Under an agreement of June, 1914, rates of wages were fixed at from 1/6 to 2/2 per day, according to the process, for women and boy cold roll workers; but " as in some districts great difficulties were experienced in getting cold roll labour, such works were allowed to make the best terms they could." These rates were increased by 80 per cent. during the war, whilst women were introduced as unskilled labourers and as crane-drivers. The terms of the statutory orders, issued by the Minister of Munitions, were rejected by the British Steel Smelters as unsatisfactory, and " substituted " women secured men's full rates of wages, amounting to 46/- plus 12½ per cent. on earnings for labourers, and 51/6 plus 12½ per cent. on earnings for crane-drivers, although the latter were liable to a small deduction from wages on account of extra assistance or supervision. " Substituted " women were members of the union, but they had mostly been discharged by the end of 1919. The finishing section of the tin-plate trade, where women are employed in " dipping," is mainly catered for by the Dockers' Union and the National Union of General Workers. A branch of women crane-drivers, organized by the National Federation of Women Workers, was transferred to the Amalgamated Union of Engine and Crane Drivers in 1918.

In the *foundry* trades, where women are employed in sorting castors, examining, etc., and to some extent in core-making, the Amalgamated Society of Core Makers had at one time under discussion the question of their recognition in small core making, and the possible advantages of female labour over boy labour " A lad would not be content to do this work regularly, his ambitions would naturally prompt him with a desire to become a proficient core-maker, and he would no doubt during the time he was cheap receive every encouragement from his employers But considering the number of boys that would be required to do this work, it is quite evident that eventually the number of core-makers would be increased to such an extent that our trade would be overcrowded, and that there would not be enough work in normal times to provide above half of us with anything like

regular employment ''* The Society did not, however, decide
to open its doors to women.

In the small metal trades, the Amalgamated Union of File
Trades and some small cutlery societies have included women
for many years, but the aggregate female membership does not
exceed 1,000. The Amalgamated Union of File Trades, which
includes 700 women in a total membership of 2,000, is chiefly
interesting by reason of the fact that four places are allocated
to women on its executive committee. A minimum wage for
women was finally gained by the Union in June, 1919, the rate
being fixed at 35/- a week on piece-work and 38/- on time-work
The National Union of Gold, Silver and Kindred Trades, which
admitted women in 1915, and had a female membership of about
2,000 in 1918, is the only other metal union which includes women.
Women chain-makers and other small metal workers are organized
by general labour unions.

* *Quarterly Report* December, 1915.

CHAPTER IV

TEXTILE UNIONS.

The textile unions, of whose 600,000 members over two-thirds are women, comprise even to-day about two-fifths of the female membership of all trade unions. Each separate industry is organized by a separate union or group of unions, although some small societies cater generally for textile workers, and there is a certain overlap, notably between wool and dyeing societies in the finishing departments. Outside the main textile centres, textile workers are organized by general labour unions.

Cotton unions.—The local cotton associations, which form the classic example of the joint organization, include over 300,000 members, of whom about five-sixths are women.* They fall into four main groups, viz., associations of weavers, warpers and winders, which organize all women employed in the weaving departments, and have an aggregate female membership of nearly 200,000; associations of beamers, twisters and drawers-in, which include some 500 women twisters and drawers-in; associations of card and blowing room operatives, which admit all women employed in the preparing departments and also ring-spinners, the aggregate female membership being about 60,000; and operative spinners' associations, which comprise some 7,000 women in their piecers' sections. These local associations belong almost entirely to the northern counties district, which forms the centre of the cotton industry, and are federated into four central organizations, namely, the Northern Counties Amalgamated Association of Weavers, covering probably 95 per cent. of organized weavers; the Amalgamated Association of Beamers, Twisters and Drawers-in; the Amalgamated Association of Card and Blowing Room Operatives; and the Amalgamated Association of Operative Cotton Spinners. The local associations enjoy, however, a large degree of autonomy. The several amalgamations are in turn affiliated to the United Textile Workers' Associations, which represents the general body of organized cotton operatives.

Outside these centralized organizations, there are about a dozen local unions, including a few small independent societies, mainly Roman Catholic in membership, the Scottish societies, and three

* This number includes " funeral " members, viz., operatives who have retired or temporarily retired from industry. In some local associations, the percentage of " funeral " members amongst women amounts to 25 per cent.

small all-women's societies—the Manchester and Salford Power
Loom Weavers, the Manchester and Salford Ring Spinners, and
the Manchester and Salford Patent Cop Winders, Bobbin and
Hank Winders, Gassers, Doublers, Reelers and Preparers, all of
which were established under the auspices of the Manchester and
Salford Women's Trades Council. In the Bristol and other out-
lying districts a proportion of cotton operatives are organized by
general labour unions.

Taking the cotton industry as a whole, the proportion of
organized women may roughly be estimated at 75 per cent. for
all departments, or 80 per cent. for weaving departments; but
these proportions are substantially higher for some groups of
workers, being nearly 100 per cent. for weavers in certain districts, 95 per cent. for card and blowing room operatives, and
97 per cent. for twisters and drawers-in. Until recent years,
however, women were markedly behind men in organization.

The Northern Counties Amalgamated Association of Cotton
Weavers, formed from forty-one local associations of weavers,
warpers and winders, has a total membership of about 225,000,
of which over three-quarters are women. This proportion, which
has increased from about two-thirds in 1914, varies, however,
considerably from one district to another. In the Oldham, Manchester and Wigan districts, it has for many years been as high
as 90 per cent. At one time, in fact, the Wigan Association
was practically a women's society. The majority of members of
either sex are weavers, organization being less advanced amongst
warpers and winders, who are entirely composed of women.
Weaving runs in families, and the associations rely largely on
the man's influence in persuading his wife and children to join
the union. The Blackburn Association, as we have seen, provides in its rules that " no person shall be eligible for any official
position in the Society, whose wife and children (if working) are
not members of the union." About one-third of the female members are married women, and young girls mostly expect to return
to industry after marriage. They take their trade almost as
seriously as men, and undergo the same period of several years'
apprenticeship.

The rules of the local associations vary considerably in detail
from one district to another, but follow broadly the same lines.
These are no distinctions of sex, and men and women join the
union on the same scales of contribution and benefits. In some
districts it is remarked that although their earnings are the same,
women tend to make a lower payment than men. In backward
areas, a 3d. contribution was common until recently, and the
old-fashioned 1d. contributor was hardly extinct. The present
vigorous campaign to level up contributions has, however, resulted

in a minimum rate of 4d per week, which is now to be raised to 6d. or more. Hundreds of women already pay from 9d. to 1/-, and compare in this well with men. The high cost of the house-to-house collection, which in straggling districts amounts to 12½ per cent. of the takings, has sometimes been charged against the female members. The system no doubt originated in women's reluctance to leave home in the evening or to enter the public-house, which in the early days of organization was the usual meeting-place, but it has long been adopted by members of either sex. Women are said to be otherwise regular and punctual contributors. The benefits include trade protection,* and generally breakdown and funeral pay, but apart from statutory schemes, no unemployment or sickness benefit. The cotton unions have not been affected to the same extent as some other societies by the problem of excessive sickness amongst women.

Women enjoy full rights of membership in all associations without exception. By the rules of some societies, the low-scale contributor is disqualified for office—a provision by which women have been sometimes affected in the past, but these rules have practically ceased to be operative with the recent rise in the rate of contribution. Women are backward in attending branch meetings, and to this cause alone is mainly attributed their failure to be nominated for election to responsible posts. The executive committee of the Amalgamated Association is entirely composed of men In the Oldham, Manchester and Wigan districts, where women form a large majority of the members, they have always sat on local committees. A woman president has held office both at Oldham and Wigan But, outside these districts, women were rarely elected even on local committees until the men's absence during the war practically compelled them to come forward and take their share in affairs. At Chorley, where a first woman was elected in 1916, six women were elected the next year, other women being appointed as collectors and one woman as auditor. The various devices adopted by modern societies, in order to ensure representation to women, find no favour amongst the cotton unions. By the rule of the Blackburn Association, two places are reserved on the executive committee to a *warper* and *winder*, which has incidentally the effect of reserving two places to women, but the distinction refers to the *trade* and not to the *sex* of the worker. No place is reserved to women weavers, whose trade interests are identical with men's.

The local secretaries, who mostly represent their associations on the central executive, exercise necessarily great influence on local committees, but the important post of secretary, although in

* Under this head may be included strike, lock-out, and victimization pay and free legal advice.

theory open to either sex, is in practice closed to women. The duties of this office combine, with those of secretary, those of rate-fixer and organizer, and the necessary degree of technical qualification is said to be lacking in women. In some districts, women are appointed as "collectors," and assist in organizing work, but even such minor posts were reserved until recently to men.

Men and women have always worked together as cotton weavers. In normal times, more men are employed on four or six-loom machines, and more women on two or four looms, but there are no lines of sex division and no restrictions on female labour. "The complaint is unfair," writes a trade union correspondent, "that women are excluded from the best paid section of the trade." It is, moreover, against the rule of their union that some men steal a march on women, and clean their machines out of the legal factory hours. "We object to men doing work overtime," declares a local official, "it acts unfairly to the women who are not allowed to do it, but who will risk being penalized before they will be behind the pace-makers." Women are, however, not encouraged to tune their own machines, or in any way to qualify for the post of overlooker. The duties of the overlooker include the lifting of the heavy "beam," and women could not in any case be employed unless the factory was equipped with up-to-date lifting apparatus and trucks. Contrary to official opinion, however, some women of practical experience believe themselves capable of tuning their machines and would prefer to do so instead of losing time in waiting for the overlooker.

The piece-work lists of the cotton weaver, the earliest of which dates from 1853, make no distinction of sex or age. Men and women, girls and boys, receive the same rate for the same job, and women earn as much as men, and "imagine themselves in quite a higher class or grade than the ring-spinner or card-room hand." Before the war, the average earnings of four-loom weavers were estimated by trade unionists at from 28/- to 32/- on fine counts, and from 22/- to 28/- on coarse counts * According to the Board of Trade figures for 1906, the earnings of men and women cotton weavers, although employed on the same machines, show a slight difference in amount. The reasons most usually given are delay in waiting for the overlooker who tunes the women's machines, and additional assistance required from "tenters" or learners, whose wages are paid by the weaver. It is possible, however, that other conditions were not exactly equal, and that differences could have been discovered in the cloth as well as a difference in age, which was twenty years and

* Mr. Greenhaugh, former secretary of the Rishton Weavers' Association, and witness before the War Cabinet Committee on Women in Industry

over for men, but only eighteen years and over for women. In some establishments, where the operatives are assisted by labourers in removing the full "spools" from the sheds, the extra wage cost is similarly charged against them; but this charge would almost certainly be compensated for to the weaver by increased output and additional earnings on the looms. Men and women, moreover, enjoy the same assistance. A difference in output between men and women cotton weavers is not at present remarked by trade unionists, or by employers, who "would be inclined, if there was sufficient female labour, to give the women the preference."*

Of the "substituted" women employed in cotton manufacture during the war, about two-thirds were weavers, women being promoted from three or four-loom to five or six-loom machines, and young girls from two or three-looms to three or four-looms. No safeguards were required as to restoration or wages, but some signs of overstrain were remarked amongst young girls promoted to adult machines, who were "off sick more often than other workers with the inevitable effect on output." Owing to slackness of trade in the early part of the war, wages failed at first completely to keep pace with prices, whilst workers were exposed to almost continuous short time. A first advance of 5 per cent. was received in January, 1916, and a similar sum in January, 1917. Progress was afterwards more rapid, and the aggregate war advances amounted to 110 per cent. on pre-war rates in December, 1918, and to 140 per cent. at the end of the following year.† At the same time, a movement was started to reduce hours of work, and a forty-eight instead of a fifty-five-hour week was secured in the summer of 1919. For the first time in history a demand now arose amongst cotton operatives for a weekly *minimum time wage,* to be guaranteed irrespective of *piece earnings.* The demand has not yet taken definite shape, but members would certainly oppose a differential rate for men and women weavers employed on the same machines. Women cotton weavers were, indeed, by no means content with the differential scale of unemployment benefit provided under the scheme of the Cotton Control Board.‡ This scheme, which was adopted in the summer of 1917, gave a benefit of 25/- a week to men, but one of only 15/- to women (raised to 18/- in August, 1918), with an extra 1/- a week for each dependent child. At one time, the Board had actually decided to grant the men's full amount to "substituted" youths who were promoted to four-loom machines, but it refused

* *Report of War Cabinet Committee on Women in Industry.* Page 89.
† Raised to 210 per cent. in May 1920.
‡ The Board was composed of seven representatives of the manufacturers and merchants and four trade unionists.

the same concession to women, and their acute resentment obliged it to reverse its decision as to youths. " If the Cotton Control Board," wrote a correspondent of the *Cotton Factory Times* in November, 1917, " could just have a few minutes' interview with those of our members who are drawing allowances which in some cases only represents 50 per cent. of their previous earnings, it would do more to convince the Board of an absolute need of a rise in the scale of pay than any number of appeals made by representatives on their behalf." The writer, consciously or unconsciously, touches a vital matter. Why was no women appointed on the Cotton Control Board?

The Amalgamated Association of Beamers, Twisters and Drawers-in, formed in 1890, comprises thirty-nine local associations and some 6,500 members, of whom 500 are women. In constitution, the local associations follow broadly the same lines as the weavers' unions. The rules make no distinction of sex, and women are eligible for every official post. The executive committee is entirely composed of men, but a woman was elected to the Hyde district committee in 1911, and many branch committees include women. In view of the small proportion of female members, women's share in management compares well with that of other cotton unions.

Women are not employed as " beamers," being unable to handle the heavy " beams "; but, in some districts, such as Hyde, Stockport, Wigan, Hadfield and Macclesfield, they have always been recognized by the union as " twisters " and " drawers-in." The work is light and delicate in character, and admittedly well-suited to women. Elsewhere female labour is prohibited; and, in more than one district during the war, men members reaffirmed their decision not to teach girl " reachers " or apprentices. This policy, however, was reconsidered later, and women were temporarily admitted in prohibited districts. Nor does the men's policy of prohibition seem to have its usual justification in the case of " twisters " and " drawers-in," in that women receive the same piece-rates, and earn as much as men. Women require, it is true, assistance from men in lifting the heavy " beams," but no deductions are allowed from the rate, and the women pay the men for this assistance a small fee of about 1/- a week. The pre-war weekly earnings averaged from £2 to £2 10/-, to which sum must be added the war bonus of 140 per cent. (December, 1919).

The Amalgamated Association of Card and Blowing Room Operatives comprises fourteen local associations and nearly 79,000 members, of whom over three-quarters are women. The female members are mainly composed of card and blowing room operatives, but include a section of ring-spinners. Ring-spinning, as we have seen, was first introduced in the 'eighties, but these

women were refused admission to the spinners' unions, and they
remained practically unorganized until the end of the century,
when they were admitted to the card and blowing room associations.   Organization made, however, comparatively little progress amongst them until recent years.   There are no sex distinctions in the rules of any association, but, owing to the difference in wages, men and women are admitted on different scales
of contribution and benefits.   In the typical Bolton district, men
pay 6d. to 1/-, according as they earn more or less than 20/- per
week, whilst women pay 4d or 6d , according as they earn more
or less than 12/-, whilst benefits, which include trade, accident,
breakdown and funeral, vary in proportion   There are no women
on the executive committee, but women serve on district and
branch committees.   In the important Bolton district, the local
committees were entirely composed of men until 1913, when some
of the better-paid women, who had failed to benefit by a certain
agreement, felt themselves aggrieved and came forward in consequence as candidates for election.   Women mostly prefer, however, to leave the management to men.

Unlike men and women weavers, men and women card and
blowing room operatives are employed in different departments,
men being practically confined to the rough and somewhat dangerous processes of the card-room, or else to posts as overlookers or
labourers.   During the war, various attempts were made to introduce women on men's work; and, in February, 1917, the Association entered into an agreement with the Master Spinners' Association, by which women's employment was temporarily permitted
in a scheduled list of occupations. Preference was given to women
members of the union, and a clause laid down that "the aggregate wage shall in all cases be the full list rate of wages."   The
experiment met, however, with no great success.   Women were
only employed as assistants, two women taking the place of one
man, or they were confined to lighter parts of the work, so that
an extra burden was thrown on the men.   The difference in wages
worked out at about 60 per cent.   In the blowing-room, where
the majority of workers are women, earnings on the whole are
below the standard for weavers   In 1914, wages averaged about
16/- a week for time-workers, and from 20/- to 24/- for piece-
workers, whilst ring-spinners, whether time or piece-workers,
received from 16/- to 22/- according to the number of spindles,
these earnings being subsequently increased by the war bonus of
145 per cent   In spite of the substantial advances of recent years,
the standard of women ring-spinners still remains a comparatively low one   In skill, they are little behind men mule-spinners,
and it is suggested by more than one trade union authority
that had women been admitted at once to the spinners' unions,

instead of being allowed to establish themselves under " non-union " conditions, their standard might have been almost as high as the men's, or twice as high as their present one. The tendency remarked in some districts for the process of ring-spinning to encroach on that of mule-spinning is directly attributed by trade unionists to the low wages of women ring-spinners.

The Bolton Provincial Association of Operative Cotton Spinners, established in 1837, has always included women in its " piecer " section. The present female membership is about 3,000. The " piecer " or spinner's assistant, who is employed and paid by the mule-spinner or minder, stands in a somewhat anomalous position. The rules of the union lay down that a majority of the " piecers " or " creelers " in each mill shall have the right to say whether they will join the Association or not, but in the event of a majority deciding to become members, the minority will be expected to conform to that decision, whilst another clause provides that " each member will be held responsible for the contribution to be paid weekly by each and every piecer and creeler employed by him, viz., big piecers and side piecers, 3d. per week; full-timers and creelers, 2d. per week; half-timers, 1d. per week," the benefits including trade and funeral benefit, and in the case of 3d members, breakdown in addition. The same rule applies to either sex, but men " piecers " have at least the opportunity of promotion to the rank of spinner—an opportunity denied to women.

The uncompromising attitude of the spinners' unions in prohibiting female labour, which has been described in previous chapters, remains practically unchanged. Men mule-spinners maintain that this work is too exhausting for women, and they are opposed on " moral " grounds to joint-workshops, but their root objection is to " cheap labour." In the Bolton district, where young men and boys are attracted by high wages to the mines and foundries, the shortage of male labour has caused women to be recognized as " piecers," but not as spinners, although the " big piecer " does actually the same work as the spinner. The promotion of older women as spinners would, moreover, remove the men's moral objection to employing young girls in the mule-spinning sheds. In view, however, of the awkward size of the mule, it would seem at least doubtful whether women under any circumstances would be employed in large numbers In the one or two non-union mills, from which the unions have failed to evict them, the machines are said to belong to a small and old-fashioned type.* During the war, renewed attempts were made by employers to introduce women in the mule-spinning sheds;

* In America, where there are no similar trade union restrictions, the experiment of female labour on self-acting mules has been tried and given up

and the Oldham, Preston and other local societies followed the Bolton example and admitted women as " piecers " for the period of the war, but not as " minders " or " joiner-minders." Agreements varied in detail, but the terms commonly laid down were that " substituted " women should be paid the usual rates of wages after a period of four or six weeks' probation, during which period the remuneration should be " and in no case shall it exceed 7/- per week." This was raised by bonus to about 14/- at end of 1918.

Wool and worsted unions —Of the twenty-seven societies belonging to the wool and worsted trades, seven include women with an aggregate female membership of over 50,000 at the end of 1918   Some nine-tenths of these belong to the General Union of Textile Workers, which at present represents three-quarters of the men and two-thirds of the women employed in the West Riding woollen industry. Organization amongst women developed enormously during the war. The National Union of Machine Woolcombers is the only other important organization which has women members, these belonging to the Bradford worsted trade. Other wool and worsted societies are men's small craft unions for which women are ineligible. The General Union of Textile Workers includes a few thousand women in the West Country (Stroud and Wellington), but outside the Yorkshire districts wool and worsted workers are mostly catered for by general labour unions. Not only in Scotland, but in Oxfordshire and the West of England, the Workers' Union and the National Union of General Workers both include large numbers of these women. In the Huddersfield district there is some overlapping between the General Union of Textile Workers and the National Society of Dyers, which has recently opened a women's branch of " knotters " and " burlers." Wool and worsted unions are mostly affiliated to the National Association of Unions in the Textile Trades, but are separately represented on the National Wool Industrial Council   The latter body includes one woman on the workers' side—a member of the General Union of Textile Workers.

The General Union of Textile Workers, formed in 1881 from a number of local associations of men and women weavers, admits men and women on the same scales of contribution, whilst benefits include trade protection, out-of-work and compensation against accident, but, apart from the National Health Insurance Act, no sickness pay. About one-third of the female members are married women. A woman representative of the Bradford district was elected to the executive committee in 1914. She was the first of her sex to hold office since the early days of organization, but her example was soon followed by others, three women being elected in 1918. The appointment of two women organizers dates from about the same year. The keen desire to conduct their own affairs which animated women in the 'seventies seems, however, to have generally vanished. Except at times of excitement, women are said to be slack in attending branch meetings, and seldom count more than 10 per cent. of members present. The Yorkshire woollen weaver is apparently harder to organize than the Lancashire cotton operative. The difficulties in Yorkshire are said to be casual employment amongst married women, and also the comparatively little influence exercised by fathers on their daughters, who start work at a later age than in Lancashire.

Both men and women are employed as weavers, warpers and winders (women and boys), condenser minders and feeders (women and boys), but only men as willeyers and fettlers, and only women as "burlers," "knotters" and "menders," or in "cap and fly" spinning. Weavers form, however, the majority of the members, organization being most advanced in Huddersfield, where as early as 1883 a piece-work list was drawn up for men and women weavers. This list, which is very elaborate, consists of two scales, one for men and another for women. The items are the same, but the piece-rate is reduced by 10 per cent in the case of women. This policy is upheld by employers on the ground that women require additional assistance in tuning their machines, and are further subject to legal restrictions in regard to overtime and night-work, but it is severely criticized by trade unionists, who attribute to it the aggravated conditions of unemployment amongst men weavers. Not only do these bear the whole brunt of overtime and night-work, but they are the first to be discharged in periods of slack trade, so that they rely on their wives and daughters for support. For these reasons, the "list" of 1883, although in operation for so long, has never been signed by any representative of the union. Outside the Huddersfield district, women's wages until recently were in the main unregulated, and the low rates had practically driven men weavers from employment. Conditions were so depressed amongst "burlers," "knotters," and "menders," that in 1915 a movement was made by the union to bring these workers under the Trade Boards Act.

The outbreak of war brought an immediate demand for female labour; and, in February, 1916, some sixteen employers' associations and some nineteen trade unions entered an important general agreement, laying down the following terms of "dilution"·—

"That where women are employed to take the place of men the rate of wages for such women shall be:—

(a) If at piece-rates the same as for men, unless women's rates are already established for that class of work (as for the Huddersfield weavers), provided no woman shall receive less than the district rate for women.

(b) If at time-rates for day-time work, and one or more women replace an equal number of men, they shall be paid the same rate of wages now being paid to males for an equivalent amount of work, and in any case not less than four-fifths of the rate previously paid to the men they replace.

(c) If at time-rates for day-time work, and a larger number of women are required to replace a smaller number of men, the aggregate wages paid to the women shall not be less than the aggregate wages paid to the men they replace, and in no case shall the wage paid to an individual woman be less than four-fifths of the wage previously paid to the men replaced."

Under this agreement, the terms of which were strictly confined to the period of the war, a number of women were introduced on men's work, but not in new fields of employment to any large extent. Men's work was mostly too rough and heavy for women, who could not " so efficiently execute their duties on account of their physical disabilities " " Substituted " women were admitted to membership, but few remained employed at the end of 1919.

Wages were otherwise regulated by awards of the Committee on Production, and in December, 1918, advances amounted to 104¾ per cent. on time-rates, with a limit of 31/5 for men, but without a limit for women—the provision being no doubt unnecessary; whilst, on piece-work, men received 83½ per cent , and women 89 per cent., on pre-war rates. It was not until February, 1919, that it was possible to fix a national minimum or *basic* rate of 17/- per week, which with the various bonuses (10 per cent. on basic rates, plus 125 per cent. for time-workers and 106½ per cent for piece-workers, who also received 15½ per cent in compensation for a reduction of hours from fifty-five and a half to forty-eight a week) amounted to a minimum wage of 39/11 in December, 1919.

The National Society of Machine Woolcombers, which represents 90 per cent of the workers of either sex employed in the Bradford worsted trade, includes 11,000 members, of whom one-half are women The rules make no distinction of sex except in the usual matter of contribution and benefits. Men pay 6d per week, and women 4d , these sums having been raised by 2d and 1d. respectively during the war, whilst benefits comprise trade, funeral and accident pay, the amount being estimated in strict proportion to the contribution Apart from the National Insurance Act, there is no sickness benefit.

In 1912, two women were elected to the executive committee, but the election was unpopular with a certain section of the men, and the experiment was not repeated Women are said to have been difficult to organize in the past, and more than once men have been obliged to strike in order to compel them to join the union. At branch meetings, the female attendance is often less than one per cent. In the first year of the war, at the important conferences on " dilution "—a subject directly affecting female labour—it is said that only three women were present amongst 500 members, but a keener interest was remarked later.

The time-work " list " of the wool-combers, which was drawn up in 1914, lays down a graduated scale of minimum rates according to the machine or process. These rates range from 26/- to 32/- per week for men, and from 14/6 to 19/6 per week for women, but the sexes are normally employed on different work. For example, in the case of "breakers off" men are employed on three or four " lapps " and women on two or three "lapps." Or again, in the case of " backwash," " strong box," " punch," and " comb-minders," women are employed on day turn (ten-hour shift until 1919) and men on night turn (eleven and half-hour shift until 1919). Under ordinary circumstances, any attempt made by employers to extend the area of female employment is strenuously resisted by the union. Men complain bitterly that women's competition has not only dragged down wages, but has also practically confined them to rough or dangerous operations, or else to night-work The society was, however, a party to the general agreement of February, 1916,* and women were temporarily admitted according to a list of " suitable " occupations. On day turn, there was little " suitable " work upon which they were not already employed, but several hundred women were introduced on night turn and received in this case men's full rates of wages. Members are strongly opposed to any relaxation of the night-work prohibition clauses of the Factory and Workshops Act, and only gave way during the war upon securing elaborate provisions for the protection of women night workers. These included notification by the Home Office to the union of all firms to whom permission was given to employ women on night shift, the appointment of a factory inspector for the Bradford district, whose special duty it would be to inspect wool-combing sheds and enforce the terms of the agreement, the appointment of responsible women supervisors, the provision of separate meal rooms, washing accommodation and seats; whilst workshop temperature should not be higher than 85 degrees, and " women with young children not to be employed at night." The union, moreover, insisted that all women should be discharged from night-work immediately after the war. At the end of 1918, war advances amounted to 30/6 for all workers rated at over 21/- per week, or in effect for men, and 20/- for all workers rated below 21/- per week, or in effect for women, with the exception of those who were promoted to night work and entitled in consequence to men's rates of wages.

* See pages 127-8

Flax and jute unions.—These societies may be divided into two separate Scottish and Irish groups. Of the thirteen societies which form the *Scottish* group, ten include women with an aggregate female membership of nearly 29,000 The most important body is the Dundee Union of Jute and Flax Workers, which would seem to have expanded recently at the expense of the old-fashioned Dundee Mill and Factory Operatives' Union. Both societies enrol skilled as well as unskilled workers, but skilled men belong generally to separate craft unions. The Scottish societies, although local in character, are mostly affiliated to the Scottish Council of Textile Trade Unions, but there was no general machinery for fixing wages until 1919, when the jute trade was brought under the Trade Boards Act.

The Dundee Union of Jute and Flax Workers, established as the result of a lock-out in 1906, has some 20,000 members, of whom 75 per cent. are women The constitution was originally modelled on the lines of the Lancashire cotton unions, contributions for either sex being 4d., 6d., and 8d. (raised from 3d , 4½d., and 6d. during the war), and benefits including trade and breakdown, but no " friendly " benefits The union followed the same example in adopting the expensive system of " house-to-house " collection, the cost sometimes amounting to 17½ per cent. of the takings. The rule as to the executive committee departs, however, from its precedent, and lays down that " the Union should be under the direction of the President, Vice-President, Secretary, Assistant Secretary, Treasurer, and not less than sixteen members of a committee, *one-half of which to consist of women, where possible.*" The proportion was two-thirds until 1913, when it was reduced in consequence of the women's failure to come forward in sufficient numbers The present committee is composed of men and women in due proportion, a woman acting as vice-president and another as treasurer.

Membership is open to " any person engaged in any way with the jute and flax trade," excepting " skilled artisans having a previously established union catering for their interests." Men and women are generally employed on different work, women being prohibited as " tenters " and mechanics, whilst men are not employed as spinners. The latter are, however, employed with women to a small extent as weavers and warpers, and in certain processes in the preparing and batching departments. The first scale of minimum rates, " to be known as the basis," was drawn up for the spinning and preparing departments in June, 1912 At the end of 1914, these rates amounted to from 13/11 to 23/6 per week of fifty-five hours for spinners, according to the size of the bobbins and the number of spindles, and from 13/- to 19/- in the preparing departments. Since then advances have been secured amounting to 18/- a week in November, 1918. An attempt was made to fix similar *basic* rates for weavers, but, with the exception of one large firm, employers refused to come to terms. A minimum wage of 32/- a week of forty-eight hours for women jute workers was, however, proposed under the Trade Boards Act in February, 1920.

The interest attached to the Dundee and District Mill and Factory Workers is chiefly historic. The society dates from 1885, when it was formed largely by the efforts of the Rev Henry Wilkinson, who continued as president of the union until October, 1918 The original objects were " to unite mill and factory operatives under a common bond of interest and to have an organization which shall be a power for the prevention of strikes and lock-outs; and in case of members being locked out or a strike being forced upon them by unjustifiable demands on the part of the employers, they may have a fund to support them." Nor are strikes viewed with favour to-day " I have tried to point out to the employers," wrote the Rev. Henry Wilkinson in June, 1914, " that the locking out of all the workers in Dundee, because a few in one mill or factory refuse to work, is altogether unjust and unreasonable. The rule must have contemplated the old state of things where it was customary to collect money at the gate of mills working to help those on strike in another works. But this is not now the practice " Strike benefit is not paid, except to strikers out-of-work through no fault of their own. " In the event of a reduction of wages taking place, the secretary is empowered to call a general meeting of members. No member is allowed to strike work without the sanction of the committee and any member infringing this rule will receive no support. But, in the event of a strike or lock-out taking place in any mill or factory where the members of this Union are in a minority and thereby forced idle against their will, the Union will support its members, provided that they take no part in the dispute." Between 1914 and 1918, the union lost over 3,000 women through strikes.

The executive committee consists of twelve women and eight men, a woman being also appointed as general secretary. The Union would seem to be specially successful in its method of collecting contributions. " It is very much to be preferred that members should attend personally and pay their contributions," state the annual reports, " but as some are indisposed to do this, collectors may be directed to call upon such members regularly." In response to this appeal, the cost of collection is not more than 4½ per cent. of the takings, and compares favourably with that of any other textile society.

The *Irish* group is composed of six local societies, mainly belonging to Belfast, with an aggregate female membership of about 20,000, this number having increased from a little over 3,000 in 1914. From the women's point of view the most important society is the Textile Operatives of Ireland (Belfast), which is practically an all-women's society, not more than 5 per cent. of its 10,000 members being men. It is entirely officered by women. Contributions are from 1d. to 4d. a week, according to the amount of benefits, which include dispute and breakdown pay, on a scale varying from 6/- to 12/- a week.

Next in importance is the Flax Roughers' and Yarn Spinners' Trade Union (Belfast), which has over 10,000 women members similarly employed in linen mills. During the war, the two societies, it would seem, acted independently in the matter of wage advances. The Textile Operatives' Union secured in four years an aggregate advance of 130 per cent., pre-war earnings being about 11/- a week for mill and factory operatives, but not more than 43 per cent. for warehouse women; whilst women members of the Flax Roughers' and Yarn Spinners' Union obtained 18/- a week on a pre-war rate of 12/6, bringing the standard up to 30/6. The trade was subsequently scheduled under the Trade Boards Act, but the Irish Board did not meet until the spring of 1920 Men and women linen workers are mainly employed on different work, although a few men are engaged as weavers at women's rates of wages. Women's employment is prohibited by the union in " flax dressing " and " roughing," on the ground that this work is unsuitable to them Employers succeeded, nevertheless, in introducing a few women as " scabs " during the war.

Hosiery unions.—Of the dozen small societies belonging to the hosiery trades, ten include women, with an aggregate membership of about 22,000 at the end of 1918. The most important body is the Leicester Amalgamated Hosiery Union, which was formed from local men's and women's societies in 1885. The Nottingham Women Hosiery Workers, established in 1890, similarly decided to amalgamate with the Rotary Power Framework Knitters' Society in 1917; but another all-women's society —the Hinckley and District Hosiery Menders'—was established in 1915. Hosiery unions have all a merely local character, but they group together for the purpose of negotiation with employers, one group for Leicestershire and others for the Nottinghamshire and Derbyshire districts. Organization is most advanced at Leicester, where the Amalgamated Hosiery Union has a membership of 9,000 women and 3,000 men, representing a large proportion of the workers of either sex employed in this district

This important society admits men at 6d a week and women at 3d., with an optional ½d for unemployment benefit. Other benefits include trade, sickness and compensation for breakdown, etc.

There are no sex disqualifications, and one woman and five men compose the executive committee. '' Some women, but not many, take an interest in our meetings,'' writes the secretary of the Union; '' we have appealed to them hundreds of times, but in the main they only come when the business is personal ''

Women are mostly employed on light machines, upon which they are said to equal or excel men in output. Where they are employed on men's machines, they do not usually mind the full number, e.g., four instead of six machines. Cotton's patent frames are reserved to men. These old-fashioned frames (which in recent years have been largely replaced by light Griswald's and other women's machines) belong to a comparatively heavy type, which is held by men to be too heavy for women. At Hawick, in Scotland, where women are commonly employed in this way, the recent tendency to replace them by men would seem at least to lend colour to the trade union point of view. The method of payment is both time and piece-work. Before the war, it was usual for piece-rates to be fixed so as to work out broadly at a minimum of 8d. per hour for men and 4d. per hour for women. Women employed on men's machines received, however, men's piece-rates subject to a deduction of not more than 5 per cent. These rates were increased during the war by a bonus of 6½d. in the shilling for men and women alike, whilst a further increase was granted in the spring of 1919 in order to compensate for a reduction of hours from 53 to 48, and another at the end of the year, amounting to 10/- for men and 6/- for women, and 3/- for youths.

In December, 1915, an agreement was reached between the Leicester societies and the Leicestershire Masters' Associations, by which women were admitted '' upon certain operations hitherto ordinarily restricted to male labour,'' provided that these operations were such as they were '' physically fit to perform,'' and that they were paid '' the same rates of wages as are now paid to males for an equivalent quantity of work.'' A similar agreement was reached for Nottinghamshire, and large numbers of women were introduced on these terms to Cotton's patent frames and other men's machines. '' Substituted '' women were, however, mostly discharged by the end of 1919. '' Of course women on men's jobs don't like leaving them,'' writes the secretary of the Leicester Union, '' or that is generally speaking Others have said that the machines are too heavy, and they are glad to return to their old ones, but with few exceptions the arrangement has worked smoothly, and I don't know of one instance but what the women have been found work in some other department.''

Miscellaneous textile unions.—Unions belonging to these trades may be divided into three groups of local societies, namely, carpet unions, lace unions, and silk unions.

Of the *carpet* unions, with an aggregate female membership of about 4,000, only the Northern Counties Carpet Trades Association included women before the war, but the most important in respect of numbers is the Kidderminster Power-Loom Carpet Weavers' Association, established in 1866, and admitting women to membership in 1917. By the end of the following year, it included no less than 3,700 women out of a total membership of 4,500. Women do not, however, enjoy full rights of membership, and one vote is shared between twenty-five women, who pay 3d. a week instead of the full contribution of 7½d. "The females are members," writes the secretary of the Association, "and if they have any cause for complaint, they at once bring the matter before the executive committee, who take action to put the matter right." No less than four women have been elected to the executive committee, and others are appointed to act as assistant-secretaries. The policy of the Association is opposed to women's employment on "jacquard" looms, which are said by men to be unsuited to women, and members include no "substituted" workers. Women members earn from 30/- to 50/- a week, including the war bonus of 105 per cent. (December 1919), whilst the fixing of a standard rate for women was at once considered by the recently-appointed Industrial Council for the Carpet Industry.

The four *lace* societies have an aggregate female membership of between 3,000 and 4,000. The Newmilns and District Textile Workers, which is the most important, has always included women, who form at present more than one-half of its 4,000 members. In the important Nottingham district, on the other hand, men and women are organized in separate societies. The Nottingham Female Lace Workers, with a membership of 750 women and a contribution of 2d. a week (1d. before the war) dates from 1891. The Long Eaton and District Operative Lace Makers decided to open its doors to women in March, 1918, and 600 joined the Union during the year, and count nearly one-half its membership. Women are nominally full members, having a right to attend and vote at quarterly meetings, and the "women's auxiliary committee" forms part of the executive, but women "are not specially invited by post-card" to attend members' meetings. Lace-finishers are organized by the National Federation of Women Workers.

The Amalgamated Society of Braid Workers, the Amalgamated Society of Women Workers, and other small societies of *silk* and allied textile workers, which belong to the Leek and neighbouring districts, amalgamated in 1919, forming the Amalgamated Society of Textile and Kindred Workers. Women members number some 7,400 women, and represent about two-thirds of the membership. Contributions are 5d. for men, and 3d. for women, but there are no sex disqualifications, and women count

3 out of 12 members of the executive committee, and 12 out of 40 members of the delegate board. As early as 1911, a scale of women's time-rates was agreed between the Amalgamated Society of Braid Workers and Kindred Trades and the Leek Chamber of Commerce. These rates ranged from 5/- to 12/6 a week for women between the ages of thirteen and nineteen, with higher rates amounting to 15/- for special classes of workers; whilst men's rates for corresponding work ranged from 5/- to 23/-. Men braid-knitters and tenters were largely employed on piece-work, but were opposed to a similar system for women. The scales remained in operation until August 1914, and since then advances have been secured amounting to 36/- a week for women over the age of 18, with a provision that adult "learners" should receive a starting-rate of 24/-, rising to the full rate in the eighth month of experience. Corresponding rates for men range from 34/6 to 60/6 between the ages of 18 and 22. It is interesting to remark that for six months between the ages of 18 and 18½ women actually receive a higher rate than men of the same age.

Men and women are both employed as braid-knitters and tenters, and to some extent as silk weavers. In the latter case, however, women's competition has practically driven men from employment. Men weavers are confined to one or two highly organized districts, where they have been successful in prohibiting female labour, or are employed on hand-looms. For this reason, the former National Silk Workers' Association, and other societies of men silk workers, refused to admit women to membership who were employed " in twisting and weaving," and organization amongst this class of worker was seriously delayed until about 1915. There was little or no " substitution " during the war, women being already employed in practically all departments of silk manufacture, excepting as overlookers or labourers.

Textile printing, bleaching, dyeing, finishing and warehousing unions.—In this group, ten out of seventeen societies include women, with an aggregate female membership of 23,000, representing over two-thirds of women employed in these trades. The most important unions are the Amalgamated Society of Dyers, Bleachers and Kindred Trades, the National Society of Dyers and Finishers, and the Bolton Amalgamation, Bleachers', Dyers' and Finishers' Association. The two former, although primarily concerned with the Yorkshire woollen industries, organize throughout England and Scotland, whilst the Bolton society is mainly confined to the Lancashire and Cheshire cotton districts. The National Society of Dyers has further organized at Huddersfield a section of " burlers," " knotters " and " menders," on the ground that these women belong to the finishing branches of the woollen industry. There is even said to be a case for an amalgamation of all woollen and worsted unions, so as to include printers and dyers, as well as the manufacturing section of this industry   On the other hand, many firms are engaged in both cotton and woollen dying, and an amalgamation on these lines would lead to other complications. Of the seven small societies of dyers, one belongs to Dundee and the rest to the Leicestershire and Nottinghamshire hosiery trades.   Organization is most advanced in Yorkshire, where comparatively few women are employed, and least advanced in Scotland where female employment is most extensive, and in rural districts

The Amalgamated Society of Dyers, Bleachers and Finishers, which was established at Bradford in 1878, and admitted women to membership about 1912, has a total membership of over 28,000 (December, 1918), of which 9,000 are women.   More than one-half of the latter belong to Scotland, a branch of the National Federation of Women Workers being transferred to the society in 1912.   Men and women enjoy equal rights of membership, and are enrolled in the same branches, but form separate sections in respect of finance.   The men's contribution is 9d. a week and the women's 3d., whilst women's benefits comprise trade protection and funeral, but not superannuation or sickness pay.   There are no women on the executive committee, or on local committees in Yorkshire, where they form only two per cent. of the members, but local committees in Scotland are largely composed of women. The secretary of the society writes that he finds women " very intelligent and enthusiastic," especially in the Scottish area. " We have female presidents, secretaries and treasurers, also members of committees. On our Scottish executive council, which has the responsibility for the whole of the Scottish business, we have 50 per cent. of females, and the same state of things exists in our London district; the reason why there are so few in office in Yorkshire, is, in my opinion, due to the fact that there are so few employed, and that they are mostly daughters or sisters of our male members, and leave the work of the trade unions to the men "

The National Society of Dyers and Finishers which is composed of over 15,000 members, counts nearly 3,500 women. Contributions are 4d., 6d. and 9d. a week for men and 4d. for women, and women's benefits include trade and funeral. They differ in this from those of men 4d. contributors, who are not entitled to funeral benefit, but to a higher scale of dispute pay. Women enjoy full rights of membership, and in most districts are enrolled in the same branches as men. The Huddersfield " female section " is exceptional, and has its own women's committee, assisted by one or two men representatives and a man secretary.

The experiment is said to be successful on the whole, members being more than usually keen in attending branch meetings. Local committees elsewhere include about a score of women members, but no woman has as yet been elected to the executive committee, or appointed to any responsible official position beyond that of delegate to members' meetings. At the Annual Delegate Board Meeting of 1919, six women attended amongst about fifty delegates.

The Bolton Amalgamation, Bleachers', Dyers' and Finishers' Association, which was established in 1866, and began to organize women about 1900, has some 28,000 members, of whom 7,600 are women. The latter figure has increased from 2,800 since 1914. The rules of the union lay down that " any female employed in the trade having arrived at the age of thirteen, and not more than fifty years of age, shall be permitted to become a member . . . and shall be allowed to do so free of charge." Women are, however, liable to certain disabilities as low-scale contributors. In the election of officers, and in all branch business, all members have equal votes, but in order to estimate the number of delegates to be elected by the branches *men* count as *full members, boys* as *half-members,* and *women* as *one-third members.* The voting power follows roughly the amount of contribution, which at present is 3d per week for women against 8d for men, but until recently was 2d against 6d. Women's benefits, which are estimated on a generous scale, comprise trade, infectious diseases and funeral benefit, but not superannuation or accident pay. The cost of collection is sometimes exceptionally heavy amongst women, amounting to 20 per cent. of the takings; but the expensive house-to-house collection, which at one time was thought to be necessary in their case, is said to be no longer desired by women, many of whom deliberately prefer to follow the men's example, and to bring their contributions to the office or workshop. Local committees include a small proportion of women members, but the national executive is entirely in the hands of men. At one time it was proposed to form a " women's council," in order to encourage women to come forward, but the proposal did not materialize.

In Yorkshire and Lancashire, when times are normal, women are confined to certain light operations in the warehouse, and are strictly prohibited on wet processes in the dyeing and bleaching house; but, in Scotland, " female employment is unlimited," with the usual reaction on wages. In Scotland before the war, men were earning as little as 18s. a week, and women as low as 8/- and 10/- on work similar to that for which the rate was, 28/- in Yorkshire. Great efforts were made to raise wages, but success was hard to maintain An important strike in 1912, which brought an increase of 35 per cent. to 120 women, and cost £2,000 in strike pay, did not prevent all except two women from leaving the union before the end of the year. With another Scotch firm in 1913, whilst substantial advances were secured for men, the men's union was obliged to acquiesce in a *maximum* rate of 10/- a week for non-union women employed in the " black-stentering and airing departments." Women's wages, when organization began, were almost as low in Bradford, where a first minimum wage of 12/- a week for adult women was agreed between the Amalgamated Society and the Master Dyers' Association in 1912. Piece-workers earned a few shillings more, or from 16/- to 18/- in Yorkshire, and from 12/- to 16/6 in Lancashire. A movement was made by the Bolton Amalgamation in 1914 to fix a minimum wage of 18/- a week for adult women, but such a rate was quite impossible to enforce.

In January, 1916, in order to meet the growing shortage of male labour, a central committee was appointed by the Home Office, consisting of nine representatives of employers' associations and nine of trade unions, to consider the matter of " dilution," and " to decide what occupations were suitable for women " The result was the following agreement :—

" In the event of an absolute labour shortage, females may be employed to perform work previously done by men which does not entail undue physical strain or danger to health from either heat fumes or dust

" If females work in stoves, the temperature of the stove shall not exceed 80 degrees, and no room in which females are employed shall be below fifty degrees.

" No female shall drag or push waggons from place to place upon which there is a weight approximately exceeding 120 lbs."

To this agreement was appended a schedule of some 150 separate processes upon which women might be employed during the period of the war. Further important provisions related to rates of wages, consolidating previous local agreements. It was provided, for instance, that " women entering a piece-work set shall be paid at a rate to be agreed upon between the employers and the society, and periodical advances shall be given until she arrives at the rate paid to the remainder of the set, which shall be so soon as she exhibits equal efficiency " Later, a clause was added that, " in fixing the bases of payment to women taking the places of men, either on piece or day rates, regard shall be had to the quantity of work done as contrasted with that formerly done by adult males." In point of fact, the women's earnings worked out at considerably below the men's. In some cases, an intermediate rate was agreed amounting to 85 per cent. of the men's standard. At the time of the armistice, average piece-work earnings were estimated by trade union representatives at 65/- to 80/- per week for men, and from 36/- to 40/- for women, including " substituted " workers. These earnings were inclusive of the war bonus, which was adjusted each quarter according to the rise in the cost of living, and amounted to 30/- for men and 18/10 for women per week of 55½ hours in November, 1918. In no case did " substituted " women receive more than women's war advances. They were, however, generally confined to the lighter parts of men's work, or four women took the place of three men. According to trade unionists, women were already employed to the full extent to which their employment was economically sound, and employers would only be tempted to retain them for the sake of cheap labour. As a matter of fact, " substituted " women were mostly discharged during 1919. They formed at no time a large proportion of members.

A new effort to standardize wages was made in 1919, when it was at last possible to establish a women's minimum or basic wage of 18/- a week (15/- in Scotland), whilst the war bonus amounted to another 120 per cent. at the end of the year. Hours of work at the same time were reduced from 55½ to 48 a week, with compensating increases for piece-workers. Further, an elaborate piece-work price list was drawn up by the National Society of Dyers and agreed with the Employers' Association for the underpaid " knotters," " burlers " and " menders " who belong to the Huddersfield district

In the *textile warehousing* group, four small societies include women members, of which the most interesting is the Female Workers in the Shipping Industry This society, which is run in connection with the men's Societies of Makers-up and affiliated to the Kindred Trades Federation in the Shipping Industry, includes nearly 2,000 women. It is nominally an independent organization, but both its president and secretary are members of the allied men's trade unions, whose offices it also shares. Members are chiefly employed as " markers-off," " stitchers," " cutters," " parcellers," " sorters," " tyers-on," etc., and to some extent as " hookers " and " stampers." At one time men were engaged as " hookers," but the low rates of wages have since driven them from employment. Both sexes are employed as " stampers," and women in this case are recognized by the men's societies on weights below 8 ozs. In April, 1916, the Joint Board of Inside Warehouse Workers entered an agreement with the Master Packers' Federation, by which women were admitted for the period of the war " to do work which is considered suitable for females " The agreement further provided that employment on men's work should be confined to " females of the regular staff," who were to be guaranteed their late positions on the termination of the war, and to be paid " the same rates as paid to males for equal work," with a minimum rate of 4d. per hour, raised to 8d. at the end of 1918. The number of "substituted" women did not, however, exceed 150.

The scale of minimum rates, which forms the women's standard or basic wage, dates from July, 1914. These rates range from 12/- a week (52½ hours in 1914) for " dhootie hookers " to 14/- for " general hookers," " parcellers," etc., 15/- for " stitchers," and 17/- for " markers-off," overtime being paid extra. The actual method of payment is a form of " piece-work." Women are paid so much a share, but no member may earn more than her share so long as other women are unemployed. There is no separate scale for young girls, but "learners " are " entitled to the minimum upon proving themselves to be capable of doing a full share for six months," and young girls " temporarily employed on higher grade work shall be paid at the rate appertaining for such grade." The object of other provisions is to protect women from overstrain. " On account of the difficulties found to exist in fixing a maximum weight to be carried or lifted, it is agreed that no girl shall be asked to lift or carry weights considered to be injurious to her health. Any complaints in reference to the above to be considered by the management and the Society." During the war, the Kindred Trades Federation agreed with the Master Packers' Federation to a sliding scale, under which further advances were received, amounting to 17/6 for a week of 46½ hours in December, 1918, and each woman was entitled to twelve days' holiday on full pay.

CHAPTER V.

CLOTHING UNIONS.

Societies belonging to the clothing trades may be broadly divided into tailors' unions, boot and shoe unions, and small local societies of hat and cap makers, fur workers, and glove makers.

Tailors' unions.—The tailors' unions practically all include women, with an aggregate female membership of about 100,000, of which over three-quarters belong to the United Garment Workers, and about 18,000 to the Amalgamated Society of Tailors and Tailoresses. Other societies, including the Royal Army Clothing Department Employees, with a female membership of 25,000, have a merely local character. The United Garment Workers' Union, formed in 1915 from an amalgamation between the Amalgamated Union of Clothiers, the Clothiers' Cutters Union, the London Society of Tailors and Tailoresses, and various Jewish Societies, was joined by the Scottish Society of Tailors and Tailoresses in 1920 It admits to membership any workers, " male or female, who are engaged in any of the occupations incidental to the manufacture of male and female clothing or attire." Organization amongst women was comparatively backward until the war, but in many clothing centres to-day, such as Leeds, Bristol, Glasgow, Wigan, and Manchester, it is estimated that 90 per cent of the workers of either sex are organized. The Amalgamated Society of Tailors and Tailoresses, on the other hand, for many years confined its membership to the *craftsman* or *journeyman* tailor; but the old rule, by which any tailor employed by another must be expelled from the union, was never enforced in the case of women, and the society has now extended the scope of its membership so as to be practically commensurate with that of the United Garment Workers. It includes, not only factory operatives of either sex, but also dressmakers, milliners, and even corset-makers. Its members are, however, not yet prepared to accept the invitation of the United Garment Workers to complete the process of amalgamation A certain number of garment workers are included in general labour unions, but this class of member has been transferred by the National Federation of Women Workers to the United Garment Workers. The Federation now confines its membership to women's clothes makers employed in small shops, whilst a similar transfer of members has been agreed with the Dockers' Union.

Men and women members of the United Garment Workers enjoy in every way equal rights of membership   Tailoresses, who at one time complained of insufficient strike pay, were even invited to exchange from the women's to the men's scale of contribution and benefits, but the offer met no response and was afterwards withdrawn   Contributions are from 6d. to 11d. a week for men, and from 2d to 5d for women, whilst benefits include trade, sickness (three months) and funeral.   There is a common fund, and women's benefits were at one time partly paid for by men's contributions, but branches composed mainly of women are now said to be as financially sound as those composed entirely of men.   Men and women are mostly enrolled in the same branches; but, in the London West End district, where tailoresses are habitually employed by tailors as their assistants, women form a separate branch.   They do not hesitate in this case to call in the aid of the union in order to enforce the prescribed rates of wages on men members.   The system of sub-employment is, however, viewed by members of either sex as objectionable, and the present aim is to abolish it.   One woman serves on the executive committee, and another acts as assistant general organizer, but women are confined for the most part in their activities to local affairs   In so far as they are appointed as responsible district organizers, they enjoy the same status and receive the same salaries as men.

The old-established Amalgamated Society of Tailors and Tailoresses similarly makes special provision for women.   The contribution, which is from 4d. to 8d a week for men, is from 2d. to 4d. for women, with corresponding variations in benefits, and the full cost of administration is not borne by the women's section.   It was, indeed, not unusual in past years for a special levy to be called for, amounting to several hundred pounds in the year, in order to make good the insolvency of the women's section, whose generous scale of benefits and excessive claims on sick pay could not otherwise be provided for   Women are eligible for every office of the union and the general staff includes a woman organizer and a woman assistant secretary (daughter of the late and wife of the present general secretary), who takes a prominent part in the affairs of the union, but women have not yet been elected on the executive committee, nor on district committees.   Moreover, low-scale, or 4d., contributors count only as half-members at delegate meetings.   The one-time distinction between men and women low-scale contributions, by which men counted as half members and women as full members, does not now exist

Wages are regulated under the Trade Boards Act, but trade unionists have by no means ceased to rely on their own efforts. The policy of the United Garment Workers is to push up wages beyond the legal minimum in well-organized districts, and then to use this advantage as a lever in order to secure the extension of the trade union rate to the whole trade. At the outbreak of war, the minimum rate was 6d. an hour for men and 3¼d. for women (3½d. had just been proposed). The women's minimum was subsequently raised by steps to 5d. in March, 1918, whilst additional advances were secured by means of arbitration, amounting to 3d. beyond the legal minimum in the spring of 1919. Finally, these advantages were consolidated under the Trade Boards Act in December, 1919, the legal minimum being raised to 8½d. an hour for women over the age of eighteen, whilst piece-rates had to be fixed so as to yield at least 9½d. an hour to ordinary workers. Other provisions related to overtime and to annual holidays. Further, women over the age of twenty employed on men's work as " cutters," " trimmers," or " fitters-up " must receive a minimum time-rate of 9½d. an hour

The Amalgamated Society of Tailors and Tailoresses prohibits female labour in high-class cutting and pressing, but no similar restrictions are imposed by the United Garment Workers, provided that women are paid men's rates of wages. Women trouser and waistcoat-makers, who are employed to some extent in the London West End district, receive the same " log " rates as men. West End women costume-cutters are equally fortunate in securing " equal pay." The rule as to " equal pay " was, however, relaxed in clothing factories during the war. Under the Home Office agreement of 1916, " substituted " women, who were largely employed as " cutters," " trimmers," and " fitters-up," and to a less extent as " pressers," were entitled to men's piece-rates, but only to a minimum time-rate of 6d. an hour. As a matter of fact, they received on an average from 50 per cent. to 70 per cent. of men's wages, which at the end of 1918 amounted to about 1/5 an hour, but they did not do the most skilled or heaviest parts of men's work. In trade union opinion, women are already employed in all suitable branches of wholesale tailoring, and " substitution " is not in the interest of employers, who " seldom require to be urged to replace women by men in spite of the differences in wages."

Boot and shoe unions.—In this group, which has an aggregate female membership of 28,000, and represents about 40 per cent of women employed in these trades, the principal society is the National Union of Boot and Shoe Operatives, established at Leicester in 1874, and admitting women in 1884. At the end of 1918, it had a total membership of 69,000, of which 20,000 were

women.   Contributions are 9d. a week for men and 4½d. for
women, and benefits include trade, out-of-work, sickness and
funeral, the amount varying in proportion to the contribution
There are no sex disqualifications, and men and women mix
in the branches   The Leicester women's branch, with 4,000 members, forms an important exception.   Its president is the one and
only woman representative on the executive committee, or on
the National Industrial Council for the Boot and Shoe Industry.
Women are not appointed as organizers, it being said that they
prefer to vote for men, but the woman member of the executive
committee takes her share in organizing work, and women serve
on district committees and assist here in the same way.

Women members belong mainly to the closing departments,
and to the stock and showrooms.   A first scale of minimum
rates was fixed by means of arbitration in July, 1912.   The terms
related only to the Nottingham district, but were soon extended
elsewhere, and finally embodied in a national agreement in June
1914.   This agreement fixed a minimum wage of 18/- a
week of 53½ hours for women of twenty years of age and over
employed on first-class operations, with a rising scale of from
14/- and 16/- for young girls from eighteen to nineteen years
respectively, and a minimum of 17/- a week for women employed
on second-class operations, with a rising scale of from 14/- to
15/- for young girls.   Women employed on certain low-grade
work were expressly excluded from the agreement.   The same
agreement laid down that " in the opinion of this Conference it is undesirable that females should be employed amongst
male operatives in the clicking, press, lasting and finishing departments of the trade, in which male labour is now almost exclusively employed, and the Conference therefore recommends that
where females are now so employed, such conditions shall
gradually cease by the effluxion of time, and that in future no
fresh female labour shall be employed in the aforesaid departments, but nothing in this clause shall prevent employers having
specified operations done by female labour in, or in connection
with, the clicking or press departments under separate working
conditions; such operations to be defined by the local arbitration
boards for their respective districts in consultation with the standing committee of the Conference "   In June, 1915, however, in
order to meet the shortage of male labour, the rule was relaxed,
and women were admitted for the period of the war in the clicking, press, lasting and finishing departments on such operations
" as they were physically fitted to perform," whilst they should
be paid " the same rates of wages as are now paid to males for
an equivalent quantity of work "   As a matter of fact, they received men's piece-rates, enjoying the advantage of the men's

elaborate piece-work statement, but only women's war advances, or 8/- instead of 15/- a week (November 1918). Another clause of the agreement prescribed that "due regard shall be paid to the desirability, where possible, of separate working conditions where male and female operatives are employed in the same department." "Substituted" women were, however, mostly employed on youths' work, the common opinion being that they were unable to maintain output on men's heavy machines. It was further objected by trade unionists that, owing to new subdivisions of labour, men were confined to unduly hard parts of the work. In the agreement of February, 1919, the old provisions restricting female labour were reinserted, whilst minimum rates were readjusted in the women's departments, the new scales ranging from 15/- to 30/- a week of 48 hours for women from sixteen to twenty years of age. The previous distinction between women employed on first-class and second-class operations was omitted, but certain low-grade workers were excluded as before. "Substituted" women were largely members of the union, and every effort was made to facilitate their return to their own departments.

In consequence of an unfortunate dispute between the National Union of Boot and Shoe Operatives and the Leicester women's branch in 1911, the latter body seceded from the union, forming the present Independent National Union of Boot and Shoe Women Workers (1,300 members). The dispute was no doubt aggravated by personal animosities, but there would seem to have been a real division of opinion on the question of piece-work, and the absence of a piece-work statement for women. Members of the women's union declare that a minimum wage of 30/- a week offers no protection to workers, many of whom earn 44/- a week on time-work and 60/- a week on piece-work. The piece-work statements drawn up by the women's union have been accepted by local firms, and some interesting provisions have been added relating to girl workers. For example, girls under the age of eighteen may remain on time-work, but they must be taught at least six separate series of operations. Again, no woman may be "kept waiting or sent home while girls are doing the same work." Further, "women and girls must all make the same *time,* and no woman must be displaced for girls." Other clauses lay down "that no operative be subject to any undue pressure or speeding up," the object being to maintain "the competency of the operatives," but, on the other hand, there must be "no restriction of output." In other respects, the women's union supports the men's policy, and members have no desire to break down the present line of demarcation between men's and women's departments.

In Lancashire, the Rossendale Boot, Shoe and Slipper Operatives, which includes a few thousand women, forms a separate local organization.

Other clothing unions.—Of these small societies, the most interesting is the Amalgamated Felt Trimmers and Wool Formers, established by the Amalgamated Society of Journeymen Felt Hatters as an allied women's union in 1884. For many years it has included between 2,000 and 3,000 women, but remains dependent to a large extent on the men's organization. Not only is it entirely officered by officials of the men's union, with which it shares an office, but the branches are represented on its executive committee by four men secretaries. Funds are kept strictly apart, but more than once the women's union has received substantial assistance from the men's fund, or has been absolved from debt incurred during unsuccessful strikes. At one time, women were said to be reluctant to join the union, and were only persuaded to do so by men who " refused to make hats for them." A rule of the union provides that one member out of five, chosen by ballot, must attend branch meetings, or else pay a fine of 3d. It is, however, not unusual for older women, who are generally uninterested except in matters of wage advances, to bribe young girls to attend in their place.

Women are mainly employed as " trimmers " The method of payment is piece-work, and before the war a good trimmer might earn from 15/- to 20/- a week. She ought rightly to have earned more, but women are careless in reporting such " nibbling at wages " by employers as the gradual insertion of extra stitches. Pre-war rates were increased by 120 per cent. by the end of 1919. Female labour is prohibited by the men's society in the felting departments, although women were at one time employed by their husbands in domestic workshops. The rule is rigidly enforced in the well-organized Lancashire districts, and was not relaxed during the war on the ground that " substitution " was unnecessary. In Warwickshire, however, women have been employed in felting since 1892, when a disastrous strike against " cheap female labour " resulted in men being practically expelled from the district. These women remained unrecognized by the union until 1915, when it was finally decided to admit them to membership.

Other hat and cap workers are organized by distributive and general labour unions. Fur workers form a group of small societies, of which two include women, but these workers are mostly unorganized. Glove makers are mainly organized by the Workers' Union, since the failure of small local societies during the war.

CHAPTER VI.

TRANSPORT UNIONS.

Transport unions fall broadly into three groups, the railway unions, the vehicle workers' unions, and the dockers' unions. Before the war, comparatively few women were employed in transport, and practically none included in transport unions, the few hundred women members of the Dockers' Union being mainly factory workers. All the principal societies, however, opened their doors to " substituted " women during the war. The aggregate female membership was about 68,000 at the time of the armistice, or 54,000 excluding clerks, and the number rose steadily until the discharge of " substituted " women during the following year reduced it again to a few thousands. The societies chiefly concerned were the National Union of Railwaymen, and the two Societies of Vehicle Workers (at present the United Vehicle Workers). The latter societies are affiliated to the National Transport Workers' Federation.

At its Annual General Meeting of June, 1915, the National Union of Railwaymen decided by 33 to 23 votes to admit women to membership. As temporary workers, they were confined to the lowest scale of contribution (3d. a week), by which they were only entitled to trade benefits. They enjoyed full rights of membership; but women were not elected to any national or district committee, and they played practically no part in management. The female membership, which was almost entirely composed of " substituted " women, was about 30,000* at the time of the armistice, but this number was probably reduced to one-tenth at the end of 1919. An arrangement was made by the union with the National Federation of Women Workers, by which members could be transferred to the latter body as they passed into other industries.

A small proportion of women have always been employed on railways as waiting-room attendants, charwomen, etc.; and, in 1913, the companies made the experiment of employing women as carriage-cleaners. They received 15/- a week, as compared with the men's standard of 21/-, it being ruled by the Conciliation Board that the latter rate did not apply to women. As a matter of fact, women worked a nine-hours' instead of a ten-hours'

* The N.U.R. makes no separate returns for men and women members, so that the figure is only a rough estimate.

147

shift, and deliberately preferred to do so, although they received less wages in return. They refused, moreover, to accept the men's piece-work system, by which the 21/- was paid for a certain number of carriages, and extra payment made for any number beyond. Their output was generally held to be limited in quantity, although good in quality.

Following the outbreak of war, women were introduced as porters, checkers, ticket-collectors, engine-cleaners, signal and points women, gate-keepers, labourers, etc., more women being employed—at least in the first instance—than the number of men whom they replaced. The union at once decided to recognize "substituted" women, but claimed that they should receive men's wages, and that their employment should in no way prejudice the men's return. Members further held that women should not be used in manipulating traffic, either as gate-keepers or in signalling or shunting. In spite, however, of repeated protests, the union failed to secure more than a part of its demands. Broadly speaking, women received the men's minimum wage in each grade, ranging from 16/- for porters to 27/- for district examiners, but only a women's scale of war advances amounting in November, 1918, to 20/6, against 33/- received by men.

Similarly, the United Vehicle Workers has now lost all except a handful of women members, but the two societies from which it was formed counted between them over 20,000 at the time of the armistice, nearly all being "substituted" workers. Women enjoyed full rights of membership, paying the usual contribution of 4d to 7d a week, and being entitled to the usual benefits. A movement was at one time started by the London Society for Women's Suffrage to form a separate Society of Women Motor Drivers. It was not intended to compete in any way with the men's organizations, but these women, many of whom had had no previous industrial experience, were notoriously difficult to organize; and an all-women's society was believed to be the best means of approaching them. After some months of more or less unsuccessful effort, however, the little society decided to accept the men's invitation to join their union. It formed the Central London women's branch, but afterwards merged with the men's branch. Generally speaking, members of either sex preferred to mix in the branches. Women were eligible for every office, but were not elected to the executive committee, nor appointed to any responsible post.

The large majority of women members were tram and 'bus conductors, who had been practically compelled by men members to join the union. The understanding was that they should be employed on exactly the same terms as men, whilst their employment must terminate at the end of the war. In some cases women were employed on short shifts, but this policy was opposed by the union. It was feared that any relief of this kind would not only give employers an excuse for deductions from wages, but add to men's hours of work. It might even have the undesirable effect of encouraging women's employment in future ! Women drivers, who were entirely composed of commercial or private employees, formed a comparatively small section of members, probably less than one-eighth. The large number of women drivers enrolled for auxiliary war service were not encouraged by the Government to join trade unions.

Women tram and 'bus conductors, who were well organized from the start, had little difficulty in obtaining men's minimum rates of wages, but the question of war advances was a matter of constant dispute. The important national award of February, 1918, by which men received an aggregate advance of 20/- a week on pre-war rates, laid down that " where agreements or awards already exist providing for the same rates to be paid to women as to men, such agreements or awards are to hold good, and an increase to be paid accordingly " In the absence of such agreements, women were to receive only an advance of 4/- on current rates. The London women 'bus conductors were at once accorded the full bonus, and a subsequent decision of the Committee on Production, by which they were refused a further advance of 5/-, met with such determined resistance that this decision was reversed. All women were, however, by no means so successful   At the time of the armistice, there were no less than four different methods of fixing wages for women conductors, viz. :—

(1) Men's full rates of wages plus men's full war advances. This method obtained with the London 'bus companies, rates amounting to 68/- a week of 54 to 60 hours, and also in Leicester.

(2) Men's full rates of wages, plus men's full war advances, the latter being subject to a period of twelve months' probation. This method was peculiar to the L.C.C.

(3) Men's full rates of wages, but only a proportion of men's war advances, this proportion being about two-thirds.

(4) Men's minimum rates of wages, but not men's customary grade increases, nor their full war advances. This method was typical of Yorkshire.

In commercial motor-driving, where women were largely unorganized, wages varied indefinitely. In some cases, the Union was able to enforce " equal pay," and in all cases to secure for its members substantial advances of wages, but for unorganized women wages remained as low as 30/- to 40/- a week, or about one-half the men's standard   This failure was all the more serious in that at least some proportion of such women might be expected to remain as drivers of light commercial and private cars.

CHAPTER VII.

PRINTING AND KINDRED UNIONS.

Of the thirty or more societies which belong to the printing and allied trades, six are open to women, with an aggregate female membership of nearly 39,000 at the end of 1918. This figure, which is still rapidly rising, represents nearly 30 per cent. of women employed in these trades, the proportion being considerably higher in London and other well-organized districts.

Amongst the skilled men's societies, the important Typographical Association, which caters outside London for men compositors and machine operators, frankly refuses to recognize the growing number of women who compete with men in unorganized districts; but the London Society of Compositors, which opened its doors to women in 1886 " provided always that females are paid strictly in accordance with scale," counts one woman compositor and nine women monotype operators, who have been able to observe these terms. They pay the men's contribution and rank in every respect as full members. The lawful entry to the trade is nevertheless closed to women by the men's refusal to teach girl apprentices. It is probable that the number of women belonging to this branch of the trade does not amount in all London to more than 100, of whom about a score are employed at non-union rates by the Women's Printing Society. The men's success in excluding women from employment may, however, be at least partly traced to the nature of the London work. The important newspaper trade is practically closed to women by legal restrictions on night-work, whilst the skilled " jobbing " trade is unadapted except to apprenticed tradesmen. The " book " trade, for which female labour is best suited, has passed to a great extent from London to the provinces, attracted by low rents as well as by cheap labour. Various attempts were made by employers to introduce women during the war; but on the ground of slack trade, " substitution " was successfully resisted by members, who called on the executive " to use the whole strength of the society to prevent the unwarranted step."

The Scottish Typographical Association includes a " female section " of some 450 members in Edinburgh, representing about 95 per cent. of women employed in this district, whilst a second " female section " was opened in Aberdeen in 1918. Owing to their low payment, women were not at first promoted to full rights of membership, but these were granted in 1918 on condition that they paid the men's full *trade* contribution, raising the rate from 3d. to 5½d. a week. The famous Edinburgh agreement of 1910 laid down that " no female apprentice compositors should be taken on until June 30th, 1916, that " all new key-boards during the same period be operated by male labour," and that " the master printers further agree to give 50 per cent. of all corrections of machine-set matter to males." This agreement, which was supported by women as well as men, terminated in 1916, but its main object would seem to have been achieved, and the question of women apprentices has not been reopened. " There is not the same demand for ' cheap female labour,' " writes the secretary of the union, " as the woman worker is being displaced by the new monotype machine, which does the work even more cheaply." Outside Edinburgh, women's employment as compositors was prohibited before the war, and few were in fact employed. The rule was afterwards relaxed, and " substituted " women were employed at Perth, Hawick, Galashiels, Dunfermline and elsewhere; but members were determined that the Edinburgh experience should not repeat itself, and agreements were concluded with individual firms, under which " substituted " women must receive men's full rates of wages. Failure to secure " equal pay," was practically confined to Aberdeen, where women were already employed by one or two firms.

In the bookbinding section, the National Union of Bookbinders and Machine Rulers, which started to organize women in 1915, included 11,000 at the end of 1919, and women actually formed a majority of members   Men and women are organized in separate branches, but enjoy equal rights of membership, whilst a rule of the union provides that places shall be reserved to women on the executive committee " in the proportion of one woman to every group where there are 1,000 women members, but no group shall be entitled to more than one women's representative." Four women were elected by this means to the executive committee in 1919. The old agreement of the London Journeymen Bookbinders, by which female or unskilled labour was restricted to certain simple operations, or "to carrying loads about the workshop," has practically ceased to be operative, but women's employment is still prohibited in the skilled branches of bookbinding or machine-ruling. In response to Government pressure, an agreement for the London district was concluded with employers in November, 1914, by which " female labour was admitted to the extent of 10 per cent. of the men and boys in the shops " on a scheduled list of skilled and semi-skilled operations, whilst a minimum rate of 7d. per hour should be paid after six months' probation; but these terms were apparently not satisfactory to employers, who took practically no advantage of the agreement.

The majority of women in these trades belong, however, not to any craft union, but to the National Union of Printing and Paper Workers, which caters for all women employed in printing and bookbinding—and includes skilled women compositors and bookbinders with bookfolders and sewers, layers-on or operatives' assistants, warehouse women, paper makers, paper bag and box makers. This society, which was formed in 1915 from an amalgamation between the National Union of Printers' Warehousemen and Cutters, a small Society of Cardboard Box Makers, and the National Union of Paper Mill Workers, has a female membership of 37,000 (1919), of which about one-third are paper-makers The old rule of the Printers' Warehousemen and Cutters, by which women as half-contributors counted only as half-members at general delegate meetings, was rescinded at the time of the amalgamation   Women enjoy full rights of membership, and are entitled to half the benefits of 9d. members, together with a marriage dowry, in return for a contribution of 4d. a week.   Branches are open to either sex.   The London women's branch, once the National Union of Women Bookfolders, forms an important exception, and has two places reserved to its members on the executive committee.   It covers over 75 per cent of women employed in this district, and in active interest in trade union affairs, in regular attendance at branch meetings and in punctuality of payment, its members are said to compare well with any other branch of the union.   For many years its representatives were the only women to serve on the executive committee, but the Edinburgh and Derby nominees have recently comprised women. The general staff includes five whole-time women organizers

The printers' warehousemen and cutters impose no formal restrictions on female labour, but women's employment is not encouraged as cutters, or on men's heavy machines.   Nor is it encouraged on night-work, men being employed at night on women's machines   The demand repeatedly made by employers during the war that the Factory and Workshops Act should be relaxed, and women employed on night-work, was vigorously opposed by members of either sex; but a certain number of women were introduced on men's warehouse and bench work.   In this case, special agreements were concluded with individual firms, under which " substituted " women received men's rates less 3/- a week (London).   These terms were, however, rejected by " jobbing " members of the London women's branch, who stood out and secured " equal pay "   Promotion to men's work was so far as possible confined by the union to its own members.

The National Union of Operative Printers' Assistants, with

a female membership of between 3,000 and 4,000, similarly caters for all women employed in printing and bookbinding. There are no sex disqualifications, but men and women elect separate representatives to delegate meetings. They mostly join on different scales of contribution and benefits, but well-paid classes of " substituted " women are expected to pay the men's full contribution of 1/- instead of 3½d. Women serve on local committees and one woman has been elected to the national executive, whilst local women's advisory committees, which sit together or separately with the branch executives, have been appointed for the discussion of women's questions. The printers' assistants, who are opposed to women's employment as " layers-on " on men's heavy machines, criticize severely the policy of the Typographical Association, which prohibits women as machine operatives, but encourages them as assistants on the ground that a " cul-de-sac " trade is well adapted to a " meantime " class of worker. With regard to " substituted " women, the same policy was adopted during the war as that of the Printing and Paper Workers.

The Manchester Society of Women Employed in Printing and Bookbinding, established under the auspices of the Manchester Women's Trades Union Council in 1896, opens its doors in the same way to all classes of women printers and bookbinders. At the invitation of the Printing and Kindred Trades Federation, branches have recently been opened, one in Warrington and another in the Potteries, but its 2,000 members belong mainly to the Manchester district The contribution is 2d., 4d. or 6d., according to wages, the higher sum being due from members earning over 24/- a week The women's union acts together with the men's societies in matters of wage advances, but members are not without criticism for the policy of trade union restrictions on female labour They ridicule especially the nice distinctions made by men bookbinders For example, women may be employed on quarter-binding, but the edges must be *cut flush* and not *turned in,* or they are allowed to draw on the book-cover, but the cover must be made of paper and not cloth; whilst the pasting on of end papers—a process " within the capacity of a child "—must not be done by women at all. The practice varies again from one district to another. Machine-ruling is strictly reserved to men in Manchester, but women are commonly employed in this way at Crewe and Wolverton. Members are at one with men trade unionists on the subject of " equal pay," but they keenly resent any suggestion that they are otherwise unfitted for skilled trades, and would gladly undergo the necessary degree of training.

The delay of the old-established craft unions in organizing women, so that their place was taken by other societies which stepped in before them, has caused the problem of demarcation to be more than usually complicated in the printing trades In organizing women of a class not recognized by skilled men's societies, the National Union of Printing and Paper Workers draws a definite distinction between women who have already established themselves in unorganized districts and women introduced for the first time in " union " shops   In the latter case, they are not admitted to membership, whilst support is given to the skilled men in resisting further female encroachment.   The position is, however, a delicate one, and tends to become acute when the skilled men's society elects at last to change its mind and to organize women. The Edinburgh " female section " of the Scottish Typographical Association, which was originally organized by the Printers' Warehousemen and Cutters, was transferred with comparatively little difficulty; but the recent action of the Association in forming an auxiliary women's section, composed of women other than compositors, has not unnaturally led to friction. Similar disputes have taken place between the National Union of Printing and Paper Workers and the National Union of Bookbinders and Machine Rulers.   Until 1915, the latter society absolutely refused to open its doors to women   It advised warehousemen and cutters " to refrain from organizing a class of worker whom we do not recognize," and drew attention " to the pronounced opinions expressed at previous meetings of the General Council in opposition to organizing females in the bookbinding trade."   During the unfortunate Burns strike of 1913-14, when men bookbinders were displaced by women, it was the National Union of Printing and Paper Workers which organized the women and brought them out in support of the men.   The cost of maintaining the strikers was, however, mainly borne by the Bookbinders' Union; and, in 1915, its London branch decided to form a women's section, members taking advantage of their close association with women bookfolders and sewers in order to persuade them to join the union. The National Union of Printing and Paper Workers, whose own branch was consequently reduced from 2,000 to 500 women, naturally resented the change of policy.   The matter was referred to the Printing and Kindred Trades Federation, which advised the Bookbinders' Union " to hand over such membership to those organizations chiefly catering for females employed in the printing and bookbinding trades." Members refused to comply, whereupon the Federation urged as a compromise that the union should " confine its organizing activities to those females engaged upon men's work."   The Bookbinders' Union similarly refused to content itself with organizing a mere handful of " substituted " women The action of the London branch was endorsed by the general council, and women were formally admitted to membership in 1917. In the spring of 1920, however, the two societies fortunately came to the only possible conclusion and approached each other with a view to amalgamation.

There is again some overlap between the Printing and Paper Workers and the Operative Printers' Assistants, and between the men's trade unions and the Manchester women's society. The relationship in this case is on the whole harmonious, each society confining itself so far as possible within certain limits. For example, the Printing and Paper Workers' Union has a monopoly of women in Derby, and the Printers' Assistants' Union a monopoly of women in Sheffield. Again, in London, one society organizes all women belonging to the warehouse and bindery departments, and the other society all women belonging to the letterpress departments. The position is nevertheless an unsatisfactory one, and is not made easier in Manchester by the policy of employers, who deliberately prefer to negotiate with the women's society to the exclusion of the men's trade unions For these reasons, a general amalgamation of all societies is coming to be more and more advocated by trade unionists as the only real solution of the present difficulties of demarcation. Nor is the principle of amalgamation opposed by the women's society, but members prefer to delay their decision until they feel themselves strong enough to hold their own within a men's organization.

Women members of the London Society of Compositors, as we have seen, receive full trade union rates of wages, amounting to £3 17s. 6d. per week of forty-eight hours at the end of 1918. Similarly, men's rates are secured by the Scottish Typographical Association for "substituted" women outside Edinburgh and Aberdeen. In Edinburgh, where a minimum wage of 17/- a week was fixed for women compositors in 1914, this rate was subsequently raised to 37/- at the end of 1918, the men's standard being 66/-; whilst further advances amounting to 7/- were received during 1919. "The time is not far distant we hope," declare members of the Association, "when the Edinburgh compositor will take her courage in both hands and demand the same rate as men." A move was made in this direction in the case of certain women compositors who took men's places in connection with the general election of 1918. It was not possible to secure "equal pay," but rates were secured amounting to about 70 per cent. instead of 50 per cent. of men's wages. The difference in wages between men and women compositors is upheld by employers on the grounds that women do not serve the full period of apprenticeship, and are mostly confined to comparatively easy work, whilst they require additional supervision and assistance in lifting the heavy "formes"; but the facts are disputed by trade unionists, who maintain that men are not always better-qualified, or that they receive similar assistance. Members of the Manchester Women's Society even deny that women are unable to lift the heavy " formes " " Four girls," writes the secretary of the society, " take each a corner of the forme and lift it quite easily without much loss of time."

Apart from special rates enjoyed by some groups of women compositors, wages are regulated by national agreements concluded between the Printing and Kindred Trades Federation, to which body the several unions are affiliated, and the Master Printers' and Bookbinders' Associations. Before the war, wages were indefinitely low, women earning from 10/- to 16/- a week. A first wages statement was drawn up by the London women's branch of the Printing and Paper Workers in 1914, fixing a rate of 17/- per week of fifty-one hours for time workers, 18/- for vellum sewers, 20/- to 30/- for forewomen, time-and-a-quarter overtime, and a corresponding piece-work price list for piece-workers; whilst another clause provided that the number of " learners " should be restricted to one for every ten adults—a rare provision in the case of women. These terms were not formally agreed by the Master Printers' Association, but in practice they were generally enforced. A general movement to standardize wages began about 1916, and by the time of the armistice minimum rates had been fixed in most important printing centres, amounting to 37/- a week of 48/- hours in London, and from 22/- to 30/- in the provinces. Finally, a national agreement was reached at the end of 1919, by which districts were grouped into London and six separate provincial *grades*. The London rate was raised to 45/6, whilst provincial rates varied from 31/- to 37/6 after four years employment, with graduated scales for young girls In the same year, a national minimum wage of 32/- a week of forty-eight hours was fixed for women paper workers. The printing unions prefer to remain outside the Trade Boards Act on the grounds that organization is sufficiently advanced not to need this protection, and members no longer belong to the class of " sweated " workers. In July, 1919, however, it was decided to form a National Industrial Council for the Printing and Allied Trades, five women being appointed from the workers' side

Paper-bag and *box-makers* are mainly organized by the National Federation of Women Workers, and their section was brought under the Trade Boards Act in the first batch of scheduled trades. The legal rate, which was fixed at 3d an hour in 1912, was advanced to 4¾d. at the end of 1918, and to 8d in November 1919

CHAPTER VIII.

WOOD WORKING UNIONS.

Societies belonging to the furnishing trades may be divided into two groups, viz , the National Amalgamated Furnishing Trades Association, which admits persons employed in any branch of the industry, and " craft " unions composed of persons engaged in particular occupations, viz., societies of carpenters, joiners and cabinet-makers, French polishers, upholsterers, organ builders, packing-case-makers, etc. The latter societies mostly prohibit women in their own branches of the industry, and women are consequently not admitted to membership. Of the " craft " societies, only the Upholsterers' and Packing-Case Makers' Unions have women members, whilst the little Manchester Society of Women Wood Workers is an all-women's union The bulk of women wood workers belong to the National Amalgamated Furnishing Trades Association or to one or other of the general labour unions, which recruited many thousand aircraft wood workers during the war. The little Liverpool Society of Upholstresses has recently joined the Workers' Union, and the Amalgamated Upholsterers' Union has been joined by the Manchester Society of Upholstresses

The National Amalgamated Furnishing Trades Association, formed in 1912 from an amalgamation of earlier societies, had a female membership of nearly 3,000 at the end of 1918, forming about 12 per cent. of all members The subsequent discharge of women munition workers caused many hundreds of these to leave the union, but women members numbered probably not less than 2,500 at the end of the following year. A " women's section " was originally formed by the Association, with a contribution of 3d. a week; but this section is now practically obsolete, and women join the " partial benefit section," which is open to members of either sex " who are not earning the minimum wage of any town or district " The contribution is 6d. a week, whilst benefits include trade, out-of-work, and funeral, but not sick pay. Members of this section are " entitled to all rights of membership," and are eligible for office, but women are not represented on the executive committee or on the general staff. They confine their activities to the branches, of which some are " all-women's " and some are " mixed "

L

Women members are mostly either French polishers or upholstresses. The Association is opposed to the use of edge tools by women, or to their employment on wood-cutting. A circular issued by the Minister of Munitions in 1916, by which employers were urged to take on female labour, met with so much opposition that it had to be withdrawn; and a subsequent resolution of the National Aircraft Committee laid down that " women should not be permitted to use edge tools," or to be employed " on any wood-cutting processes connected with aircraft " " Substituted " women in aircraft wood-working were mainly employed in " assembling " or in making small parts   The Association raised no objection in this case, and in some districts extended its permit to chair-making, provided that no men were unemployed and women's employment was recognized as strictly temporary.   Rates of wages for aircraft wood-workers were fixed by statutory order, amounting to 6d. an hour plus 11/- a week at the end of 1918; but French polishers and upholstresses are covered by local agreements with employers.   The policy of the Association is to secure a flat minimum rate, covering so far as possible all classes of workers.   In London the first women's minimum was fixed in 1919, amounting in May, 1920, to 1/4½ an hour for French polishers and 1/2 for upholstresses, whilst men of all classes received a minimum of 2/3½.   Similar rates on a somewhat lower basis were fixed in Manchester, and one or two other organized districts.   It is not uncommon for men French polishers and upholsterers to receive rates substantially higher than the minimum, but this case is very rare amongst women.

Chapter IX.

Chemical and Pottery Trades.

Eight small local societies of chemical workers, salt workers (women bag stitchers and salt packers), and oil workers (women candle makers and packers), include a proportion of women, but the aggregate female membership barely reaches one thousand, chemical and drug workers being mainly catered for by general labour unions. The pottery unions are more important in membership, men and women being mainly organized by the National Society of Male and Female Pottery Workers.

This society, formed in 1906 from earlier local organizations, has some 25,000 women members (1919), representing about three-quarters of the total membership, and 50 to 60 per cent. of women employed in the Stoke-on-Trent district. The number of women has increased from a little over 2,000 at the outbreak of war. Men and women have equal rights of membership, but there are separate scales of contributions and benefits, men paying 6d. a week and women 2d. or 3d. This scale provides for trade benefits only, but some women afford an extra 1d. a week for out-of-work or " no situation " benefit Widows receiving strike pay are entitled to the men's allowance of 1/- a week for each dependent child. There are no women on the executive committee, but several on district committees The Society has recently appointed a woman organizer, and for many years has employed women collectors, who collect from members of either sex. Men and women mix in the branches, the experiment of all-women's branches has been tried and failed.

Women are mainly employed in certain departments of their own, as decorators, aerographers, transferers, potters' attendants or dippers' helpers, etc., and in the warehouse; but they compete to some extent with men as cup-jolliers, bowl-makers, plate and saucer makers, dippers and casters, the tendency in each case being for women to displace men. The Society has not been able to enforce any definite lines of demarcation, but on grounds of health men members are opposed to women's employment as placers and dippers, or in making or casting large pieces of earthenware or sanitary ware.

The method of payment is mainly piece-work, and women's earnings averaged before the war from 11/- to 12/- a week on ordinary work to about £1 for women employed on certain new processes. Warehouse women employed on time received from 9/- to 12/- a week. In the case of "substituted" women, it was usual for men's piece-rates to be reduced by one-third, or by two-thirds in the case of young girls. The old system of "allowances" to employers was by no means extinct, and women employed on men's work, and nominally receiving men's piece-rates, were obliged to return to their employer a fixed proportion of their earnings.

In April, 1915, an agreement was reached between the Society and the Manufacturers' Association by which "substituted" women should "be employed at the same prices and under the same conditions as those of the men whose places they have filled, provided that such work has generally been regarded by the trade as men's work and on the distinct understanding that the men on their return should have the first claim on the old places." Under this agreement, a number of women were employed on men's work, so that in the Stoke Newington area the proportion of female to male pottery workers rose from an approximately even number in 1914 to about three to one at the end of 1918, women potters being allowed for the first time to employ attendants. The term "essentially men's work" led, however, to considerable evasion of the clauses relating to wages, for employers maintained that women were already employed in one district or another in practically every process which was discussed. In some cases, the Society was able to enforce journeymen's full rates, but generally speaking "substituted" women were obliged to "allow" to employers about one-third of their earnings In the case of "placers," there were considerable readjustments of process, one man being replaced by two women, who were not permitted to carry the full saggars, or to lift saggars above the level of their shoulders, or to enter ovens. It was therefore agreed that "substituted" women should receive a minimum wage of 18/- a week of forty-eight hours, rising after six months to 20/- (including 20 per cent bonus), plus 33⅓ per cent ; whilst the difference in amount between the wages of two women or one man (receiving 6/3 a day plus 20 per cent plus 33⅓ on earnings) should be paid to men placers, who did those parts of the work from which women were relieved   "Substituted" women, who are largely members of the union, still remain to some extent employed on men's work.

The war advances of 20 per cent on rates and 33⅓ on gross earnings (roughly 60 per cent.) applied to both sexes alike; and in August, 1919, the Society finally succeeded in its object of securing a standard for practically all classes of women workers. The award fixed broadly three scales, viz., 22/- a week of forty-seven hours for warehouse women, 25/- for dipping-house women, and

2/- extra for women hand scourers, with a bonus of 20 per cent in each case. It was further agreed that women transferers and enamellers should receive 4d. and 4½d. an hour respectively (plus 20 per cent.); whilst women " flat makers " should be paid men's piece-rates, or men's piece-rates less 10 per cent. in certain departments of flat pressing. At the same time, minimum rates were fixed for potters' attendants, ranging from 10/6 to 24/- for women from the age of thirteen to twenty-one. Another clause provided that "any adjustment in the piece-work rates to enable the journeymen or journeywomen to pay the above minimum rates to be arranged at individual works."

CHAPTER X

FOOD AND TOBACCO TRADES.

Men and women *food* workers are mainly catered for by general labour unions, the women members of all food unions numbering substantially less than 4,000. The Amalgamated Union of Operative Bakers, which opened its doors to women in 1915, has the most important female membership, or about 2,000 women, mainly employed as confectioners and bakers (tea-cakes, etc.). Wages are agreed between the union and employers separately for each district, women's rates being generally fixed on a two-thirds basis. In this way, a minimum wage of 45/6 a week of 48 hours was fixed for the London district in August, 1919. At one time, some 20 per cent. of female members were "substituted" women employed in breadmaking, but these women, who received about two-thirds of men's wages, were mostly discharged during 1919. The policy of the union in normal times is to exclude women from breadmaking. "Both employers and ourselves," the secretary of the Union writes, "agree that the process is too heavy." The Dublin Guild of Female Biscuit Operatives, established in 1916, comes next in importance, with a female membership of about 1,000, and a contribution of 3d. a week (raised to 6d. in 1920). Members succeeded in raising wages from about 15/- a week in 1914 to about 30/- at the end of 1919. Other organizations which include women are the Journeymen Butchers' Federation, the National Union of Millers, and the National Union of Brewery Workers, but the female membership in each case is negligible.

In the skilled branches of the *tobacco* trades, four societies cater for women with an aggregate female membership of about 3,000 The only important body is the National Union of Cigar Makers. The Cigar Sorters and Bundlers, the Cigar Box Makers and Paperers, and the Cigarette Makers are confined to London, and represent between them only a few hundred women. Unskilled men and women tobacco workers are catered for by the National Union of General Workers and other general labour unions.

The National Union of Cigar Makers, which admitted women to membership in 1895, amalgamated with the Nottingham Female Cigar Makers in 1918, women numbering over three-quarters of the members at the end of the year. Men pay 1/3 a week, London women 8d., and provincial women 4d., whilst benefits include trade, out-of-work, " lost time " and funeral. There are no sex disqualifications, and women's interest in the union is becoming increasingly active. Three women out of seven members serve on the executive committee, and a woman president was elected in 1919. As unofficial organizers, women are said by the secretary to show considerable ability, especially in dealing with their own sex; but members on the whole prefer that a man should be at the head of affairs. A predominant male element on the executive committee is believed to be necessary in order to maintain the present comparatively high level of wages.

Men cigar-makers are practically confined to London, where they make the best brands of cigars. Women are mostly employed on cheap brands, but compete with men to some extent. The method of payment is piece-work. " Substituted " women before the war received about four-fifths of men's piece-rates; whilst rates were fixed on a definitely lower basis in women's branches of work. A movement was, however, started in London about 1915 to secure men's wages for new classes of " substituted " women. The shortage of labour caused one firm after another to come to terms, and other employers were soon obliged to follow suit. At the end of 1918, not only war workers, but women previously employed on men's work, were receiving full trade union rates of wages, including the war bonus of 50 per cent., so that they earned up to £3 a week. It was, indeed, the success of the London movement which decided the Nottingham Female Cigar Makers to join the men's union, and a similar campaign was immediately started in the provinces, where rates were 20 per cent. below the London standard for identical brands of cigars. At the end of 1919, the advance on women's pre-war rates amounted to 122½ per cent. in London and 130 per cent. in the provinces, whilst men received only 97½ per cent.

For women tobacco strippers and other unskilled workers, some of whom are included in the National Union of Cigar Makers, wages are comparatively low, and the several·trade unions concerned recently joined in claiming the protection of the Trade Boards Act. By this means, a minimum wage of 30/- a week of 48 hours was fixed in May, 1919, which rate was raised to 35/- in the following August.

CHAPTER XI.

DISTRIBUTIVE AND KINDRED UNIONS.

The two important societies belonging to the distributive trades are, first of all, the National Amalgamated Union of Shop Assistants, which caters generally for the distributive workers, and for dressmakers, milliners and other productive workers employed by distributive firms, and secondly the Amalgamated Union of Co-operative Employees and Commercial Workers, whose members are mainly co-operative employees, including productive as well as distributive workers * The Irish Drapers' Assistants, an offshoot of the National Union of Shop Assistants, and modelled on the same plan, further includes some 1,500 women, and the National Union of Grocers' Assistants something less than a hundred. The large influx of women into grocery shops during the war caused such alarm to be taken by the latter society that its members decided to withdraw their previous recognition of female labour, and to admit no new women members The five small Hairdressers' Unions are similarly reserved to men The aggregate female membership of all distributive societies, which was about 18,000 in 1914, rose to over 60,000 in 1918, and probably to about 80,000 at the end of 1919. Of this number over 35,000 belong to the National Union of Shop Assistants, and rather less than this figure to the Amalgamated Union of Co-operative Employees The Shop Assistants' Union, which also includes many thousand co-operative workers, is in favour of one common organization for all distributive workers, and maintains that " co-operative employees should not stand apart from their less fortunate fellows." The two societies were, however, unable to come to terms and an amalgamation is now taking place between the Amalgamated Union of Co-operative Employees and the National Union of Warehouse and General Workers, which is mainly a general labour union.

In the allied *catering* trades, five small societies are reserved to men, whilst the National Union of Café Workers (Liverpool and Manchester) is an all-women's society The Amalgamated Union of Hotel, Restaurant and Club Workers, which included a few hundred women in 1914, fell practically into abeyance during the war, but revived in 1920, taking the name of the United Catering

* About one-half in the case of women

164

Trades Union.   The National Union of Shop Assistants takes the view that tea-shop girls are outside its province, except in so far as they are employed by general stores, and these workers are organized by the National Federation of Women Workers and other general labour unions, and latterly by the United Catering Trades Union.

The National Amalgamated Union of Shop Assistants, nearly one-half of whose members are women, makes no distinction of sex, except with regard to contributions and benefits.   The trade contribution, which is 4d. a week for men, is 3d. for women and 2d for dressmakers and milliners, whose wages until recently were exceptionally low.   Provident benefits, which include unemployment, sickness, funeral and marriage dowry, must be separately subscribed for.   Contributions vary from 2d. to 2/2 a week, and are the same for either sex.   Owing to the relatively high cost of administering the lower scales and the comparatively high sickness rate amongst women, the women's section stands in a less strong financial position than the men's, and the recent substantial increase in the proportion of female members gave rise at one time to some anxiety   The normal balance was, however, redressed during the war by the low claims on unemployment benefit.

Men and women are enrolled in the same branches.   The principle of sectional organization is adopted in respect of certain trade groups, such as dressmakers and milliners, hairdressers, chemists' and druggists' assistants.   The policy results in some instances in an all-men's or all-women's branch, but the distinction is one of trade and not of sex   Women shop assistants, as we have seen, are strongly opposed to sex distinctions, or to " any woman being appointed for any position (other than woman organizer) simply and solely because of sex."   One or two women generally gain election to the executive committee—Miss Talbot was president of the union in 1919—and women serve freely on local committees.   They are further represented by an active " women's advisory council." The general staff includes as a rule a woman organizer, and four whole-time women district secretaries have recently been appointed amongst responsible local officials.

Organization has been exceptionally difficult in the past.   Even in 1920 it was possible for a great draper's firm to require all new employees to sign an agreement that " they will have nothing to do with the union whilst they are in its employ."   The minimum wage committee, appointed by the union in 1908 to consider questions of wages, recommended that women's rates should be fixed on the basis of a *three-quarter* standard, or one of *four-fifths* in London.   This decision was arrived at for two reasons.

In the first place, a three-quarter standard represented considerably more than women's earnings at the time; and equality seemed impracticable, and only likely to prejudice the higher claims of men. In the second place, it was believed that a certain difference existed in the physical capacity of men and women which affected the value of their labour. The committee made, however, certain important reservations. In the case of managers, where physical capacity did not count, both sexes should receive the same wage; in the case of mantle assistants, where women's earnings were comparatively high, the women's minimum should be proportionately raised; whilst " equal pay " should be enforced for new classes of " substituted " women. " If this is not done," remarked the committee, " there would be a gradual displacement of men by women workers, with the sole object on the employer's part of reducing wage cost." The scale of wages fixed in 1910 included a women's minimum of 18/- a week, with an additional 5/- in London, deductions of 10/- to 12/- being allowed in the case of living-in   Other recommendations laid down that the number of apprentices should be limited to one junior to every ten seniors in large shops worked in departments, and one junior to every three seniors in shops not " departmentalized," and apprenticeship " should not be permitted to be entered upon after the 17th birthday." The minimum wage committee was subsequently reappointed in order to carry out its recommendations, and local committees were formed in the various districts with power to fix local rates above the national minimum, subject to sanction by the national committee. The rules of the union were further amended in 1916 to the effect that " members must not accept situations or offer their services in any district at a lower rate than the minimum fixed for the district," and the executive committee took power to suspend members from benefits unless the rule was complied with.   But even a three-quarter standard was almost impossible to enforce for women members   As late as the spring of 1918, an investigation made by the minimum wage committee revealed shockingly " sweated " conditions   Scotch members—adult women of 20 to 42 years of age—received wages from 9/- to 13/- a week (living-out), South Wales members, aged from 19 to 22 years—wages from 4/- to 10/- a week; Irish members, aged from 17 to 26 years —wages from 2/6 to 12/- a week   " These figures," declared Miss Talbot at the Annual General Meeting, " represent actual wages at present being paid to women, some of them occupying responsible positions in shops and show rooms.   There is a much larger section untouched by organization receiving wages lower than those quoted."

In the case of " substituted " women, however, largely grocers' assistants, the union was able to start afresh. The minimum wage committee still believed it impracticable to claim " equal pay," but recommended a *four-fifths* instead of a *three-quarter* standard, and this policy was widely enforced. A certain section of members, led by Mrs. Bessie Ward, took the view that the union should have gone for " equal pay," and resolutions to this effect were moved at two consecutive Annual General Meetings. Mrs. Ward urged that in many instances " substituted " women were doing the whole work of men, or else were doing other work equally valuable to the employer, but in each case her resolution fell to the ground. It was not until the Annual General Meeting of 1919 that the delegates finally came to the opinion that " the national minimum wage committee should immediately consider the drafting of equal rates of pay."

Apart from " substituted " women, a general advance of wages did not begin until 1917, but from that time onwards one success followed another. The movement was most remarkable amongst down-trodden dressmakers. The Edinburgh strike alone, which involved 1,200 women and a score of firms, resulted in advances of wages amounting to £14,000 a year. The big movement came, however, after the armistice. During 1919, advances of wages were secured amounting to no less than £3,000,000. It is estimated that the wages of women members rose during this year by 80 per cent, whilst non-union women received advances of about 45 per cent. The old scales of minimum rates were revised, new ones being drawn up on a four-fifths basis for women, and these rates were now agreed by large numbers of firms, in some cases covering many thousands of non-union women as well as members. The 1919 scales laid down rates ranging from 20/- to 53/- a week of forty-eight hours for women between the ages of sixteen and twenty-eight, and a minimum of £4 a week for managers of either sex (5/- to 10/- extra in London). The union, meanwhile, succeeded in bringing the distributive trades under the new Trade Boards Act. Numbers of non-union women were still receiving wages of less than £1 a week. Members are in favour of one national minimum wage scale, which should apply to all distributive workers irrespective of trade, so that one rate would obtain in drapers' or grocers' shops, furniture or book-shops, dairies or tobacco stalls; but they were unable to gain their point, and as many as eighty separate boards are in process of being set up for different trades.

The Amalgamated Union of Co-operative Employees similarly has a large and growing female membership. In practice men pay a contribution of 6d. to 9d. a week and women one of 4d. or 5d., but the scales apply equally to either sex. Women are not yet represented on the executive committee; but, in 1915, Miss

Wilkinson was appointed organizer, and two similar appointments were made in 1919   There has been no movement such as that amongst shop assistants, to form " women's advisory councils," but a " women's department " was started by Miss Wilkinson soon after her appointment " in order to deal with the many problems, new and old, arising out of the great influx of women into the unions." It was not the intention to separate " the interests of men and women in the ordinary routine of the branches," but the object was " to care for and represent those special interests of women which are not coincident with those of men."

The famous minimum wage scale, which was drawn up by the Union in conjunction with the Women's Co-operative Guild and the Co-operative Board in 1912, laid down rates ranging from 6/- to 24/- a week for men from fourteen to twenty-one years, and from 5/- to 17/- for women from fourteen to twenty years   At the outbreak of war, this scale had been adopted by some 240 out of about 1,400 co-operative societies as well as by the Co-operative Wholesale Society, and covered no less than 12,000 women and girls   In well-organized districts, men members had secured supplementary scales of annual increments, by which the minimum was raised to 30/- at the age of twenty-seven, and in one or two cases women had followed their example.   In the South Wales and Monmouthshire district, where the movement was most advanced, not only did members of either sex receive 2/- above the scale for a week of forty-eight hours, but the women's minimum was raised to 28/- at the age of twenty-seven, or only 5/- less than the men's at the same age period   This case was, however, an exceptional one.   " Women of brains and initiative," wrote Miss Wilkinson in the *A U.C E. Journal* (September, 1917), " with responsible and arduous posts, are still hampered by that strong tradition which pervades the co-operative movement that a woman's wages are practically settled for ever when she has become twenty-one, and that however important a woman's work may be, she must be considered as assistant to some male manager." Definite progress was made during the war, although advances of wages varied considerably from one district to another.   In the West Riding, the aggregate bonus at the end of 1918 amounted to 22/6 a week for men over the age of twenty-one and women over the age of twenty, but more often women received 7/- or 7/6 less than men   The agreements of 1919-20, which vary with each district, still show a substantial difference between the sexes except in the case of managers who receive "equal pay." In the important North-Western Counties district, the women's minimum is 44/- a week of forty-eight hours at the age of twenty-one, and the men's from 60/- to 67/6 at from twenty-one to twenty-three years; whilst, in the Southern Counties district, the women's rate is 45/- and the men's 60/-   First assistants must receive from 3/- to 5/- extra, and managers of either sex a minimum of 75/-.   Special terms were secured for " substituted " women, based on the following resolution of the Annual Delegates Meeting of 1917 :

(1) That the substitution be by joint agreement between the union and the employing societies.

(2) That immediate payment of A.U.C.E. male rates of wages shall be made to experienced females; but in respect to females without experience, one month's probation on A.U.C E. female rates of wages be allowed, and after such probationary period the wages and conditions shall be individually the same as those sanctioned by the union for males

(3) That all females so substituted, unless they are already trade unionists, shall be required to immediately become so, and that membership of a trade union organization shall be the condition of their employment for temporary service.

(4) That the temporary nature of the service be intimated by the employing societies to the females engaged, and that it be agreed that the males whose labour is replaced shall be reinstated in their situations as soon as they are able to resume work.

(5) That steps be taken to secure the due observance of labour and public health laws by the Co-operative Societies employing such substituted labour.*

The period of probation was subsequently extended from one to

---

* The policy is further explained in a note issued by the Union to the Coatbridge Co-operative Society during a dispute about the same time.

(1) The Employees' Union is not opposed to females coming in on work formerly done by males, provided they are paid male wage for age rates.

(2) The Union is opposed to the idea of three females being brought in to replace two males at the wage of two males, because it immediately lowers the minimum wage for the individual and the grade of employment, and leaves open the way for the introduction of unregulated cheap labour

(3) The Union does not stipulate that each female substituted shall have exactly the same wage as the man replaced. If, for instance, a man leaves the Society, and was receiving 33/- per week at 25 years of age or over, and is replaced by a woman of 21 years of age, the Union does not ask for 33/-, but for 28/-, which is the present rate at 21 years for males She is to be regarded exactly as a male in matters of wages and bonus, etc

(4) The objection of the employers that women's work is not equal in value to men's does not apply here   Their work in the shops will be made of equal value by adjustment   The females will be fully employed on counter work or other work suitable to them, and with the hearty co-operation of the men, the sum total of the duties will thus be accomplished, if male wages are paid

(5) The statement that substituted female labour is only a temporary expedient is not likely to be borne out by facts.   Many co-operative employees will not return to their employment after the war, owing to death, disablement, and other causes

three months, but with this modification, the terms were agreed by fifty-five co-operative societies, and in most instances " substituted " women received the men's bonus.   Members had reason to congratulate themselves, but the achievement had cost the unions no less than seventy strikes.   According to representatives of the union, employers had little or nothing to lose by " substitution."   In the Yorkshire district, where the places of 163 men had been taken by 164 women, the ordinary duties of the counter had been enormously increased by the complicated system of rations.   Women grocers' assistants, it is true, required some assistance in the handling of heavy goods, but in this case longer time was spent in the equally valuable and more skilled work of salesmanship.

Chapter XII.

Clerical Unions.

Organization is comparatively backward amongst clerks. Not only has it been hindered in the past by a class prejudice against trade unionism, but clerical workers belong to almost every industry, so that there are difficulties of demarcation between purely clerks' organizations of a " craft " character and the great industrial unions. Various attempts have been made at one time or another to form a general federation of clerks, but each attempt has failed. Trade unions which deal exclusively or mainly with clerks may roughly be divided into three groups, namely, commercial clerks, railway clerks and civil servants.

Commercial clerks —In this first group may be included the National Union of Clerks, the Association of Women Clerks and Secretaries, and three small societies of insurance agents, which were opened to women during the war The aggregate female membership is about 13,450 (December 1918), the large majority of women belonging to the National Union of Clerks. Apart from purely clerical unions, the Amalgamated Union of Shop Assistants, Warehousemen and Clerks and the Amalgamated Union of Co-operative Employees include a certain proportion of men and women clerks, but the number is not large. The former society confines its activities to clerks engaged in the distributive trades.

The National Union of Clerks, established in 1890, has a total membership of 43,200 (1920), of which about 10,800 are women, this figure having more than multiplied by ten since 1914. Women have always been admitted to membership on exactly the same terms as men. The trade contribution is 8d per week for either sex. An additional payment may be made for unemployment, sickness and death benefit, but comparatively few women care to afford the extra penny which is required in each case. Women members were at one time entitled to a marriage dowry in addition, but they protested against a rule which seemed to give them preferential treatment, and the provision was dropped.

Men and women mix in the branches, and women members definitely refuse to accept any privileges which are not accorded to men. An attempt was made to form a " women's league " in 1911, but it died almost at once—killed, it was said, by the

women members. A series of " national guilds " have recently
been formed in order to deal with the separate interests of different
industrial groups, viz , engineering clerks, insurance clerks,
colliery clerks, clerks in the iron and steel industry, or local
government clerks, but there is no question of sex differentiation.
Similarly, women members are opposed to reserved places on the
executive committee, and prefer to stand for election in open competition with men. One woman has so far been elected each
year, but the number hardly represents a due proportion in regard
to the female membership. Women are eligible for all official
posts, but up to now no woman has been appointed   They act,
however, as branch secretaries and take their full share in branch
work.

Wages are practically unregulated and, although all women are
not paid less than all men, it is true to say that the average rate
of payment is substantially less for women than for men   In
1912, the union laid down a rate of 35/- a week as the minimum
wage for adult clerks of either sex, but the rate was quite impossible to enforce for women. In giving evidence before the War
Cabinet Committee on Women in Industry, the general secretary
stated that before the war the average salary for clerks was 30/-
a week for men and 20/- for women; but many women employed
by insurance companies and similar commercial firms were known
to receive wages as low as 10/- a week. According to an enquiry
undertaken just before the war the highest salary paid to a
woman clerk was found to be £175 per annum, and the lowest
5/- per week *

The union tried to secure the same war advances for women as
for men; but its efforts were mostly unsuccessful, the average
bonus being somewhere about 25/- per week for women and 40/-
for men, and it happened occasionally that women were left out
altogether. " Substituted " women were not more fortunate
than others   There is no class of clerical work which can be
especially defined as women's work. Men and women are engaged in practically all branches of the clerical profession,
although a tendency may be remarked for women to be confined
to the more routine work, leaving the higher administrative posts
to men   During the war many thousands of women were employed on men's work   In banks, where " substitution " took
place on a large scale, employers alleged that it took three women
to do the work of two men, and wages were paid accordingly
As a matter of fact, women did not do exactly the same work as
men did—in some cases they did actually more—and comparisons
were not easy to make, but the general opinion amongst trade

* *Women Workers in Seven Professions* By Professor Edith Morley,
(1915) Page 281

unionists was that women's wages were quite unfairly reduced. In some few instances, it is true, women actually received a higher wage than men, but the reason was in this case that men were undergoing training, whilst women had no similar opportunities of promotion.

For these reasons, members have adopted the formula " equal pay for similar duties," in place of the more ambiguous one " equal pay for equal work." " No two workers," declares the general secretary, " can turn out exactly the same amount of work in the same time, neither is the work exactly the same quality. In fact, no employer employs the phrase ' equal pay for equal work ' to male workers. Equal pay for similar duties to men and women would not cause any displacement of female labour. In cases where equal pay has been obtained for women they take more interest and give higher output."[*]

The present trade union claim is for a minimum wage of £3 10s. a week for adult clerks of either sex, and in some cases this is enforced, but the average wage of a woman clerk is not more than about 45/-.

The Association of Women Clerks and Secretaries, formed in 1903, had a membership of about 1,200 in 1918, which figure rose to over 6,000 in 1920, largely owing to an influx of temporary civil service clerks. Membership is open to any salaried woman worker, whose main occupation consists of clerical, administrative, secretarial or organizing work, " provided that any candidate for membership, also eligible for membership of a trade union recognized by the Trades Union Congress as appropriate to her industry, is also a member of that trade union." The Association further admits honorary members and associates, but the latter class is confined to young girls or women who are undergoing training. Subscriptions are at the rate of 1/- per month for ordinary members, 5/- per annum for honorary members, and 2d. per month for associates, whilst extra payments are required for provident benefits, which include sickness, unemployment and old age.

From time to time, negotiations have been opened with the National Union of Clerks with a view to amalgamation, but the matter is for the time being in abeyance. The main point at issue is the claim by the Association for special representation of women and reserved places on the executive committee; but, in view of the opposition expressed by its women members, the National Union of Clerks does not see its way to reversing its present policy.

The Association supports the National Union of Clerks in demanding " equal pay for similar duties "; and, in order to

[*] War Cabinet Committee on Women in Industry

M

place family men and single women on an equal economic footing, further claims some form of children's pensions. Members consider that the effect of " equal pay " would be to displace women at first; but, if they were as well trained as men, they would soon be able to hold their own The Association has been especially successful in securing advances for civil service clerks.

Railway clerks.—This group is covered by the Railway Clerks Association, which caters for clerical, supervisory, administrative, professional and technical employees in all departments of the railway service. The total membership is 85,000 (December 1918), of which between 13,000 and 14,000 are women. The rules make no distinction of sex. The rate of subscription is 6d. per week, unless the salary is below £70 per annum, in which case it is reduced to 4d. Benefits include trade, unemployment, disablement, retirement and convalescent benefit. Branches, which are " mixed," are grouped into " divisions " or " districts," and each branch is represented by at least one delegate on the " divisional council," women taking their part with men. At most of the large stations, " office committees " are appointed, upon which women are represented whenever possible, but a woman has so far not been nominated for the executive committee The question of reserving places to women was raised at a special women's conference in 1917, but was voted down by women members In response to a request from the latter, two women's conferences have been held, one at Leeds in 1915, and another at Birmingham in 1917, and both were very well attended; but, having had their say, women members do not appear to have any further desire for separate conferences, and feel that they can now hold their own with men. Wholetime organizers are not appointed by the Association, but women do voluntary work in the branches.

Women's employment in railway offices was only just beginning in 1914, but the subsequent shortage of men caused an influx of something like 20,000 women during the war. They were introduced as booking clerks, account clerks, invoicing clerks, and general clerks in the goods and passenger departments. In most cases they took the place of men, but an exact comparison of work was difficult to make because of slight variations in duties. In a large staff it may be said that, roughly, women do the routine and men the more responsible work. " In railway offices," states the general secretary of the Association, " there has not been the necessity for any great modification of processes to enable women to do the work. At the outset when women took the place of trained clerks, the proportion was three women to two men, or five women to four men. At present, taking into account the increased volume of work, both in quality and quantity the women equal the men when they have acquired experience and knowledge of methods."*

Wages vary with different companies. The Association claims "equal pay"; but railway companies are all alike in refusing it The inequality begins with the method of payment, men receiving an annual salary, whilst the majority of women are paid on a weekly basis. The difference may be partly attributed to the fact that women are still regarded as temporary workers. For the same reason of uncertain tenure, they are not generally eligible for the companies' superannuation benefit, nor are they entitled to the same benefit as men during absence through sickness. Before the war, women's rates varied from 20/- to 28/- a week, according to the line and district, the amount representing about three-fifths of the men's standard; but wages were indefinitely low in unorganized offices. Speaking at the women's conference of 1917, delegates brought to light glaring instances of underpayment. In some cases women clerks of twenty-five years of age were only receiving 11/6 a week The Association took up the women's case, substantial advances were secured, and "substituted" women received the men's minimum rate in each grade, but not men's annual increases, and about one-third of the men's war bonus.† The improvement was a real one, but women's wages still remain unregulated to some extent. The important railway agreement of 1920 did not apply to women, and their case has only now come under negotiation.

No restrictions are imposed by the Association on female labour, and men clerks do not object to women's employment, provided that it is not used to pull down the trade union standard which has taken years of effort to build up. In view, however, of the large number of men clerks still serving with the colours, "substituted" women are regarded as temporary and not permanent workers.

A working agreement between the National Union of Clerks and the Railway Clerks' Association provides that clerical workers in the railway service should join the Railway Clerks' Association before they become members of the National Union of Clerks.

Civil servants.—This group is said to comprise no less than 240 societies, of which probably about one-third include women. The aggregate female membership may be estimated at 55,000

The most important body is the Union of Post Office Workers, which has an approximate membership of 115,000, about 17,000 being women. The union was formed in the spring of 1920 from an amalgamation of earlier societies, including the Postal and Telegraph Clerks' Association, the Fawcett Association and the

* War Cabinet Committee on Women in Industry.
† The war bonus was the same as that of railway manipulative workers, 33/- for men and 20/6 for women at the end of 1918

Postmen's Federation, and represents the main body of postal workers. Societies outside the union include the Federation of Sub-Postmasters, the Federation of Supervising Officers, and the Post Office Women Clerks' Association (2,600 women), whose members have always refused to associate themselves with manipulative workers, and prefer to affiliate to the Federation of Women Civil Servants. The Civil Service Sorting Assistants' Association (1,100 women), whose members are opposed to " direct action," similarly remains outside the amalgamation   Women members of the present Union of Post Office Workers are chiefly composed of telegraphists, telephonists, and sorting clerks, but also include postwomen, typists, caretakers, etc. Assistants employed wholetime in sub-postmasters' offices are allowed to join, but not subpostmasters' assistants who work half-time in shops. The latter unfortunate class of women are mainly organized by the Amalgamated Union of Co-operative Employees. Temporary workers during the war were admitted to the Postmen's Federation (about 10,000 women in 1918), but not to the Postal and Telegraph Clerks' Association, or to the Fawcett Association, until the amalgamation of the three societies in 1919. Temporary workers of the latter class were mainly organized by the Temporary Postal Workers' , , Union and other small societies of temporary workers The 2,500 women members of the Temporary Postal Workers' Union had been reduced to 500 at the end of 1919.

Post-office unions make no distinction of sex. The Union of Post Office Workers may be joined at a contribution of 3d., 4d , or 5d., according to wages, but there are no benefits other than those of membership. The question of strike pay is now under consideration, and should members decide in its favour a further subscription would be necessary. Election to the executive committee is by open ballot at the annual conference, and five women were elected in 1920. In this connection, it is interesting to record that by the rule of the old Postal and Telegraph Clerks' Association, two places on the executive committee were reserved to women telephonists (a condition of its amalgamation with the former Society of Telephone Employees), but the rule came to an end in 1918, when seven women were elected in the ordinary way The present union employs one whole-time woman organizer, and women act as voluntary organizers in the districts.

The wages of Post Office workers have been regulated in the past by means of recommendations made by periodical House of Commons Select Committees Rates vary with the character of the district. In 1914, the women's rate in London was from 18/- a week at the age of eighteen, to 40/- after sixteen years' service (compared with from 20/- to 65/- received by men); whilst, in small provincial towns, the women's rate was from 12/- to 28/-,

and the men's from 14/- to 42/-. There was great delay in securing a war bonus, and when it came at last women did not receive
more than one-half the men's sum. This proportion was, however, raised afterwards to about two-thirds, the women's bonus
amounting to 15/- a week at the end of 1918. Members have
always advocated "equal pay irrespective of sex," and, until this
principle is recognized by the Post Office, they are prepared to resist
any further displacement of men by women. "Substituted"
women during the war received only women's rates of wages, but
they were generally relieved from men's night-work, and certain
other arduous duties.

Outside the Post Office, the innumerable little societies of civil
servants are mostly affiliated to the Civil Service Federation, or
to the Civil Service Alliance; whilst civil servants of the supervisory and administrative grades are enrolled in the Society of
Civil Servants (about 200 women). The old National Joint Committee of Postal Unions was at one time affiliated to the Civil Service Federation, but the present Union of Post Office Workers
prefers to stand alone. The Civil Service Federation, which is
mainly concerned with *manipulative* workers, comprises sixty-three
small unions, of which eight include women, with an aggregate
female membership of about 12,000 Membership is open to civil
servants, either through an affiliated society, or by means of a
"central association," which is designed for persons not otherwise organized; but there are no distinctions of sex, and one
woman has been elected to the executive committee. Amongst
the most important of affiliated societies are the Civil Service Sorting Assistants' Association, which is an all-women's society, and
the Civil Service Union, which was formed by temporary workers
during the war, and includes a proportion of clerks.

The Civil Service Alliance, on the other hand, confines its activities to clerks. It was brought into existence in 1916, in order to
resist an attempt by the Government to abolish overtime without
compensation in wages, and at present comprises thirty-seven
affiliated societies, of which nine have women members. The
aggregate female membership is about 5,500, and twelve women
out of sixty-six members serve on the general council. The largest
and most interesting of the affiliated societies is the Federation of
Women Civil Servants (3,500 members), consisting of seven small
departmental unions, of which one is the Association of Post Office
Women Clerks. The policy of Government departments, which
deliberately encourages small departmental societies, is severely
criticized by trade unionists as against the interests of organization.

During the war, it was usual for regular and temporary clerks
to be enrolled in separate societies, but an effort is now being

made by the Civil Service Union and other societies of " war
workers " to break down these barriers. The Civil Service Union
caters for all grades and classes of " brain workers," men or
women, regular or temporary, employed in the civil service.

Wages before the war were practically unregulated except by
the Treasury   The standard in November, 1914, was £150 to
£200 per annum for principal women clerks, £115 to £140 per
annum for first-class clerks, £65 to £110 per annum for second-
class clerks, 26/- to 31/- per week for shorthand typists, 20/- to
26/- for typists, and 18/- to 36/- for writing assistants.   War
advances were the same as for post-office workers, or 15/- a week
for women over the age of eighteen; whilst shorthand typists and
typists received an advance on their maximum rates, raising the
figure to 42/- and 32/- respectively.   During 1919, a further all-
round increase was granted by the Government, amounting to 30
per cent. above the 1918 standard.   Finally, on the initiative of
the Civil Service Alliance, the whole body of civil service unions,
including the Union of Post Office Workers, put forward a claim
for a consolidating bonus, which should be the same for men and
women, viz., 130 per cent. on the first 35/- a week of all pre-war
salaries, 60 per cent. on the amount between 35/- a week and
£200 per annum, and 45 per cent. on the amount between £200
and £1,000 per annum.   This scale, which varies with the cost
of living and applies to civil servants in all departments, was
adopted by the National Council for the Civil Service in May 1920,
and subsequently accepted by the Treasury   " It is realized on
all sides," members of the Civil Service Alliance declare, "that the
application of the principle of equal pay furnishes the sole safeguard against a competition of cheapness which is disastrous alike
to men and women." They further advocate that methods of recruit-
ment in the civil service should be the same for either sex   The
feeling is especially strong amongst members of the Federation
of Women Civil Servants, who are restive at the delay in securing
" equal pay." The disappointing Report of the National Council
for the Civil Service, which advocated different methods of recruit-
ment and payment in the higher branches of the service, has made
them realize that new energy must be put in from the women's
side if their movement is to become a live one   The equal bonus
is a step in the right direction, but it does not make the salaries of
men and women civil servants anything like equal

Municipal clerks are mainly organized by general labour unions,
which tend to absorb the small societies of corporation workers,
but some are included in the National Union of Clerks.   The
latter society, together with the Workers' Union and the National
Association of Local Government Officers, form the workers' side
of the National Joint Council for Local Authorities' Administrative,

Technical and Clerical Services, which has actually adopted the principle of "equal pay." The scale of salaries laid down in June, 1920, ranges from £70 to £325 per annum for adult officers of either sex, plus the usual civil service bonus.

CHAPTER XIII.

VARIOUS UNIONS.

In this group may be included the National Society of Brush Makers, which admitted women to membership in May, 1918, and counted over 2,000 by the end of the year, four small societies of basket makers, amongst them the National League of the Blind (400 women), seven small unions of leather workers, comprising between them from 3,000 to 4,000 women, and the Amalgamated India Rubber Cable and Asbestos Workers The latter society has a female membership of about 4,000, but women rubber workers are largely organized by general labour unions. Other societies which cater for women in various industries are small bodies of municipal employees not yet absorbed into general labour unions, the National Theatrical Employees (about 1,000 women), the British Gardeners, the Domestic Workers of Great Britain, the two last-named societies having each a mere handful of members, and the National Laundry Workers, with a membership of something less than 1,000. Professional and artists' organizations are not included within the present survey.

CHAPTER XIV.

GENERAL LABOUR UNIONS.

Of a dozen or more general labour unions, practically all include women, and two are all-women's societies. The aggregate female membership, which was little more than 20,000 in 1914, had risen to 216,000 at the end of 1918, women forming about one-quarter of the total membership The discharge of munition workers, who composed probably 80 pe‧ cent. of women members during the war, caused a fall in number in the early part of 1919; but, as these women passed into other industries, they not only rejoined their union but brought in recruits. It is probable that at the end of 1919 the aggregate female membership was little less than at the time of the armistice.

General labour unions cater in almost every industry. Members belong mainly to unskilled or semi-skilled trades, but skilled workers are not excluded. Of the several industrial groups, one of the most important is that of women metal workers, who are almost entirely organized by general labour unions This group, which is always a large one, probably included two-thirds of all women members during the war. Other important groups of women are food and tobacco workers, chemical and rubber workers, textile and clothing workers who belong to minor industries, or are employed in unorganized districts, and latterly laundresses and to some extent domestic workers Metal, food and textile workers are fairly evenly distributed between different unions, but the National Federation of Women Workers and the Workers' Union would seem to be the principal societies for women's light clothing, laundry and domestic workers, the Workers' Union and the National Union of Warehousemen and General Workers for chemical and drug workers, the last-named society and the Dockers' Union for tobacco workers, and the Workers' Union and the National Union of General Workers for rubber workers. The Workers' Union also acts with the National Union of Agricultural Labourers as chief representatives of agricultural workers. Both societies recruited many hundreds of landswomen during the war.

General labour unions may broadly be divided into two groups, namely, all-women's societies, of which the outstanding one is the National Federation of Women Workers, and joint-organizations, the most important of these being the National Union of General Workers and the Workers' Union.

The National Federation of Women Workers has roughly a membership of 80,000 women, or about the same at the end of 1919 as at the time of the armistice.   The constitution is modelled on that of an ordinary general labour union. '' All women engaged in unorganized trades are eligible for membership,'' whilst women '' in sympathy with the objects of the Federation may become members, provided that any member eligible also for membership of a trade union recognized by the Trades Union Congress as the trade union appropriate to her craft or trade shall not be entitled to contribute for trade union benefits in the Federation unless she is also a member of that trade union.'' Further, sympathetic persons may be admitted as honorary members ''upon payment of a minimum subscription of 5/- per annum,'' but honorary members are not entitled to vote.   Members under the age of 21 have full rights of membership, but must not be elected to the executive council or appointed as officers.   The executive council is composed of a president, vice-president, treasurer, secretary, one member elected by each of the seventeen districts, together with three *advisory* members appointed by the Women's Trade Union League, '' who shall not be entitled to vote.''   Miss Gertrude Tuckwell was president until 1918, when she decided not to stand for re-election owing to her belief that '' the Federation has now reached a stage in its development when its president should be chosen from among the members of its rank and file.'' Following again the usual method of general labour unions, the factory or local industrial group is so far as possible adopted as the unit of branch organization, although for reasons of convenience branches in scattered districts may include a wide variety of workers.   Contributions range from 3d. to 8d. per week, 3d. contributors being entitled to all trade benefits, namely, strike and lock-out pay, general assistance in raising wages and free legal advice, to benevolent benefit (i e., '' any form of benefit which may be decided upon by the executive council in a particular case''), and to funeral pay, whilst, on the higher scales, benefits include sickness and unemployment.   Members are further entitled to the return of one-half the total amount of their contributions on marriage, provided that they have not at any time received sickness benefit and are leaving industry   Until recently, the low contribution, together with the high cost of organizing women, allowed little margin of income, but during the last two years the Federation has been able to build up a substantial reserve fund as well as to meet its rapidly growing expenditure. The present staff includes over a hundred persons, of whom fifty are general or district organizers   The regular staff is supplemented by a number of honorary helpers, many of whom give whole-time service The Federation is affiliated to the Labour Party, the Trades Union Congress, the General Federation of Trade Unions, and the Standing Joint-Committee of Industrial Women's Organizations. It is represented on practically all important Government committees dealing with industrial women's questions as well as on local statutory bodies. It has also representatives on a number of National Industrial Councils and on the large majority of trade boards. Following the enfranchisement of women in 1918, members decided by a vote of over 14,000 against 500 in favour of political action.

The National Union of General Workers, recently formed from an amalgamation between the National Union of Gas Workers and General Labourers and other general labour unions, has a total membership of 350,000, of whom about 60,000 are women (December 1918). The union " embraces every kind of labour and admits all workers, women as well as men, on an equal footing," but does not " accept or retain as members workers who are already members of another union, except where conditions of work make it reasonable to do so." The entrance fee is 1/- for men and 6d. for women, " save where women receive the same wages as men, when districts are empowered to receive women under the same conditions as men." This provision is, however, seldom operative. The ordinary contribution is 5d. for men and 2½d. for women, latterly raised from 3d. and 1½d., whilst women are entitled to one-half men's benefits, including trade, a proportion of unemployment benefit and grants for total disablement. Men and women are enrolled in the same branches, the factory or local industrial group being adopted as the unit of branch organization; an all-women's branch is practically confined to workers in factories or industries, where only women are employed. Any particular class of labour represented by over 100 persons has, however, " the right to apply for permission to start a branch of its own." Women are subject to no disqualifications, either on grounds of sex or as low scale contributors; but, in practice, they take no part in management. The union employs regularly one whole-time organizer, whilst " temporary staff are engaged as required."

The Workers' Union, established in 1898, has a total membership of nearly 500,000 (1919), of which about 60,000* are women. Any persons " who accept the principles, methods and objects of the Union " may become members and " shall pay a contribution of not less than 4d. a week." Women members " may pay either full or half contributions, and receive full or half benefits," or they may join " the special section for female members," and pay a con-

* The figure rose to about 100,000 during 1920

tribution of 3d. Benefits include trade, accident, total disablement and funeral, whilst members of the " women's section " are entitled to a dowry in addition, either upon marriage or upon reaching the age of fifty.   Out-of-work and sickness benefit, which are optional, require additional subscriptions.   All members have equal votes in the Union, and all are equally eligible for office. Some sixteen women organizers are employed, forming nearly one-quarter of the whole staff, but women are not represented on the executive committee, and few are elected to district committees.   Members of either sex are generally opposed to all-women's branches, which are practically confined to members employed in women's industries   " Women will never organize women," a trade union correspondent declares in the *Trade Union Worker* (December, 1916), but " workmen can and have successfully organized work women."   Branches composed entirely of women are said, on the whole, to be the most difficult to retain.   " We have had large branches started," the same correspondent writes, " when trouble has arisen, or when women have wanted higher wages, and the branches have prospered until the Union has finished negotiating with the firm; but when all is smooth again, I have been astonished at the shrinkage of members." In "mixed" branches, on the other hand, women " get into the habit of not attending branch meetings and leaving all the work in the hands of the men."   At the triennial delegate conference of 1916, the Bolton women's branch brought forward a resolution recommending that " women shall be represented on the general committee," but the motion apparently fell to the ground.

Other important general labour unions are the National Union of Warehouse and General Workers, which is on the eve of amalgamation with the Amalgamated Union of Co-operative Employees and has probably not less than 20,000 women members, and the Amalgamated Union of Labour, with about 5,000,   The remaining societies, amongst which may be mentioned the Irish Women Workers' Union, are mostly small local organizations   It is significant that, apart from the National Federation of Women Workers, women are not represented on the executive of any important general labour union.

In June, 1917, a Joint-Committee on Women's Wages and Working Conditions was set up by leading general labour unions, Miss Macarthur acting as chairman.   The object was to secure joint-action in matters of common interest, but its function has since been largely taken over by the National Federation of General Workers.   This body, which is composed of all important general labour unions excepting the National Federation of Women Workers, is assisted by a women's advisory council, but women are not represented on its executive committee.   The National

Federation of Women Workers is invited to take part in its deliberations on matters affecting women; but affiliation was refused, .as we have seen, on the ground of its constitution as an all-women's society Some representatives of affiliated societies further took exception to its alliance during the war with the Amalgamated Society of Engineers. Co-operation between general labour unions and skilled men's societies, apart from joint-action on national industrial councils, is generally confined to joint-claims for advances of wages. Similarly, the policy of the National Federation of Women Workers may be distinguished from that of most general labour unions by its readiness to transfer members to their appropriate societies, as the latter are prepared to admit them. Such transfers have recently taken place between the women's union and the National Union of Printing and Paper Workers, the Amalgamated Union of Clothiers' Operatives, the Amalgamated Union of Engine and Crane Drivers and the London Packing Case Makers.

The question of co-operation between general labour unions tends, however, to lose its significance before the more important one of amalgamation. The National Union of General Workers, as we have seen, is the result of a recent movement in this direction; and the Workers' Union is now in similar process of amalgamation with the Amalgamated Union of Labour and the Municipal Employees' Association, the new body taking the name of the National Amalgamated Workers' Union. Of the 5,000 or more women members of the Municipal Employees' Association, many are clerks and even professional nurses as well as caretakers, attendants, charwomen, etc.; whilst the proposed amalgamation between the Amalgamated Union of Co-operative Employees and the National Union of Warehouse and General Workers will eventuate in a general labour union comprising large numbers of shop assistants. The area of general labour unions would seem for the moment to be encroaching on that of other forms of organization. From the women's point of view, however, the most interesting scheme is that for an amalgamation between the National Union of General Workers and the National Federation of Women Workers. The terms, which are practically agreed, propose that the women's union shall be dissolved, transforming itself into a so-called " district " to be known as the " Women Workers' District of the National Union of General Workers." According to the rules of the latter union, a " district " is not necessarily geographical, but, may be formed by any group of branches " numbering not less than 3,000 members ", whilst a branch may be formed by " any particular class of labour representing over 100 persons." The " women's district " would in this way be open to existing women members of the National Union of General Workers, who preferred to join an all-women's " district," as well as to members of the present women's union.   Each " district " elects its own representatives on the general council, and has power to make bye-laws, and also to retain any moneys which are not due to the central fund   The terms of amalgamation further provide for the special organization of women, and their separate representation at Trades Union Congresses and Labour Party Conferences.

Wages in unorganized trades are at present largely regulated by the Trade Boards Act, but trade union action is as necessary now as in the past in order to operate the Act and obtain advances. To the efforts of general labour unions may be largely attributed the recent marked improvement in unorganized women's trades. In the metal trades, so far back as 1913, an important agreement was concluded between the Workers' Union and other general labour unions on the one side, and, on the other side, the Midlands Engineering Employers' Federation, fixing rates of wages for women metal workers.   These rates, which ranged from 6/- to 12/- a week of 53 hours for women from 14 to 21 years of age (compared with 38/- for skilled tradesmen and 23/- for unskilled men labourers), set the standard for the Midlands district. Women chain-makers, who had been brought under the Trade Boards Act chiefly by the action of the National Federation of Women Workers, enjoyed in 1914 a rate of 2¾d. an hour; but small ammunition workers, for whom the efforts of Miss Macarthur had been unavailing to obtain the same protection, still received indefinitely low wages. The campaign of the National Federation of Women Workers and other societies on behalf of women munition workers has been described in a previous chapter. By means of arbitration awards and statutory orders, wages were pushed up and standardized until at the time of the armistice rates amounted to 5d. an hour plus 11/- a week, or 6d. plus 11/- for " substituted " women (as against a standard ranging round 46/- a week for skilled tradesmen, or 26/6 for labourers plus 16/6 plus 12½ per cent. on earnings), piece-rates being estimated so as to yield to ordinary workers 25 per cent. above the standard A further all-round advance of 5/- a week was received in January, 1919.   These rates represented the standard for the main body of women munition workers, but special classes of " substituted " women were entitled to special rates, rising to 7d., 8d , and in some cases 10d an hour; whilst women " employed in the place of skilled tradesmen " received men's full rates of wages (less a deduction of 10 per cent. on account of additional supervision), although not men's full war advances, or 11/- instead of 16/6 plus 12½ per cent on earnings.   These statutory orders applied only to engineering and ship-building establishments, but the 5d. and 6d. rates, together with the 11/- war advance, were afterwards extended to brass-founding, electric lamp, asbestos, cable, nail, nut and bolt, optical instruments, small tool, explosives, and rubber manufacture, and the 6d rate to general aircraft and aircraft wood-working, where rates were as low as 7/- a week before the war. The legal minimum rate for chain-makers was raised during the same period from 2¾d. to 4d. an hour in November, 1908, and to 7½d in November, 1919 Hollow-ware workers, who had been brought under the Trade Board Act in 1916, secured similar advances From 10/- a week in 1914, the legal rate was raised to 3d. an hour, or 13/- a week, in 1916, rising again by steps to 30/9 in December, 1919, whilst another 6/6 a week was secured by trade union agreement.

In the food-preserving trades, which are mainly organized by general labour unions, women members received 11/- or 12/- a week in 1914, but there was no common standard. It is significant that at Sheffield in this year the Amalgamated Union of Labour was unable to secure a rate higher than 8/- a week for fifty women brewery workers, and this sum represented an advance of at least 1/- a week ' The main food-preserving trades, viz., cocoa and chocolate, jam and sugar confectionery, were brought under the Trade Boards Act in 1915. The minimum rate, which was first of all fixed at 3d. an hour, was gradually raised to 6½d. in March, 1919, whilst additional advances were secured by agreement between the unions and federated firms, bringing up the minimum to 9d. in January, 1920. "Substituted" women, employed on a scheduled list of processes, were even promoted to men's full rates of wages, or 11d an hour. Similar advances were secured for unorganized groups of textile and clothing workers. Rope and net workers, who received an average of from 8/- to 12/- a week in 1914, now received the usual rates of munition workers. Lace finishers, who were amongst the first to enjoy the protection of the Trade Boards Act, advanced in four years from 2¾d. to 5½d an hour Shirt-makers, whose wages were indefinitely low until 1915, similarly were brought under the Trade Boards Act; the legal minimum was pushed up from 3d. an hour in 1915 to 8d. in November, 1919, the latter rate consolidating previous trade union advances. Button-makers, who before the war earned 8/- a week on piece-work, now received 20/- on time-work, and 23/- to 24/- on piece-work The trade passed under the Trade Boards Act early in 1920, the legal rate being fixed at 8½d. per hour. Laundresses, whose wages averaged about 12/- a week in 1914, were brought under the Trade Boards Act in the autumn of 1919, but the legal minimum of 28/- a week had already been forestalled by trade union action in London and other organized districts.

Special restrictions on female labour are not imposed by general labour unions; but, where the interests of men members are concerned, the union claims " equal pay " for " substituted " women. In the food preserving trades, as we have seen, this claim has been actually enforced under the Trade Boards Act. Not more than a few women were concerned, but the triumph was none the less a real one. In tobacco manufacture, the National Union of General Workers similarly concluded an agreement with employers that " substituted " women should be paid " the same wages as are now paid to males for an equivalent amount of work done," together with the usual provision that " female operatives shall only be employed in substitution of male labour where and so long as it is not found possible to obtain male operatives," but, in practice, women tobacco workers received only about two-thirds of men's wages.

PART III

PROBLEMS OF WOMEN IN TRADE UNIONS

CHAPTER I.

WOMAN'S PLACE IN INDUSTRY.

BEFORE discussing the problems of women in trade unions, it is first of all well to define woman's place in industry. In view of the wide variety of occupations, any classification must be to some extent an artificial one, and the following short analysis does not pretend to be other than very rough and incomplete in character. Its object is merely to indicate the main types of wage-earning occupation and the broad lines of sex demarcation. With this qualification in mind, industrial occupations may be classified under four main headings, i e., labouring work, craft work, process work, and clerical work.

(1) *Labouring work.*—This group of occupations, which so far as concerns women is largely composed of unskilled warehouse and domestic workers, may be said to cover all manual occupations of a mainly undefined or "general" character. In normal times, the sexes are separated by a broad line of demarcation, men being employed on the heavier or outdoor work and women on the lighter or indoor work. The line is chiefly determined by the physical capacity of the worker. In occupations involving severe physical strain, women's labour is uneconomical, offering little or no advantage to employers even at comparatively low rates of wages Men have a natural monopoly of physical strength. Nor are women attracted as a rule to rough or heavy work of this kind. As new trades are opened up to them, indeed, the census figures seem to suggest that general labouring is more and more left to men Between 1881 and 1911, the number of men to each woman rose from 20 to 47 in agricultural work, from 68 to 188 in the mines, where women have always been and are still employed to some extent at the pit-head. In up-to-date factorie there is a similar tendency, and where women are employ

189

N

operatives, men are not uncommonly introduced as labourers. Even amongst general domestic and unskilled hotel and restaurant workers, it appears that the proportion of men is slightly increasing. During the war, owing to the shortage of male labour, this movement was temporarily reversed, women being introduced to various forms of outdoor labouring commonly done by men, but these experiments were only very partially successful. More workers were required for the same job, or women were subjected to undue physical strain, or else an unfair share of heavy duties was thrown on the men who were employed with them. The result in nearly all cases was a reduction of output. Apart from the question of trade union restrictions, it is improbable that any large number of " substituted " women would have remained permanently employed in these trades except at extremely low rates of wages.

The worker of either sex is, however, strictly limited in physical capacity, so that compared with mechanical power manual labour is in the main uneconomical Both in outdoor and indoor trades, unskilled labouring is coming to be more and more done by machinery. The labourer has already been displaced to some extent by the motor or crane driver—occupations, it may be observed, not unsuited to women Even in domestic service, where machinery is most backward in development, the "vacuum house-cleaner" and the " household motor " have begun to compete with the old-fashioned charwoman This group of occupations, although still a large one, forms in consequence a relatively contracting section of industry. Moreover, with each advance of wages by which the cost of unskilled labour is raised above that of machinery, this movement tends to be accelerated.

(2) *Craft work* —In this group, to which belongs the fully-skilled or " journeyman " tradesman, may be included all manual occupations of a mainly "jobbing" or "individual" character. In normal times, here again the sexes are separated by a broad line of demarcation The large majority of skilled trades are reserved to men, whilst women are confined to the domestic arts and needle-craft. The question of physical capacity counts for comparatively little, nor is there any reason to suppose that women are deficient in a sense of craft, but men are protected by another form of monopoly, of which the causes are less physical than social. In order to make an article or to perform a job throughout, the worker requires an all-round expert knowledge and experience, from which women are usually debarred by their failure to undergo a long apprenticeship. The average young girl who looks forward to leaving industry on marriage is not prepared, nor is her employer, to make a large outlay on technical training Whilst a boy is willing to serve a five or seven years' apprenticeship, and becomes

qualified in every branch of his trade, a girl will be content with a period of two or three years, and is qualified in only one or two branches. During the war, numbers of women took the places of fully-qualified tradesmen; but, generally speaking, they did only a part and not the whole of the job, so that its "individual" character was lost. The growing desire for economic independence amongst all classes of women is leading them to attach new importance to industrial qualifications. There is no doubt that an increasing number of women are looking forward to professional careers; but, until the average young girl expects to remain in industry after marriage, a long apprenticeship will almost certainly be the exception and not the rule.

Domestic industry and needlework form a class apart.* By immemorial tradition, these trades belong to women. No cooking or dressmaking is so fine, and no housework or washing so rough, that it is held by employers or trade unionists to be too skilled or too laborious for women. Nor is the expectation of young girls to leave industry on marriage regarded as a bar to technical training. On the contrary, such training is commonly believed to be an essential part of their education as future wives and mothers. It is significant that no education authority thinks it worth while to provide technical training for women in normal times except in housewifery and needle-craft. To what extent these occupations are specially congenial to women raises another question. It is a fact that they are not unwilling to leave these as new ones are opened to them. Since 1881, the number of domestic workers is known to have considerably decreased in relation to the general female population. This decrease is most remarkable at the earlier ages and may be at least partly attributed to the objection of the younger generation of industrial women to the living-in system. This objection does not apply to the same extent to the needlework trade, but until recently the low rates of wages and long hours of work received by dressmakers and milliners offered little inducement to employment in view of the skilled character of the work. During the war, thousands of domestic servants and needlewomen eagerly took the opportunity of escape to men's trades, and their present return to their own is apparently only compelled by necessity.

Under "individual" methods of production, the standard of output is high in quality, but for obvious reasons limited in quantity. This group of occupations forms, not only a small, but also a constantly contracting section of industry. The desire of employers to increase production, as well as their anxiety to employ semi-qualified and consequently cheaper classes of workers,

* Infant care is not included under this heading. The trained children's nurse should rank as a professional.

both tend to the same result; and the job of the fully-skilled tradesman is coming to be more and more split up amongst a host of
semi-qualified machinists and machines. In most modern industries
a long apprenticeship is practically confined to small groups of
workers specially selected for promotion. In up-to-date factories,
indeed, it is not unknown for the duties of the foreman or overlooker to be almost as specialized as those of the operative, and
for only one or two real experts to be employed in a staff of
several hundred workers. In munition factories, inexperienced
women were promoted as forewomen and " tool setters " after a
few weeks' or a few months' experience. Some subsidiary processes of manufacture, carried on inside or outside the factory, still
require in the worker an all-round knowledge and experience, but
these processes are comparatively few. By the use of standardized
parts, even such work as repairing may lose much of its "jobbing"
character. This tendency towards simplification of process is least
marked in domestic industry, but is not entirely absent Food-
preparing and clothes-making are constantly passing from the
home to the factory; whilst experiments in large scale or co-operative housekeeping have already reached the practical stage. The
reform of domestic service may in time be expected, not only to
bring such assistance within reach of working-women who are
now unable to afford it, but to release thousands of workers from
paid or unpaid domestic service for more productive and apparently more congenial employment.

Process work.—This group, which is mainly composed of semi-
skilled factory operatives, may be said to cover all manual occupations of a mainly " specialized " or " sectional " character, Here,
once more, the sexes are separated in normal times by a broad
line of division, men being employed on the heavier or more
skilled, and women on the lighter or less skilled work, but the
line is drawn by artificial as well as by natural causes. In many
" process " trades, not only the power, but also the skill is mainly
inherent in the machine, or the worker is confined by sub-division
of labour to one or a short series of operations. Men's monopolies
of physical strength and expert training count for comparatively
little, and the line may be partly or mainly drawn by trade union
restrictions on female labour Where organization is strong and
rates of wages are in consequence comparatively high, operations
may be reserved to fully-qualified tradesmen which, if not " within
the capacity of a child," may yet be learned by inexperienced
women in the course of a few weeks or a few months; whilst,
where organization is weak and low rates of wages have driven
men from employment, women may be employed on work at least
as skilled or laborious as that from which they are ordinarily excluded. In some textile trades, where women habitually remain

at work after marriage, they even undergo a comparatively long period of apprenticeship.   It is also true to say that men's trades are relatively *well-organized* and *highly-paid,* and women's trades relatively *ill-organized* and *badly-paid,* This artificial line is, however, constantly shifting, and there would seem to be a gradual displacement of men by women in the " process " type of trade. It is not necessarily a question of direct sex competition, for men and women are mostly employed in different processes or in different districts.   But women are introduced together with a new mechanical device, or a new sub-division of labour, bringing the job within the reach of a less skilled or robust class of worker, and the *women's* process tends to take the place of the *men's* process.   Or women are introduced in unorganized districts, and the trade tends to pass from the *men's* district to the *women's* district.   In the textile trades, where both sexes have been employed for over a century and women form the majority of the workers, a certain point of equilibrium would seem to have been reached.   The relative position of male and female labour has been almost stationary for a generation.   In many factories, men's employment is practically confined to posts as overlookers or as labourers, or to certain subsidiary processes for which women are unsuited, or else to night-work.   But, in other industries of a " process " or mainly " process " type, the movement is not without significance.   Between 1881 and 1911, the number of men to each woman fell from two to one in tailoring, from 26 to 5.2 in printing, from 3.7 to 2.8 in china and earthenware, from 1.3 to 0.6 in tobacco, from 20 to 16 in the metal trades.   In the latter case, the chief increase has taken place since 1900, when women came in with the general adoption of automatic machinery.   During the same thirty years, indeed, the proportion of men to women rose only in one or two industries, such as in paper-making, where the work is largely general labouring, or in lace-making, where machines are of a large and expensive type and the high overhead cost is partly met by means of habitual night-work   During the war, the relaxation of trade union rules and regulations allowed this movement free play.   The effect was most remarkable in the engineering trades, where the vast output of war munitions and new methods of " mass " production offered exceptional opportunities for the employment of inexperienced women. Owing to more or less changed conditions, an exact comparison of output was seldom possible, but the general opinion would seem to have confirmed the long experience of the cotton weavers.   On light or moderately light work, women compared well with men in output; on simple " repetition " work, they actually excelled them and were better able to bear the strain of monotony. Their shorter experience was, indeed, in some cases a positive advantage.   The restoration of trade union practices, together with the return of industry to normal channels, caused the movement to be reversed afterwards, but there is no reason to suppose that this reverse will be a more than temporary one. The question of trade union restrictions on female labour is discussed in a later chapter; but, artificial causes apart, the normal progress of industry may be expected to act in future as it has done in the past, and to bring men's trades more and more within reach of women.

There are no limits, or none within sight, to the physical capacity of machinery or mechanical methods of production. This group of occupations forms a large and expanding section of industry.   An exchange from hand-work to machine-work, from "individual" to "sectional" methods, has almost invariably the effect of enormously increasing output, and the semi-skilled factory operative has a comparatively high productive value. Not only the expectation of high profits on the part of employers, but the growing demand for commodities amongst all classes of consumers will cause industry to flow in these productive channels.

Clerical work.—In this group of occupations, which is mainly composed of clerks and shop assistants, may be included all non-manual occupations of a mainly clerical or routine character. The same broad features reappear as in the previous groups. Men's monopolies of physical strength and expert training count for comparatively little, but women are mostly confined to inferior posts not requiring in the worker an all-round expert knowledge, or a long experience. There are other barriers of social tradition, by which in normal times women are excluded from certain fields of employment. Owing, however, to the relatively slow growth of trade unionism, trade union restrictions do not practically exist, and the line of sex demarcation is a less definite one in consequence, and one easier to overstep than that in organized industries of the factory type. With the growth of the "big business" and the development of mechanical or routine methods of organization, the tendency of women to displace men has been even more pronounced than in the "process" trades. Between 1881 and 1911, the number of men to each woman fell from 29 to 3 1 amongst commercial clerks, whilst a not much less remarkable movement seems to have taken place amongst shop assistants.*   During the war, owing to the shortage of male labour, this movement was further accelerated, nor has it since been reversed to the same extent as in the "process" trades. This group of occupations forms another great and expanding field of industry, although the clerk and shop assistant tend to displace the small merchant or shopkeeper rather than other groups of wage-earners.

* The census figures for shop assistants are not exactly comparable.

Broadly speaking, it is probably true to say of men and women in industry that men can do all things which are done by women—men are even supreme in the domestic arts and needlecraft—and some things which are not. This admission on the part of women is not so humiliating as it may appear to men. Industry is not the whole of life. Moreover, those things which cannot be done by women are a diminishing quantity. Not only do they hold their own with men in some of the most productive and progressive fields of industry, but each advance of wages or improvement in working conditions may be a means of further redressing the present balance against them. The sound economy of high wages was once more proved during the war, and unexpected powers of physical endurance, as well as capacity for fine workmanship, were revealed amongst well-paid classes of " substituted " women. Other factors tend in the same way towards a greater sex equality in industry. The present trade union claim is that workers of either sex should be relieved so far as possible from excessive overtime and night-work, or any unduly laborious or injurious conditions, and new protective laws which apply to men and women alike are now superseding the old legal restrictions on female labour. Women appear, moreover, to be more susceptible than men to good or bad working conditions, which susceptibility reacts on output. This effect was especially remarked during the war in relation to hours of work It was conclusively shown in munition factories that the shift for maximum efficiency was definitely shorter in the case of women than men; whilst, on moderately heavy work, women could hold their own with men on short shifts, but not on long shifts. The general adoption of a 44-hour week would probably make for an increase in the relative efficiency of women. Similarly, irregular timekeeping, which is one of the most serious charges made by employers against women, and commonly attributed to temporary indisposition or domestic requirements, may be remedied to a large extent. Not only should hours of work be short enough to allow of reasonable leisure for home life to workers of either sex, but the wages of women who are employed whole-time in industry should be sufficient to assure them at least that modicum of domestic assistance which is commonly provided to men by their wives. In this connection, the device of the " sick worker," by which in the cotton industry one operative arranges with another —probably a married woman who has retired, or semi-retired, from wage-earning—to take her place on emergency in the factory, deserves the consideration of other groups of industrial women Amongst women cotton operatives, irregular timekeeping is not remarked even by employers.

Nor has the progress of education been altogether without

influence in the breaking down of old barriers to skilled trades. Many processes commonly reserved to skilled tradesmen, although their character is so specialized that they can be learned by inexperienced men and women in the course of a few weeks or a few months, may yet require in the operative such qualities of accuracy and nice judgment as are not usually found except in apprenticed or fully-qualified workers. Skilled domestic servants, dressmakers and milliners, clerks and shop assistants, were notoriously in high demand in munition factories. For employment as skilled mechanics, many employers deliberately selected women of secondary education who had no previous industrial experience. Not less significant are the apparent effects of education in the cotton industry. Before the passing of the first Education Act of 1871, it was the general opinion of employers that, in order to maintain efficiency, children should be trained in the mills almost from infancy. Until the outbreak of war, it was believed that the training of young children could not be safely postponed beyond the age of 12, or at the latest 14. After four years' experience of "substitution," however, the Home Office was able to report that "some slight period must elapse before full efficiency is reached, more especially in the ring room, on the mules and some subsidiary processes of weaving, but the necessary skill may be readily acquired by an intelligent worker" When school age is raised from 14 to 18, or still better to 21, and a general knowledge of mechanics is included as part of a liberal education, industrial efficiency will no doubt be maintained, or may be actually improved, although no worker from the operative to the manager has had more than a few weeks' or a few months' special training

Methods of "mass" production are condemned by the craftsman as mechanical. The craftsman is akin to the artist, and his desire to express his ideal can, perhaps, find only complete satisfaction in individual performance. The spread of true education and the awakening of new artistic sensibilities amongst all classes of consumers may be expected to bring a partial revival of "individual" methods of production in the making of articles for intimate personal consumption. Similarly, a revolution in the objective of industry, so that goods were directly made for *use* and not for *profit,* would almost certainly lead to the setting of a new value on good workmanship. But it takes all sorts to make a world, quantity as well as quality. No person can desire to cook his dinner on an "individual" stove, or to cross the seas in a hand-made boat. So far as the large majority of workers are concerned, there can be little prospect of return to conditions of a past age. Methods of "mass" production are, however, not necessarily inhuman. As control of industry passes eventually from the hands of an autocratic employer into those of a workers' democracy, indeed, these methods, from being mechanical, may become co-operative; and they may express, if not the passion of the artist, at least the human instinct to share in the common service of humanity. Nor is it a necessary condition of scientific management that the mechanic should be reduced to a a common measure with the machine. Democratic control of industry—even mere advances of wages—may bring, on the contrary, such a new respect for human labour that the worker will in time be relieved of practically all duties except those of a " directing intelligence," and the mere " hewing of wood " and " drawing of water," or the " purely automatic operations " against which he rightly rebels, will be almost entirely delegated to machinery.

CHAPTER II.

OBSTACLES TO ORGANIZATION.

The relatively backward state of organization amongst women remains even to-day a conspicuous feature of trade unionism Its causes may be briefly discussed under the six following headings.

(1) *The character of women's occupations.*—In each industry, as we have seen, women form seldom more than a section of semi-skilled or unskilled workers, amongst whom trade unionism was late to develop. Not only were semi-qualified women ineligible for the skilled men s "craft" unions, which were the primitive form of organization, but they were unable to form similar societies of their own. The strength of the old-fashioned "craft" union, whose membership was confined to workers in one or a small group of skilled trades, lay almost entirely in the ability of its members to control the entry to these trades, and so to maintain them a close preserve This ability depended in turn on the length of period required for qualification. A five or seven years' apprenticeship might offer a real security against illicit competition; but one of a few weeks or a few months—a common period in semi-skilled and women's trades—it is clear could afford practically none. Hence, semi-skilled and unskilled workers had to seek for other forms of organization Nor did the sense of "craft" fellowship, which was one of the earliest incentives to combination, extend to the semi-qualified woman who crept into industry, it might be as the unpaid assistant of her father or husband. The early achievement of women cotton weavers may be at least partly attributed to the comparatively skilled character of their work. Thus, the problem of women in trade unions does not only refer to their sex, but forms also part of the larger problem of organizing semi-skilled or unskilled labour. From the earliest efforts at combination in the beginning of last century down to the rapid growth of the great industrial and general labour unions in recent years, the women's movement has closely followed, if it has not kept pace with, that of semi-skilled and unskilled men. The decay of apprenticeship tends, indeed, to undermine the former strong position of the skilled men, and many old-established "craft" unions have been forced by circumstances to enlarge the basis of their membership so as to

include one class after another of less qualified competitors. Nor
is it particularly desirable that a monopoly of skill, except as a
weapon against the dangerous force of capital, should be held
by small select groups of workers. The problem broadly is how
to find the right type of organization This subject is discussed
in a later chapter, but it may be remarked here that women's
progress in organization has, generally speaking, coincided with
that of the " industrial " and general labour unions, whose members include all classes of workers employed in one or more
industries and rely on no monopoly except that of numbers

In the traditional women's trades, there are similar difficulties
to overcome Amongst domestic workers and needle-women, the
skill seldom amounts to more than the normal feminine ability to
cook, or wash, or sew. Here can be no question of monopoly.
In the skilled or luxury branches of these trades, organization
is inevitably prejudiced by the close personal contact of the
worker with a social class which is not her own, but in whose
luxury she shares to some extent. In small dressmakers' or
milliners' shops, the comparative ease with which the worker
passes from the rank of employee to that of employer is equally
prejudicial to organization The isolated conditions of home-
work, or those dependent ones of living-in, by which women are
chiefly affected, are likewise unfavourable to a robust growth of
trade unionism. The new demand, however, which is coming
from the younger generation of industrial women, that working
conditions in the traditional women's trades shall be brought into
line with those of less backward industries, together with changes
in social relationships, makes it probable that these sources of
weakness in organization will not be permanent ones

(2) *Low wages.*—Low wages, according to Miss Mary Macarthur, are at once the cause and effect of women's backwardness
in organization. The point does not need to be insisted upon.
A body of " sweated " workers lacks obviously, not only the
energy, but the actual material means of organization. Before
the war, thousands of women were barely able to afford the
lowest contribution of a penny or twopence a week, and threepence
was about the maximum. Living from hand to mouth, women
again were handicapped by an aggravated fear of victimization.
In the cotton industry, organization has progressed step by step
with advances of wages. In the worst " sweated " trades, it
could not even begin until the worker had secured the protection
of the Trade Boards Act and a legal minimum wage. During
the war, well-paid classes of " substituted " women had notoriously the best character as trade unionists. These facts all point
to one conclusion. When women receive men's wages, then and
not before, they will gain men's full strength in organization.

(3) *Delay in recognizing women on the part of men's trade unions.*—The necessity for organizing women is at present generally acknowledged by men trade unionists. For nearly half a century, following the example of the cotton weavers, one union after another has decided to admit women to membership. The old prejudice, which would exclude them on no other ground than that of sex, has practically ceased to exist. The question of trade union restrictions on female labour is discussed in a later chapter, but it may be pointed out here that, until women are recognized in men's trades, they obviously cannot be admitted to men's trade unions. Organization can only follow and not precede recognition. It was for this reason, as we have seen, that during the war the Amalgamated Society of Engineers decided not to admit women to membership, but to enter into a temporary alliance with the National Federation of Women Workers. Delay of this kind is probably inevitable, but it is none the less unfortunate. The action of the men's trade unions in refusing to recognize women does not necessarily achieve its end of excluding them from employment, but too often the result is only to leave them unorganized or to be organized by other societies, which have not the same trade interests to protect. In either case, women establish themselves in the trade or industry under " non-union " instead of " union " conditions, and develop a bad instead of a good tradition, whilst employers on their side build up a vested interest in " cheap and docile " female labour. Before organization has properly begun, the problem of unfair female competition has grown to unmanageable proportions, and the lost ground is doubly hard to recover. The cotton weavers' unions certainly owe part of their success in enforcing " equal pay " to their prompt action in organizing women. Similarly, the transport unions, which were faced for the first time during the war with the problem of " substituted " women and at once decided to organize them, had a comparatively easy task. It is safe to say that the London women 'bus conductors would never have won their case for " equal pay " had other women been already employed on 'buses at low rates of wages. The present cause for delay in organizing women will, however, be only removed with that of trade union restrictions on female labour.

(4) *Antagonism on the part of employers*—Trade unionism receives to-day at least lip-service from employers. Respect is paid by one power to another; but, unfortunately, women have until recently been comparatively weak in organization, and they still have to face in consequence something of the old bitter hostility of their employer, who sees in each attempt to organize them a direct attack on his vested interest in " cheap and docile " female labour. During the war, it was not unknown for a great firm,

which habitually negotiated with the men's trade unions, deliberately to refuse similar recognition to organized women. Another and more subtle form of the same policy is that by which employers try to encourage a weak type of women's organization —preferably a small " sectional " all-women's society. Employers are, however, discovering a new respect for women as these are coming to trade union power.

(5) *The broken term of industrial life.*—Most women are wage-earners at one time or another, but few women are employed in industry for the whole of their lives, or ever escape entirely from domestic duties. Comparatively little importance is attached to trade conditions and, in consequence, to trade unionism. For the same reason of " mortality by marriage," industrial women are largely young people, who are notoriously more difficult to organize than adults. The reliable qualities of women cotton operatives would seem to be by no means unconnected with the large proportion of married women in this group, so that the average young girl has more than the normal expectation of returning to industry after marriage. Weaving runs in families, and women have a more than usually permanent interest in a trade which is also that of their fathers or husbands. The married woman, however, who deliberately remains in industry must not be confused with the unfortunate young mother who is suddenly forced into wage-earning by the death or unemployment of her husband. This latter type of worker is one whom it is practically impossible to organize. Her release from industry is urgently called for, not only for the sake of herself and her children, but also in the interests of her fellow-workers. A Mothers' Pensions Bill has already been drafted by the Labour Party with this object. Unless the race is to come to an end, the industrial life of the average woman must always be more or less a broken one, but there are signs that she is developing a more permanent stake in industry. The outlook of the girl worker can hardly fail to be influenced, not only by the growing desire amongst industrial women for economic independence, but by the opening up of men's trades to women, whereby the industrial interests of man and wife are brought into more and more direct line

(6) *Tradition.*—Women have never been backward in strikes. They are, on the contrary, more often accused by their officials of being too forward, so that they " down tools " for frivolous reasons and drag out the men after them. It is a fact that the courage and loyalty of unorganized women in supporting organized men have been amongst the principal factors in deciding the latter to organize them. A more than usual prejudice against trade unionism may nevertheless be remarked amongst certain " genteel " classes of women   It is the part of a " lady " to be

exclusive and inconspicuous, and such qualities are not conducive to active trade unionism. The various forms of snobbishness, which would ape the customs of a superior social class, refuse to associate with social inferiors, deprecate as bad taste the open discussion of incomes or trade concerns, and hide poverty as a vice, would seem to be more characteristic of women than men. Another and not less grave source of weakness is the low value set by women on their own labour—a modesty inherited, perhaps, from a past generation who acted as unpaid assistants to their fathers or husbands. Nor is the exclusive attachment of women to the home and family, which is unfortunately encouraged in them by their men-folk, always compatible with generous labour sympathies. To the good influence of husband or father in this matter, indeed, the cotton unions attach such great importance that they make him so far as possible responsible for the action of his wife and children in joining the union! Old traditions are, however, giving place to new ones. The typical young girl of to-day is as healthily " unladylike " as her brother, as self-confident, and almost as undomesticated. Trade unionism during the war, from being " bad form," became actually fashionable in West End shops and City offices. These difficulties, which belong to an older generation, are in natural course of solution.

In conclusion, it may be said that women are faced with more than usual difficulties of organization. These do not, however, refer primarily to sex, but to the fact that women mostly belong to a class of semi-qualified and badly-paid workers. No obstacles, moreover, are really insuperable, but these tend, on the contrary, to disappear spontaneously with changes in economic and social conditions.

CHAPTER III.

TYPES OF WOMEN'S ORGANIZATIONS

Women's organizations, which are largely identical with men's, vary to the same degree in structure; but, for the purpose of the present discussion, this variety may be divided into three significant types, namely, the *all-women's society*, the *joint "industrial" union*, and the *general labour union*

(1) *The all-women's society.*—Of some 200 women's societies established during half a century in every variety of industry or trade, hardly a score have counted more than a few hundred women, or have survived longer than a few years Success, although rapid and sometimes dramatic in its effects, was mostly short-lived, and members left the union almost as quickly as they had joined it. The reasons are not far to seek. Forming in each industry only a section of semi-skilled or unskilled workers, without monopoly of skill or numbers, women lacked the means of either a sound " craft " or a sound " industrial " unionism. Other difficulties of organization were aggravated in the same way. The financial weakness of a small group of underpaid workers was in itself an almost hopeless handicap. The substantial friendly benefits, which formed the cement of the men's early societies, were clearly beyond reach of women; whilst, without outside assistance, strikes led straight to bankruptcy. Expenses of office and staff were necessarily cut down to a minimum. Nor was it easy to maintain efficiency of management in a society mainly composed of young people, or of married women heavily burdened by domestic duties; and responsible officers were as hard to keep as to find. The most valuable purpose served by the all-women's society has probably been as a nucleus for organization, so that women have learned to hold their own before joining a men's trade union It is for this reason that such comparatively successful societies as the Manchester Society of Women Employed in Printing and Bookbinding or the Association of Women Clerks and Secretaries, whilst acknowledging the advantages of the joint-organization, prefer to continue for the present as independent bodies, or are not prepared to amalgamate except on special terms.

The allied women's society, subject to control by a men's trade union, would appear to have the character of an all-women's branch rather than that of an independent society. This form of organization has no doubt been suited in the past to the particular circumstances under which it took shape, but generally speaking it would seem to offer neither the educational advantages of the all-women's society, which oblige women to stand on their own feet, nor the more material benefits of the joint-organization.

(2) The *joint " industrial " union* —Following the classic example of the cotton weavers, men and women, who are employed in the same workshops, are mostly organized in the same trade unions. Men and women are, however, not generally employed in the same trade or " craft," women being confined to certain inferior branches of work, or forming an inferior class of worker. The old-fashioned " craft " union, whose members belong to a skilled trade or to a small group of skilled trades, is in consequence seldom adapted for the purpose of a joint-organization. Apart from any question of sex, women are ineligible for membership. The case of the cotton unions is a peculiar one; but, as a matter of fact, these associations cannot rightly be described as " craft " unions. It is true that the basis of membership is not so broad as that of the industry, but neither is it so narrow as that of the single trade. Thus, the weavers' associations include, not only weavers, but all workers employed in the weaving departments; whilst the card and blowing-room associations comprise, not merely one or two groups of operatives, but all workers employed in the preparing departments. The type may be best described as a " divisional form of industrial union." Some joint-organizations present, indeed, the curious phenomenon of a " craft " basis for men, but an " industrial " basis for women Thus, the National Union of Printers' Warehousemen and Cutters (now incorporated in the National Union of Printing and Paper Workers), and the National Union of Operative Printers' Assistants, each confines its activities in the case of men to the class of worker indicated by the name of the union, but both cater for all women employed in printing and bookbinding. This anomaly may be directly traced to the policy of the skilled men's societies, which have refused in the past to recognize women in their own branches of the industry, so that these women were left to be organized by outside bodies, none of which had a special claim to this duty. Nor was the situation improved by the subsequent decision of the skilled men's societies to reverse their policy and to admit women to membership. The present state of overlapping, which unfortunately exists between rival printing societies, can only be remedied by means of amalgamation.

Women's progress in organization has then mainly followed the growth of the great " industrial " and general labour unions. The advantages of the "industrial" type of union, which admits to membership all the workers employed in an industry, against those of other forms of organization, cannot be discussed here in detail. It is enough to point out that the primary object of trade unionism is to free the workers from the tyranny of employers. Hence, the best type of organization is that which is best adapted to win this freedom; and every argument in favour of " industrial " unionism, which applies to semi-skilled and unskilled men, may be applied with added force to women in proportion to their greater weakness in organization. Without support from the skilled men who are employed with them, semi-skilled and unskilled women are practically defenceless against the aggression of employers; whilst the skilled men are exposed to almost equally grave risks by leaving unorganized the semi-skilled and unskilled women from whose numbers may be drawn their most dangerous trade competitors. Loyalty to and understanding of each other's interests are essential on both sides, and experience shows that these conditions may be best realized where men and women are intimately associated within a common organization. Women who are backward in trade unionism can, moreover, be approached and influenced with more than usual facility by men fellow-workers. Persuasion may, indeed, reach the point of actual compulsion. For these reasons, the joint " industrial " union is commonly advocated by trade unionists as the best form of women s organization.

The general labour union —There are, however, important industries which are not effectively covered by " industrial " unions In the engineering trades, where the skilled men societies have not yet decided to recognize women; in domestic service, and similar women's industries, where it is apparently still impossible to form stable " industrial " organizations; in many food preparing trades, where the workers of either sex are equally unskilled and unorganized; in the textile and other trades, where organization is confined to the main industrial centres, there is a great host of women for whom no appropriate societies are available. General labour unions may be divided into two groups, namely, the great joint-organizations and the National Federation of Women Workers.

The National Federation of Women Workers, which is entirely composed of women, differs from the normal type of general labour union in constitution and to some extent in policy. Uniting so far as possible in one body all classes of women for whom there are no appropriate trade unions, and so pooling their slender resources of funds and personnel, it has overcome the extraordinary difficulties of organization, and enjoys the unique distinction of being a successful all-women's society. In power of numbers, in the variety and substance of its benefits, in financial stability,

O

in the wisdom of its counsels and the distinction of its leadership, in negotiation or disputes with the employers, in public influence and in its status as a trade union, the Federation loses nothing by comparison with any other general labour union, yet it retains the advantages of an all-women's organization. Not only are women obliged to come forward and manage their own affairs, but the concentration of its members on women's problems has led to the formation of an exceptionally matured women's opinion, and a policy whose broad statesmanship and practical effectiveness has caused it to be adopted by women far outside members of the union. At Trades Union Congresses and Labour Party Conferences, on Government and statutory bodies, at public meetings or demonstrations, it is recognized by common consent as the leading authority on women's questions, and fills a place in the trade union world which could be filled in no other way. Without its initiative, indeed, it would seem that women's interests and point of view would be too often entirely overlooked.

Nor is it purely an accident, but the outcome of its essentially feminine and adaptable character, that a harmonious relationship has always been preserved between the Federation and the skilled men's societies. The rivalry and differences as to demarcation, which unfortunately exist between some " industrial " or " semi-industrial " and general labour unions, have been notably absent Adopting the policy of the Women's Trade Union League, the Federation has strictly observed the principle of the joint-organization for men and women employed in the same trade or industry; and, as one or other of the skilled men's societies has decided to open its doors to women, it has not hesitated to transfer to it a branch of its members. It is significant of this special relationship that during the war the only alliance which was entered into between the great engineering societies and the general labour unions was that between the Amalgamated Society of Engineers and the National Federation of Women Workers The point is not an unimportant one. Even in normal times, large numbers of unrecognized women may be employed in semi-organized districts, where the men's trade unions, although not prepared to admit them to membership, have admittedly no means of preventing their employment The general labour unions have here a free hand, but the position is nevertheless a delicate one and may at any time reach a critical stage Similarly, an all-women's federation would seem to be better qualified than most general labour unions to make an appeal to the skilled workers who are included in the body of unorganized women. A union which is mainly composed of general labourers of the opposite sex, for good reasons as well as for bad ones, has no particular attractions to offer to skilled dressmakers or milliners, skilled domestic servants, or skilled women mechanics. During the war, indeed, the claim of certain groups of engineering women to join the men's societies, or else to form similar ones of their own, was felt by middle-class women to be so strong that it led to their advocacy of all-women's " craft " unions. With the subsequent discharge of " substituted " women, this movement came naturally to an end; but, apart from any check of this kind, it was almost certainly doomed to failure. The type of skilled trade which was adapted to " substitution " during the war was one which could obviously be entered by inexperienced women after a comparatively short period of training; and such women, although technically classed as " skilled," yet lacked the essential means of a sound " craft " organization. Nor is it generally practicable in a modern industry, such as engineering, to draw a hard and fast line between skilled and semi-skilled, semi-skilled and unskilled workers, and there would seem to be no reason beyond that of a narrow trade or class prejudice why all concerned should not join the same union. Moreover, where any group of members had a separate " craft " or " industrial " consciousness but no means of forming a strong separate organization, it would be not impossible to devise some form of sectional representation within the general labour union, which would meet its reasonable claim that its special interests should not be overlooked Such a development on the part of industrial groups would be in no way at variance with the constitution of general labour unions, whose branches are already largely formed on the basis of the factory or local industrial group.

The modern movement towards amalgamation is now extending to general labour unions, and the National Federation of Women Workers has decided not to stand aloof. The argument in favour of one union for men and women loses, perhaps, something of its point where the object is to unite every variety of unorganized worker and not all the workers employed in one trade or industry, but the need for economy and consolidation of forces is none the less a vital one. Terms of amalgamation, as we have seen, have already been practically agreed between the Federation and the National Union of General Workers. It is proposed that the women's union should form a women's " district " or section within the latter body, with considerable powers of autonomy and the right to elect its own representatives on the executive committee; whilst provision would be made for continuing the special organization of women and for separate representation at Labour Party Conferences and Trades Union Congresses. The object is that, although forming an integral part of the common organization, the Federation should preserve so far as possible its present individuality as an all-women's society.

Without this assurance, members rightly feel that the loss to the women's movement would more than outweigh the gain in trade union strength.   The small part played by women in management with the joint-organization is discussed in a later chapter. This part may be not unreasonably expected to become in future a more important one.   It is possible that women will one day be well represented by great unions of shop assistants, garment workers, domestic and laundry workers, of which they will form the large majority of members and directly control the policies. But, in the meantime, the management of the joint-organizations is for all practical purposes in the hands of the men.   Under such circumstances, it is almost inevitable that women's interests and point of view should be, if not actually overlooked, yet accounted as matters of only secondary importance.   For the Federation to give up its present task of voicing women before these are effectively represented by joint-organizations would mean a loss to the industrial women's movement, of which the gravity is almost impossible to over-estimate.   Lines of demarcation are mainly determined by history and it is idle to lay down general principles.   But, in a great amalgamation or federation of general labour unions containing within itself more or less autonomous " industrial " groups, a natural line of demarcation would seem to be indicated, which would give to the women's " district " or section as its special field the traditional women's industries—this section forming, perhaps, the nucleus of future " industrial " unions—and also those organized trades where women were not yet recognized by their appropriate societies; whilst other " districts," which included members of either sex, would operate in industries where men and women were both employed, but were equally unorganized.

The Women's Trade Union League.—No single union, it is clear, can claim to represent the whole body of organized women. This duty has been performed to a great extent in the past by the Women's Trade Union League, which is open to affiliation by the female members of any recognized trade union.   As the women's trade union movement ceases to be dependent on " persons of wealth and leisure," its task in organizing women will necessarily come to an end, but it would still seem to have an important duty to perform in promoting discussion and forming opinion on women's questions.   In matters affecting industrial women as a whole, the chief authority is now passing to the Standing Joint-Committee of Industrial Women's Organizations, which includes representatives of married women co-operators as well as of women trade unionists; but, in matters of purely trade union concern, the claim to represent women would seem to belong to the League

Nor is there any apparent reason why the League should not so enlarge its constitution as to include professional women's organizations. Thousands of professional women are employed to-day—teachers, doctors, dentists, nurses, journalists, civil servants—who are not only wage-earners, but whose incomes are little if at all higher than those of industrial women. The narrow line which separates the interests of workers by hand and by brain can be said hardly to exist amongst women. One of the significant effects of the war was to break down the old artificial barriers, by which two social classes are segregated into hand and brain workers, regardless of natural aptitude or inclination, or even of education; and hundreds of middle-class women found useful and congenial occupation for the first time in their lives. The experiment was only a temporary one, but no experience can be entirely without influence on the future course of events. To the making of the new world of labour all workers must contribute, and this world will be richer and not poorer because the contribution of each will be different. The forward attack by labour on capital, which aims at giving a new and nobler direction to industry, will almost certainly be led by men, but the less dramatic yet equally vital movement whose object is to secure a full share of wealth, not only to the poorest of the workers, but to the least of all citizens, may not improbably find its leaders amongst women

To sum up, it may be said that, owing to the aggravation of ordinary difficulties of organization, the all-women's society is a failure. Women are not generally eligible for the men's "craft" unions, the sexes belonging to different trades; but, for men and women employed in the same industry, the joint "industrial" organization would seem to offer the greatest advantages. These unions, however, for one reason or another do not cover all women's industries. In this case, the National Federation of Women Workers or the "Women's District" of the National Union of General Workers, acting if necessary in co-operation with the skilled men's societies, would seem to be the best alternative, leaving other general labour unions or "districts" to operate in those industries where workers of both sexes are unorganized.

CHAPTER IV.

THE WOMEN'S SECTION WITHIN THE JOINT-ORGANIZATION.

The female members of the joint-organization are faced with three main problems, namely, their low-scale contribution, the minor part played by them in management, and the subordinate position of the woman official.

(1) *The low-scale contribution.*—Women who are admitted to men's trade unions enjoy, with few exceptions, full rights of membership. Generally speaking, it is correct to say in this respect that rules make no distinction as to sex except in the matter of contribution and benefits The reason for this distinction is obvious. The scale of contribution and benefits must necessarily bear a relationship to the member's capacity to pay, and few women earn men's rates of wages. Women are usually admitted at a half-scale or a three-quarter scale contribution, ranking not uncommonly as young people, and are entitled in return to a proportionately reduced scale of benefits. In some few instances, mostly amongst old-fashioned societies, the low-scale contributor does not rank as a full member at delegate meetings, or is disqualified for responsible office, but it is not a question of sex disability. Under similar circumstances, men are subject to the same rule It has, indeed, been not unknown in the past for men who are low-scale contributors to rank as half-members, but women as full members, because " they do not take advantage of their opportunities."

But, although sex disabilities do not practically exist, yet it is almost inevitable that the position of the low-scale contributor should be prejudiced to some extent. The case of women who receive less than their due share of benefits is so rare as to be almost unknown; but it is by no means uncommon for the female section of the union to be partially dependent on men's funds. The marriage dowry, to which in some societies women are entitled in addition to their ordinary benefits, may be supposed to be compensated for by the low claims on funeral benefit incidental to a comparatively youthful section of members; but, this case apart, women tend to contribute on so low a scale that, in order to provide them with an attractive list of benefits, these latter are deliberately calculated on an unduly high basis. Other societies, whose members are largely married women, complain of the excessive claims on sickness benefit made by the female section. The relatively high cost of administering the lower scales of contribution and benefits has, moreover, a similar tendency, and women for this reason alone are comparatively expensive members. At the outbreak of war, the National Union of Shop Assistants was faced by actual financial embarrassment for no other reason than that a change had taken place in the relative proportions of its male and female members. Similarly, the expense of a house-to-house collection—a method still common amongst old-fashioned textile unions—has been charged against women, who are said to be reluctant to follow the men's example and to bring their contributions to the office; but most societies now adopt the method of " shop-collectors " for members of either sex, so that the point tends to lose such importance as it might once have had. In other respects, women bear a good character as regular and punctual contributors.

The problem of the low-scale contribution is bound up with that of wages; but, as the women's standard approximates to the men's, it would seem to be desirable that both sexes should pay at least the same " trade " contribution. As a preliminary to promoting women to full membership, this principle has already been adopted by more than one important society. Friendly benefits must obviously vary with the needs of different groups of members, but the contribution here should be optional, and not compulsory, and each section should be self-supporting. The cotton unions, whose efforts in organizing women have been more than usually successful, provide no sickness or unemployment benefits. Most societies, however, attach a high importance to these benefits as a means of binding members to the union, and it is claimed by trade unionists that not only voluntary but state or national schemes should be administered through the trade unions. Trade union opinion further demands that benefits provided under the latter schemes shall be adequate for maintenance and granted on a non-contributory basis, the full cost being charged on the state or industry as a whole. It may be expected that " friendly " benefits provided by individual societies will eventually be confined to extras or to special cases.

It has sometimes been remarked that, irrespective of ability to pay, the sound economy of a generous trade union contribution is less appreciated by women than men. The accusation may, perhaps, be not altogether unjust Habits of penury are as hard to unlearn as those of luxury During the war, most societies succeeded in raising their scales of contribution both for men and women to some extent, but this rise has seldom kept pace with advances in wages   The importance of an adequate trade union contribution cannot be too urgently insisted upon.   Trade unions depend largely for their success on the soundness of their financial position, and the outlay of a few extra pennies a week in contribution may be repaid a hundred-fold in advances of wages.

(2) *The minor part played by women in management.*—Women who are admitted to men's trade unions enjoy, as we have seen, full rights of membership, and are eligible for every office of the union.   Exceptions to this rule are rare and confined to unimportant societies.   Nevertheless, the failure of women to play an effective part in management, which was remarked by Mrs. Paterson nearly half a century ago, remains a conspicuous feature of their movement to-day.   The old prejudices and prudishness which led men members to condemn as unwomanly the " go-to-meetings " woman, or to suspect moral danger in joint meetings —an attitude, it is said, deliberately encouraged by their wives— tend fortunately to disappear.   The most deeply-rooted traditions were shaken during the war, when the absence of men on service obliged women to come forward and take an active part at least in local affairs.   Nor ought men to be blamed because women do not use their opportunities.   Women members are clearly responsible beings.   As a matter of fact, little blame can be attached to either side, and the real causes of failure are to be found in the same complex of circumstances which handicap women in organization.   The inferior grade of worker to which women members mostly belong, their poor wages and consequently low-scale contribution, their not infrequently illicit entry to the trade and late admission to the trade union, their comparative youth and inexperience, the tradition of social and economic dependence, and until recently their political disabilities, one or all of these factors have contributed to place them in a subordinate position in the union   The burden of home duties, from which young girls are by no means exempt, further hampers them seriously in active public work.   Except at times of excitement, they are backward in attending branch meetings, and for this reason alone tend to lose their chance of nomination for responsible office.   The present movement towards a greater sex equality in industry, together with changes in social and economic conditions, will no doubt have their influence on women's position within the joint-organizations.   That women are capable of playing a leading part in trade union affairs has been abundantly proved by the experience of the National Federation of Women Workers.   Nevertheless, it is probable that for many years to come men will dominate in management.   The mere advantage in age and experience throws the weight on their side.   How to ensure adequate means of expression to women forms then

an important trade union problem. Moreover, no section of trade unionists, as no class of citizens, can afford to choose its representatives entirely from persons of another tradition and outlook than its own. This fact is, or ought to be, well known to labour men and women. With the best intentions in the world, as we have seen, women's interests and point of view tend to be, if not actually overlooked, yet accounted as of secondary importance, and trade unionists of either sex are at one in advocating some means by which women may be associated in management. Of these various devices, those most commonly adopted are the *all-women's branch,* the *reservation of places to women on committees of management,* and the *women's advisory council.*

The device of the all-women's branch offers no doubt certain advantages in obliging women to come forward and manage their own branch affairs, but it has also serious drawbacks. A branch composed entirely of women shows inevitably something of the weakness of the all-women's society and tends to lack vitality, whilst the segregation of men and women members may lead to lack of sympathy between them and even to conflicting policies. Without intimate association between men and women in the branches, indeed, the joint-organization may fail in its principal object. Moreover, the all-women's branch can only ensure that women will take an active share in local affairs, and local committees may or may not enjoy any real authority. It is, in fact, not uncommon for an all-women's branch to be controlled by the men's branch committee, one or more of whose members have a right to sit on the women's committee. The advantage of separating men and women members in this way would seem on the whole to be outweighed by the disadvantages, and the all-women's branch is not generally advocated by trade unionists of either sex, who definitely prefer to mix in the branches. The case is altered where men and women members belong to different industrial groups. Amongst general labour unions, as we have seen, the local industrial group forms the natural unit of branch organization, and these branches, or the "districts" which they go to form, may be entirely composed of women. The proposed Women's District of the National Union of General Workers will not be confined at first to women employed in particular women's industries, but it may be expected to develop eventually along these lines. Separate branches for men and women belonging to different "craft" or trade groups, on the other hand, are not generally advocated by industrial unionists, except in the unusual case where women members are employed by men members, so that the joint-organization is in effect one of *employers* and *employed.* Under the circumstances, indeed, no form of joint-organization can be entirely free from objection, and it would seem desirable to form separate unions.

The *reservation of places to women on committees of management* is not open to the same objection of separating the sexes, and further has the advantage of ensuring direct representation to women in general management. This advantage is, however, not always so substantial as it may seem   Disability is the reverse side of privilege, and women elected by this means complain that they do not enjoy the same status as men colleagues who were elected in open competition.   Their opinion carries comparatively little weight, whilst the one or two places reserved to their sex tend to remain a maximum   It is no doubt possible in theory to reserve a number of places to women in exact proportion to the female membership, but this policy does not always work well in practice.   No trade union can afford to elect to responsible office any but those members who are best qualified for this honour, and one or other sex may be unable to put forward at the time its full complement of suitable candidates.   Nor is it satisfactory for men and women office-holders to be separately elected by members of their own sex, so that they tend to represent *sex* rather than *labour* interests.   For these reasons, women clerks and shop assistants, although keen feminists, have always rejected any proposal of their unions for reserving places to women on committees of management, and this device is only advocated by trade unionists as a temporary measure, so that women may find their feet, especially after amalgamation between an all-men's and an all-women's society   The case of the general labour union, whose men and women members belong to different industrial groups and may form separate branches and "districts," stands again apart.   The proposed Women's District of the National Union of General Workers is entitled to elect its own representatives on to the national executive committee   Similarly, in "industrial" or "semi-industrial" unions, whose members belong to distinct "craft" or trade groups, places on the executive committee are sometimes reserved to one or more of these groups, which may be entirely composed of women.   Thus, the rule of the Blackburn Association of Weavers reserves one place each to a "warper" and "winder," who are invariably women, but none to women weavers, whose trade interests are identical with men's. Where one section of members is employed by another, so that trade interests may be directly conflicting, reserved places of this kind would seem to be highly desirable; but under ordinary circumstances, some form of advisory council is usually advocated by industrial unionists as the best means of representing separate "craft" or trade interests.   In this connection, it should be observed that women stand the best chance of election in unions where more than one candidate is elected in each electoral area. In one-member areas, members of either sex generally prefer to elect a man.

The *women's advisory council*—a device invented by women shop assistants—would seem to avoid the disadvantages of sex distinction or privilege in the constitution of the union and yet to provide a real means of expression to women members. These councils, which are elected by the female members of the branches and may be formed for either national or district areas, have only advisory and no executive powers. Their object is in no way to compete with, or to take the place of official bodies, but to supplement the work of the latter, encouraging women to take an active share in branch affairs, and promoting their election to district or national committees. Their chief function is that of education and propaganda. The women's advisory council affords a practical training-ground for inexperienced women both in organizing and committee work; whilst members learn how to form and express their opinion, and to draw up a women's programme. By this means, even two or three women representatives on the executive committee, or two or three women delegates at the annual general meeting, may exercise an influence on the counsels of the union which is out of all proportion to their numbers. The women's advisory council of the National Union of Shop Assistants is entirely dependent for financial support on voluntary contributions from the branches, but its work in stimulating organization amongst women would seem to be sufficiently important to members as a whole to justify a grant from national funds.

It is sometimes suggested by men trade unionists that the women's advisory council has already fulfilled its purpose when it has secured the election of one or more women on to executive bodies, and that to prolong its existence beyond this point may only serve to develop an aggressive feminist spirit. This criticism has no doubt an element of truth *Chacun a les défauts de ses qualités,* and women who have learned to stand up to their employers, may have learned at the same time to stand up to men trade unionists; but there is no failing which one sex has so much to fear in the other as apathy or indifference to the common cause of labour. Sex consciousness, like class consciousness, thrives best by suppression; and in a temporary conflict of sex interests, the opportunity given to women members to make known their opinion—to which men members might even be converted— would act as the best form of safety valve. The women's advisory council may, in fact, play a part within the joint-organization not unlike that played by the Women's Trade Union League within the trade union world.

(3) *The subordinate position of the woman organizer.*—Although

women are eligible for every office of the union from that of " collector " or " shop steward " to that of general secretary, these official posts are commonly held by men. Amongst cotton unions, it was rare until recently for women to be appointed even to the post of " collector." Sooner or later, however, most societies have decided to appoint one or more women organizers, and few have found reason to regret their decision. Generalization on questions of sex is dangerous. The qualities of a first-class organizer are essentially personal, but it is probably safe to say that both men and women organizers do the best work amongst members of their own sex. In the matter of mere recruiting, one sex may rouse in the other as great, or even greater, enthusiasm than in its own, but its influence would seem to be of a less permanent character, and less effective in developing the solid qualities of mind and character which go to the making of a reliable and active body of trade unionists. The woman organizer, by mere force of her own example, may inspire her sex with a self-confidence which could be gained in no other way. There seems, however, to be some difficulty in finding the right type of woman. Under any circumstances, the post of organizer is one which is hard to fill. The necessary qualifications include, not only high qualities of mind and character and exceptional personal gifts, but a considerable capacity of physical endurance The perfect combination of faculties is a rare one amongst men, and an even rarer one amongst women. Choice again is limited by the fact that a comparatively small number of women remain members of the union beyond the period of youth. For various reasons, it is not unusual for a union which recruits its male staff entirely from within its own membership, to look further afield for suitable women candidates. Many women organizers are drawn from outside trades or professions, or come down straight from the university. This policy is sometimes criticized by trade unionists. Snobbishness is not peculiar to one class. Members of the union, who have a practical experience of working conditions, have undoubtedly a prior claim to appointment, and to neglect home talent would be as unfair as it was unwise in destroying a strong stimulus to activity in the branches ; but the claim of one member to preferment ought not to outweigh that of the society as a whole to be well served. Practical workshop experience is a valuable asset, but it cannot be looked upon as the only, or even the most important, qualification for office. A certain variety of attainment may, indeed, be actually desirable, and a large organizing staff should include university graduates who have some legal training and expert experience in negotiation as well as practical workers in the trade

It not infrequently occurs, especially in unions with a comparatively small female membership, that only one or two women are appointed in a large staff of men organizers. In this case, it is almost inevitable that women should hold a somewhat different position from that of men. For example, women are appointed as national organizers, moving from one district to another as occasion arises, but without fixed responsibilities; whilst men are appointed as district organizers, each of whom is in charge of his own district. In other cases, where the duties of organizer are carried out by the secretary or by members of the executive committee, all of whom happen to be men, a special post has been created so as to allow the appointment of a woman organizer. Distinctions of this kind may be inevitable; but women organizers should enjoy, so far as possible, the same status as men, and their employment should most emphatically not be confined—as it too often is—to more or less subordinate work. No policy could be so disheartening to women officials—and, incidentally, to women members of the union—than to refuse them the usual opportunities of promotion for no other reason than that of sex. Nor is it necessary, or even desirable, that women's work in organizing should be restricted to members of their own sex. It is, on the contrary, an economy of labour, and an actual relief to the organizer, to combine the harder task of organizing women with the easier task of organizing men. The best results are sometimes said to be obtained by a man and a woman working together in double harness, so that each supplements the qualities which may be lacking in the other. The trade union official, whether man or woman, should enjoy, so far as possible, security of tenure, and be appointed by the executive committee and not by means of a general election

There is no need, or ought not to be, to impress upon trade union employers that men and women officials should receive "equal pay." This principle, which should be extended so as to include all travelling and similar allowances, is universally accepted in theory, and commonly, but not invariably, observed in practice. The personal expenses of the woman organizer, who requires to exercise special care both as to her dress and place of lodging, are more than usually heavy. To lay down a standard for the trade union official is extraordinarily difficult. So long as the cause of labour makes its present appeal to fine and generous instincts, there will always be men and women of conspicuous ability who will disregard private advantage and prefer the service of the trade unions to any other advancement. Their devotion can only be repaid in the affection and respect of their fellow-members; but, because their work is largely one of love, there is no reason for trade unionists to neglect the sound economy of high wages. As a general rule, it may be said that the standard of the trade union official should approximate to that of *persons engaged in corresponding occupations* and not that of *persons organized,* who are almost certainly underpaid A small struggling society has to cut its coat according to its cloth, but salaries of four figures are now not unknown amongst high officials of great societies.   A common salary for a woman organizer is from £4 to £6 a week, with travelling expenses in addition; but, apart from officers of the National Federation of Women Workers, women do not usually hold the highest positions.   The most serious drawback of the trade union service is the habitual over-work which is apparently involved, and women who are over-conscientious, and take things less easily than men, suffer most from the strain   The frequent necessity for sick leave has, indeed, been sometimes used by trade unionists as an argument against the appointment of women organizers Long and irregular hours of work are for obvious reasons inseparable from the duties of the trade union official, who is no more able to spare himself during a trade dispute than is the responsible Minister of State in times of war or international crisis.   Periods of extraordinary strain should, however, be followed by extra holidays, and responsible officers ought to be relieved so far as possible from all routine duties   The most lavish expenditure on office and staff may still be reckoned a small item compared with the large sums in advances of wages, which depend upon the efficiency of trade union officials

The question of training is an equally important one. The modern woman trade union official claims that she belongs to a profession, and that she ought to undergo a professional training, which should include, not only practical experience in organizing work and in office routine, but instruction in economics, industrial history and law   Such instruction would seem to be specially desirable for practical workers in the trade, who have had little opportunity of general education.   As a means of broadening experience, it is further suggested that a period of apprenticeship should be served by young officials in at least one great organization other than their own   The National Federation of Women Workers would seem to be specially indicated as the practical training ground for women officials   In this connection, a welcome movement has been started at Ruskin College, Oxford, with the special object of providing for the needs of trade union officials.   These courses, which may extend from one to three terms, can be entered for by workers of either sex; whilst a hostel has been opened for the convenience of women students The matter of finance presents the chief difficulty   The minimum cost of training, which has nearly always to include some provision for maintenance, must necessarily be comparatively high

The union at whose expense the young organizer is trained has, moreover, no assurance that he or she will remain permanently in its service. The problem of training is, indeed, one which concerns the trade union movement as a whole, and its main cost ought to be borne by a common fund and not by individual societies.

Chapter V.

Trade Union Restrictions on Female Labour.

Trade union restrictions on female labour are the common rule in organized trades. According as the men's trade unions are strong, female labour is entirely prohibited—any future, if not the present, generation of workers—or women are restricted to certain inferior branches of the industry, or to certain unorganized districts. Variations of policy are mainly determined by circumstance, and a total absence of restrictions does not necessarily argue a difference of principle. Where women's employment is an established fact before organization begins, and men have no means of preventing it, restrictions are obviously useless. A genuine indifference to lines of sex demarcation is practically confined to cotton weavers.

This widespread character of trade union restrictions on female labour points to a common cause or causes. Men trade unionists are accused of a policy of sex privilege and prejudice, especially by middle-class women. The charge, unfortunately, has a basis of truth A belief in the divine right of every man to his job is not peculiar to kings or capitalists, and democracy is hard to practice at home. The comparatively favourable working conditions enjoyed by men in organized trades have been mainly built up by their own exertions in the past, and they are not disposed to share these advantages with a new host of women competitors. Trade unionists are, in fact, no better than other men. A more respectable motive, but one not less keenly resented by women, is the anxiety sometimes expressed by men to protect women-folk from harm, and to confine them, if not to the home, at least to " womanly " occupations. Men's claim so to dictate to women their manner of employment has at no time been admitted by women trade unionists, who maintain as jealously as men their right to earn their living in their own way. Least of all are women prepared to accept men's judgment in matters of health and morals; and they are not a little suspicious of a " chivalry " which may deliberately prohibit them from operations " within the capacity of a child," and yet expressly allow them " to carry loads about the workshop !" At Trades Union Congresses, the National Federation of Women Workers has more than once protested against men's interference in the matter of " unsuitable " occupations, and its members have urged that this question, which is chiefly a medical one, should be referred for enquiry to a responsible Government commission As a matter of fact, women's claim to earn their living in their own way is not at present seriously disputed by men trade unionists, who realize that a policy of sex privilege and prejudice can only lead to the damage of their own cause, and obscure the real issue. The true causes of trade union restrictions on female labour are economic. From a long and bitter experience, trade unionists have learned that the introduction of women into men's trades is invariably followed by a fall of wages from the men's to a women's level, so that men are finally driven from employment Like Chinamen or coolies, women are condemned as blacklegs. Nor did the experience of the war, and the general failure of " substituted " women to secure men's wages, incline men to change their opinion. It served on the contrary to rally women in support of the men's policy. It is significant that the only opposition to the Restoration of Pre-War Practices Act came from middle-class women's organizations.

To what extent, however, the prohibition of female labour has succeeded in its object of preventing women's employment raises another question. Success would seem until now to have been at most local or partial Women have been driven away from one district, but they have come back in another, and the *men's* trade has followed the *women*. Or women have been kept out from one process, but they have been brought in on another, and the *women's* process has displaced the *men's* process Men cotton spinners have been more than usually successful in their campaign against female labour, but the fact that women are not employed as mule-spinners in America, where there has been no similar opposition, suggests that they would not under any circumstances have been employed in large numbers. Nor are men mule-spinners altogether unaffected by the competition of women ring-spinners, which latter process tends to displace mule-spinning in the manufacture of coarser counts of yarn. A " blackleg proof " trade union, which was able to control every worker in the industry, could no doubt abolish female labour—it might even abolish employers—but such a union does not exist Men's refusal to recognize women, meanwhile, has the disastrous effect of delaying organization, so that women develop a " non-union " instead of a " union " tradition, and employers a vested interest in " cheap and docile " female labour. For the men, on the other hand, to withdraw their restrictions, without adequate safeguards against a fall of wages, would only be to precipitate a disaster which might be averted by delay. The problem is by no means a simple one.

P

Various solutions have been suggested by employers. One well known to trade unionists, and recently advanced by witnesses of the Engineering Employers' Federation before the War Cabinet Committee on Women in Industry, proposes that all work should be divided into two classes, namely, *men's* work and *women's* work. *Men's* work should include all occupations of a specially laborious or a genuinely "jobbing" character, this class of work being not generally suitable to female labour; whilst *women's* work should comprise all occupations of a comparatively light or "specialized" character, for which female labour is notoriously well-adapted. The former should be reserved to men and paid at *men's* rates of wages, but the latter should be freely opened to women and paid at *women's* rates of wages. In other words, employers are prepared to respect, for what they are worth in the labour market, men's monopolies of physical strength and expert training, but they claim the right in return to exploit unprotected classes of female and semi-skilled workers. They do not deny that the result of their proposal would be a considerable displacement of skilled men by women, but it is maintained that this effect would be an actual advantage, and no disadvantage to these men. To the latter, indeed, it is held out as a bribe that the lower rate paid on women's work would enable a higher rate to be paid on men's work; whilst the rapid expansion of trade, which should follow the introduction of cheap labour, would allow the displaced men to be reabsorbed as overlookers, or in certain subsidiary processes requiring special skill. At times of rapidly expanding markets, some reabsorption of this kind would no doubt take place, but could hardly do so to the extent which is supposed by the theory. The tendency of modern industry is for promotion to be reserved to comparatively small and select groups of workers. In order to reabsorb the whole body of displaced men, the expansion would have to be a phenomenal one, and such as would be very unlikely to extend in an old country beyond a few small branches of industry, or one or two small groups of firms. This expansion would, moreover, tend to be compensated by corresponding contractions in other industries, which had not the same stimulus of cheap labour. In foreign markets, where the advantage of cheap labour is claimed by employers on national as well as on private grounds, it is a fact well known to economists that the real competition lies between one home trade and another, and not between a home and a foreign trade. It is certain that the skilled tradesman of the "jobbing" class in question is disappearing from industry. A more probable result of displacement would be for men to be reabsorbed as labourers. The relative increase of female employment in "process" trades, and the corresponding decrease in labouring trades, which have taken place in past years, seem to point in this direction. Such a movement, in itself may, perhaps, be not undesirable. Labouring work, including outdoor pursuits, is probably as well-suited and at least as attractive to the average man as a simple " repetition " job. The real complaint of the labourer is that of low wages. The experience of the war has shown that, so long as rates of wages are maintained, the expansion of a comparatively well-paid industry, such as engineering, may react on other industries so as to level up wages for badly-paid classes of workers. Were this expansion to continue indefinitely, it is not impossible to imagine a state of affairs where such rough work as washing or charing, which is unattractive to women, would be paid at so high a rate that it might actually tempt some enterprising men to choose these trades in preference to the lighter branches of engineering ! The real danger to which the workers are exposed is that by means of " unfair female competition " women may precipitate the men's movement from one group of trades to another before organization is sufficiently advanced to meet the changed position This danger would be all the more serious in view of the progressive character of those trades which are classed as *women's* work. Under this ingenious scheme, indeed, the wonder would be that, in the race of employers to adapt industry to cheap labour, any work would remain which could still be classed as *men's*.

The amendment to the Restoration of Pre-War Practices Act, proposed by certain middle-class women's organizations, had it been accepted by the Government, would have exposed the workers to not dissimilar risks. The object of this amendment, as we have seen, was to exclude from the operation of the Act the new trades or processes, which had grown up within the men's field of employment, but in which women had formed the majority of workers during the war. These new trades or processes might be expected to expand in future at the expense of old ones, so that the point was by no means an unimportant one. The intention of those promoting the amendment was no doubt that women should receive men's wages, but no assurance to this effect had been given by, or was even required from, employers. In the new trades in question, as a matter of fact, employers had deliberately declared their opposition to " equal pay." At the time of the agitation, " substituted " women were, with few exceptions, receiving only *women's* or intermediate rates of wages; whilst the extensive changes of process, together with the large influx of semi-skilled workers of either sex, had so effectually obscured the skilled men's standard that in most cases there was none with which the women's rate could be compared. Not only was it in the last degree improbable that women would have received men's wages, but it was in the first degree probable that, as soon as wages were released from Government control, the comparatively high standard enjoyed by them under the exceptional circumstances of the war would have fallen to the normal level of women's wages. It is sometimes suggested by advocates of unrestricted female labour that, by the mere fact of enlarging women's field of employment, the opening up of men's trades would have the effect, of raising women's wages to a level, if not so high as the men's, at least higher than their present one. The argument may be sound to some extent; but the interests of industrial men and women cannot be separated in this way into water-tight compartments. The total sum of wages would almost certainly be reduced, and any gain on one side be outweighed by a greater loss on the other. Moreover, unless women were well-organized, their benefit might be only a temporary one, so that the final result would be merely to enlarge the area of " sweated " trades. It is significant that, in spite of the general opening up of men's trades to women during the war, wages remained almost stationary for large groups of unorganized women; whilst, notwithstanding the wholesale discharge of " substituted " workers in the year following the armistice, wages rose substantially for all classes of women, a rise which in most cases may be directly attributed to the progress of organization. Women have truly little or nothing to gain from *men's* work—except *men's* wages.

There is, indeed, no short cut out to salvation. The fear of degradation to their standard of living and of unemployment, which lies at the root of men's restrictions on women's labour, will not be removed except by removing this threat. The problem of unemployment lies outside the scope of the present subject. The broad principle may, however, be laid down that *the position of the involuntarily unemployed should be not less desirable than that of the voluntarily employed.* The problem of wages is discussed in a later chapter. It is enough to remark that *the standard of the worst-paid worker should be not so low that the best-paid worker would be unwilling to accept it.* Then at last each recruit in industry—every man or woman released from idleness or unproductive work—will bring relief and not dread to the workers whose burden he has come to share. Women of all classes are opposed to trade union restrictions on female labour, but they differ as to their mode of attack. It is claimed by middle-class women, on the one hand, that men trade unionists should now at once withdraw their restrictions, leaving it to the discretion of employers as to how far women would then receive men's wages. Industrial women demand, on the other hand, that employers should immediately pay men's wages, within women's as well as men's field of employment, trusting to the goodwill of men trade unionists that all restrictions would then be withdrawn. It is natural, perhaps, that the benefit of the doubt should be given by women in each case to men belonging to their own class. The fact is, however, significant that, in industries where "substitution" is uncontrolled, women do not receive men's wages; whilst women cotton weavers, who enjoy "equal pay," have at no time been subject to trade union restrictions There is no reason to suppose that one class is constitutionally more just than another. Employers are only more to blame than trade unionists in that they refuse to abolish a system which practically compels them to follow the sole dictates of private profit and to buy their labour, as any other commodity, in the cheapest market. From the trade union point of view, the question is primarily one of organization. Between unorganized women and organized men, no agreement is possible. Women must first of all be organized, nor can their failure to do so be excused on the plea that men decline to organize them. The National Federation of Women Workers has given practical proof that women can organize themselves Men must, however, meet women half-way. In every policy there is an element of risk, but the most daring may be the least dangerous one. If men's trade unions are strong enough to prevent women's employment, they are also strong enough to permit it on their own terms; whilst, if they are not, no policy is fraught with so many risks as one which tends to delay organization. Nor can women postpone indefinitely their entry into men's trades merely because there is no men's standard with which the women's rate may be compared Organization is essential on both sides But between organized workers of either sex, belonging to the same or to separate societies, an honourable agreement would seem to be within reach by which the interests of each would be safeguarded The real issue at stake in the case of "substituted" women is not as to which sex shall be employed, but as to what rate of wages shall be paid—a *men's* or a *women's* standard. The terms of this agreement would so far follow the lines suggested by employers that a distinction would be made between *men's* and *women's* work, but the object would be to preserve, and not to break down, present lines of demarcation until trade union restrictions could be safely withdrawn With regard to doubtful trades or new processes, to which either sex had a claim, a good rule would be that the job should be held to belong to whichever class of worker received, or would receive, the higher rate of wages. The better-paid worker is presumably the better-qualified for the job, and no party could rightly blame the decision. In *men's* trades, women would undertake not to accept employment unless they received *men's* rates of wages, or such other rates as might be fixed by *men's* consent, whilst men would agree on their side to withdraw all restrictions on female labour and to support women in their demand for "equal pay." In *women's* trades, women would be free to fix their own working conditions, but would continue their campaign for advances of wages, and men to co-operate with them, until the standard within women's field of employment should have so approximated the men's that the present need for artificial lines of demarcation would have ceased to exist So long as the majority of women are content to receive a women's standard, it will be impossible to convince employers that on men's work they are worth men's wages, or men trade unionists that they are able to secure these. The fight for " equal pay " may, indeed, be won or lost in *women's* trades.

CHAPTER VI.

" EQUAL PAY FOR EQUAL WORK."

At the Trades Union Congress of 1888, it was formally resolved for the first time that " where women do the same work as men they shall receive equal pay," and mainly with this object in view men have assisted women to organize. The principle of "equal pay " has since then received practically unanimous support from men and women trade unionists. It has further gained the general acceptance of middle-class feminists, and even at times a lip-service from the Government or from private employers. In practice, however, the policy has been rarely carried out, and men in despair have continued to exclude women so far as possible from employment. Not only do employers frankly deny that women are entitled to men's wages, but the looseness of such terms as "equal pay for equal work" has made these easy to evade. Before the war, " equal pay " was practically confined to men and women cotton weavers, and was only extended afterwards to small groups of " substituted " women who were protected by a strong trade union organization. A double standard of wages is commonly supported by employers on one or all of the following grounds ·—.

(1) *A difference in the needs of men and women workers.*— This argument is one well known to public authorities, who profess to pay " fair wages " Thus, Mr. Herbert Samuel, when Postmaster-General in 1915, declared that " equal pay for equal work," as these terms were rightly interpreted, should be " equal standard of comfort for people doing equal work." For, according to his theory, " if you pay a single woman the same wage as you pay a family man, you are giving her a much higher standard of comfort than you are giving him," and he refused to contemplate such a reversal in the natural order of things. The same theory underlies the recommendation in the Majority Report of the War Cabinet Committee on Women in Industry, that the minimum subsistence wage should be fixed on a different basis for men and women. Similarly it was implied in the awards of the Special Tribunal for Women under the Munitions of War Act, by which women employed on men's work were entitled to receive men's *basic rates* but not their *war bonus*. The latter, according to the Tribunal, was not an ordinary advance, but a special grant in order to meet the extraordinary rise in the cost of living, by which

a single woman might be supposed to be less affected than the family man   The bonus, it was argued, should be placed on a par with the *separation allowances* received by soldiers and sailors, or with the *children's allowances* granted to the police.   In controlled establishments, as a matter of fact, the cost of the war bonus was borne by the Government and not by individual employers.

The theory is sound so far as it goes.   But, unfortunately, even a Government Department cannot afford to neglect ordinary commercial considerations, whilst private employers, exposed to the keen competition of rival firms, are practically obliged to ignore all others, and to buy their labour, if not in the cheapest market, at least to their own best advantage   The worker, after all, is paid for his work, and, under present competitive conditions, a system which requires that wages should vary with the size of his family, or other personal liabilities, can only result in excluding him from employment in proportion as these liabilities are heavy. Nor are trade unionists prepared to allow such discretion to employers, or any similar interference in their private affairs.   Moreover, a system of wages, which merely distinguishes between one sex and another, fails in its express object of providing for the separate needs of different classes of workers   Between the family man and the bachelor, the widow with dependents and the wife or daughter partially supported at home, needs may vary at least as much in degree as between one sex and another   The fact should not be overlooked that there are actually more bachelors than spinsters employed in industry

For these as well as for other reasons, some form of state allowances for dependent mothers and children is now generally advocated by feminists   A Government enquiry into the whole subject of such allowances or pensions has been actually proposed by the Standing Joint-Committee of Industrial Women's Organizations, and a similar recommendation was made by Mrs. Sidney Webb in the Minority Report of the War Cabinet Committee on Women in Industry   The Majority Report of this Committee even went so far as to recommend that a system of children's allowances should be immediately considered by the Government in connection with men and women teachers, who were otherwise entitled to "equal pay."   Nor, apparently, is the principle of state allowances for dependents objected to by enlightened employers.   Mr Seebohm Rowntree, although opposed to "equal pay" for men and women, recommends that state relief should be granted to breadwinners in respect of every dependent child beyond a family of three   These various proposals cannot be discussed here in detail; but it may be remarked that a scheme, by which allowances for dependents would be provided by an independent public authority, would avoid all the usual inconveniences which attach to such provision by employers. State allowances of this kind are also advocated for their own sake. The right to an independent income would effectually protect pregnant and nursing mothers, young people and invalids, against the economic insecurity and the humiliation which may be involved by dependence of one individual upon another, whilst it would relieve all workers from the unevenly distributed and in many cases the crushingly heavy financial burden which is entailed by personal support of dependents.

(2) *A difference in the market price of male and female labour.*— The comparatively modest demands made by women who are not responsible for dependents, together with their weakness in organization, have resulted in a substantial difference in the normal rate of men's and women's wages; and it is not infrequently observed by public authorities, as well as by private employers, that the same wage or salary which attracts a certain type of woman will not necessarily attract a man of similar qualifications. This effect of " equal pay " in recruiting men and women of different education and social standing was specially emphasized by the recent Departmental Committee on Teachers' Salaries, when it recommended a double standard of wages. It is further argued by employers that, the sum of wages being a fixed quantity in each industry, any advance received by women beyond the market price of their labour can only be paid for at the expense of men belonging to the same industry. This argument has been recently used by education authorities with so much effect that it has actually scared men teachers into opposing " equal pay " Industrial men, who are more impressed by facts than theories, refuse to take alarm at so stale a red herring. Employers are naturally reluctant to pay more than its market price for any class of labour, and they also foresee a fertile source of disaffection in the fact of a double standard of wages, according as women are employed on men's or on women's work. The latter is not necessarily the least skilled or laborious. During the war, the growing discontent with their standard of living amongst all classes of industrial women was directly attributed by employers to the comparatively high rates of wages received by " substituted " workers How far, however, this new discontent amongst women should be feared as a morbid symptom of industrial disorder, or welcomed as a healthy growing pain of labour, depends on the standpoint from which it is viewed.

The Departmental Committee on Teachers' Salaries expressly qualified its recommendation for a differential rate by a reference to " present social and economic conditions." The qualification is a significant one. The present low standard of wages in women's trades, which may be largely traced to backwardness in organization, cannot be accepted by trade unionists as a necessary or permanent condition of industry. The anomalies arising from a double standard of wages may, moreover, be removed by a rise on one side as easily as by a fall on the other   The rates of wages obtaining in each industry is largely a matter of habit, and good habits may be learned as well as bad ones. In *men's* trades, where a men's standard is already established, no inconvenience is caused to employers who are obliged to pay this standard to '' substituted '' women. In *women's* trades, where a vested interest has been built up by employers in '' cheap and docile '' female labour, the position is a different one. In the words of the Minister of Munitions, when in the third year of the war he exhorted women to be patient with rates of 2½d. or 2¾d. an hour '' these trades have their own customs, their own rates of wages, all framed under the stress of national and international competition,'' and '' to interfere rashly would be like sticking a knife into the works of a clock.'' The Minister of Munitions was, therefore, obliged to '' proceed with caution '' Caution is a relative term   The inability of a particular firm or industry to meet the stress of national or international competition ought not to be borne, were it only for one day, by the poorest class of workers. No form of protective tariff or bounty, whatever were its objections, could be so grossly unfair. Trade unionists may be said to '' proceed with caution '' who recognize a distinction between men's and women's trades, but are determined to enforce a fair minimum wage in each case, and lose no opportunity of levelling up women's wages to a men's standard. The passing of the new Trade Boards Act, and its rapid extension to organized as well as to unorganized trades, have been described in previous chapters. The unfortunate clause, by which six months must elapse between one decision and the next and a serious check is placed on advances of wages, should be repealed at once, but in other respects the new Act may be said to represent a substantial improvement on the old one. A universal minimum wage, applicable to all industries and every group of workers, is not advocated by trade unionists   The latter are by no means opposed to '' equality of income,'' but they propose to abolish first of all the present gross disparities between wages and profits. The comparatively high earnings enjoyed by organized workers may act as a powerful stimulus in raising wages for other more backward-groups to whom it sets an example, and trade unionists are naturally disinclined to lose this advantage, or to trot at the pace of the slowest horse. Some means are, however, advocated by socialists, by which the protection of a statutory minimum wage may be ensured to all weak classes of workers, who for various reasons have failed to be brought under the Trade Boards Act, or to have their wages otherwise regulated. The most practicable proposal would seem to be that made by the Women's Employment Committee, which reported to the Minister of Reconstruction during the war, and proposed that no worker should be paid a wage lower than the lowest minimum rate fixed under the Trade Boards Act, except under a trade board decision. Such a provision would also have the desirable effect of making it to the interest of employers to hasten rather than to delay the extension of the Act to " sweated " trades It cannot, however, be too often repeated that the good or ill-working of all legal or other machinery for fixing wages must ultimately depend on the human will behind it; and the best means of obtaining men's wages is for women to achieve men's strength in organization. To argue, as do employers, that no worker should receive more than the market price of his or her labour, is only an argument to keep things as they are.

(3) *A difference in men's and women's output* —This argument is one commonly used by private employers, who accept the formula of " equal pay for equal work," but interpret its terms as " equal pay for equal output," or " equal payment by results." The same theory underlay the decision of the Minister of Munitions under the Treasury agreement, by which he laid down that " substituted " women were entitled to men's *piece*-rates, but not to men's *time*-rates. Similarly, it received support in the Majority Report of the War Cabinet Committee on Women in Industry, which recommended that " women doing similar or the same work as men should receive equal pay for equal work in the sense that pay should be in proportion to efficient output," but it was repudiated by Mrs. Sidney Webb in the Minority Report, who advocated that men and women employed on the same work should receive " the same occupational rates "

In piece-work trades, where output can be accurately measured, the principle of equal piece-rates, or " equal payment by results," may work well in practice. The success of the cotton weavers in enforcing " equal pay " has no doubt been facilitated by the piece-work system of payment. Many trades are, however, necessarily time-work in character, output, by the nature of the work, being practically impossible to measure; whilst in other trades, such as engineering, where processes require constant readjustment, the workers rely on the time-rate in order to protect the standard, on *piece*-work as well as on *time*-work. The piece-rate is otherwise too liable of abuse by unscrupulous employers, who are anxious to secure a piece-work effort for a time-work wage, and reduce the piece-rate at each effort made by the worker to raise his earnings above the time-work level. Trade unionists, many of whom are opposed for other reasons to methods of " payment by results " and are not prepared to see these extended, naturally ask why women, as a condition of receiving the trade union rate, should be required to prove equality of output, from which test men are exempt? Neither the long experience of the cotton weavers, nor recent experiments amongst munition workers, point to the conclusion that women are necessarily behind men in efficiency Except on work which is obviously unsuitable to their sex, even admitting some slight shortcoming on one side, the disparity between men and women workers is certainly less than that between many workers of the same sex. Nor would the problem be solved by taking as the basis of fixing wages the output of the average man or woman, for such workers are not necessarily employed. On men's heavy work, as a matter of fact, employers rightly prefer to employ a masculine type of woman.

Trade unionists, therefore, maintain that no system of payment by results, which is not allowed in the case of men, can be permitted in the case of women; and that women, who are entitled to men's *piece-rates,* are equally entitled to men's *time-rates.* The National Federation of Women Workers, as we have seen, has deliberately amended the formula of " equal ·pay for equal work " to that of " equal pay for the same job " This strict interpretation of " equal pay " would no doubt have the effect of excluding women from work for which they were definitely less well-suited than men; but this effect would be not undesirable Women of normal feminine constitution would be confined to women's occupations without the need for artificial restrictions, whilst those of masculine capacity could be freely admitted to all men's advantages. The remedy for small output is not low wages, but lies rather in the opposite direction When women are no longer either underpaid, or overworked, it is probable that in the large majority of trades the present slight disparities in output will automatically disappear

(4) *A difference in men's and women's qualifications* —Another point is, however, raised by employers, who maintain that although there is no actual deficiency of output, yet women tend to belong to an inferior grade of worker, and for this reason alone they are not entitled to men's wages. Not only, it is argued, do they lack men's physical strength and expert training, but they are subject to specific feminine weaknesses, such as mortality by marriage, bad time-keeping due to temporary indisposition or domestic emergency, prohibition from night-work and other legal or customary restrictions on female labour, by which output may be indirectly affected. In the case of workers enjoying comparative security of tenure—civil servants, railway workers, co-perative employees, and to some extent commercial clerks and

shop assistants—trade unionists are not opposed to graduated scales of wages according to the period of experience. They claim in this case, on the contrary, that " substituted " women are entitled to men's annual increments, and that they should not be treated, as they are too often now, as perpetual juveniles But, without security of tenure, graduated scales of this kind expose the workers to very obvious risks, and experienced men and women who are entitled to promotion tend to be discharged in favour of young people who are not. Some deduction from the standard rate in the case of young people, or " learners," is commonly accepted by trade unionists; but, unless this deduction forms part of a definite scheme of apprenticeship, so that employers give genuine instruction in return, the policy is open to similar abuse. This is especially so with regard to women who are less protected than men by monopolies of physical strength or expert training. Not only women and girls, but women and boys, are largely employed on the same work, and " unfair juvenile competition " is notoriously an important factor in keeping down the level of women's wages. Young persons employed under adult working conditions should clearly receive adult rates of wages. During the war, the statutory order, which related to young girls employed on men's work in engineering and ship-building establishments and actually allowed a deduction from *piece*-rates, amounting according to age from 10 per cent to 30 per cent , would have caused a general revolt in the cotton industry, where the weavers' piece-work " list " must be paid in full irrespective of sex or age. The argument of a difference in qualification is, however, most commonly used in reference to semi-qualified women employed in place of fully-skilled tradesmen; and, in this form, it is unanimously rejected by trade unionists. Apart from the fact that the absence of full technical qualifications is not necessarily a disadvantage in production—it may be a positive advantage on simple "repetition" work—it is claimed that the rate should attach to the operation, or to the machine, and not to any qualification of the worker For, if the worker is fit for his job, he is also fit to be paid for it; whilst, if he is not, he ought not to be employed in it. On work, moreover, for which men's qualifications are required—a man's physical strength, his social or domestic independence, his exemption from legal and customary restrictions—it is obvious that employers cannot and do not employ unqualified women. Or, if they can and do, it is fair to assume that their disadvantage is only a potential one. In this connection, a good story is told by Miss Mary Macarthur. In a certain Government office, some women had been introduced during the war in place of men as lift attendants The number of workers per lift remained the same as before, so that there was no question of a difference in output, and the National Federation of Women Workers put in its usual claim that women should receive men's wages. It was, however, explained by the authorities that women were unable to repair the lifts, and on this ground the claim was refused. The Federation returned to the challenge. "Was it not a fact," Miss Macarthur asked, "that men did not repair the lifts?" The reply was "Yes." "Was it not a fact that men could not repair the lifts?" Again the reply was "Yes." "Was it not a fact that if men could repair the lifts they would not be allowed to repair the lifts?" Once more the reply was "Yes" "Was it not a fact that an official notice had been posted expressly forbidding men even to try to repair the lifts?" Still the reply was "Yes" Trade unionists, unfortunately, have to fight their battles with other weapons than those of mere reason.

Too little attention has no doubt been given by women in the past to technical qualifications. That women should be worth men's wages is an obvious preliminary to "equal pay," but to pay them less than men on account of real or supposed deficiencies is to put the cart before the horse, and to place an actual premium on unqualified female labour The royal road to industrial efficiency lies through education All facilities for technical training, including those provided by the trade unions, should be open to workers of either sex. To discourage a professional spirit in women is certainly not to encourage them to be serious trade unionists The present tendency seems, however, to be against a long period of apprenticeship or technical training, except for a comparatively small number of technical experts. The chief asset of the worker is a high standard of general education, which is not less important to young girls because they may change their occupation on marriage. Education should include, not only the fullest possible degree of physical and mental development and a general equipment for social and industrial life, but also that exercise of initiative and responsibility which is the most valuable part of the teaching in our misnamed " public " schools. The worker of to-morrow has to learn, not only how to serve, but how to govern.

(5) *A difference in the job done by men and women.*—Men and women, as we have seen, are not generally employed on the same job, but women are introduced into men's trades together with a new mechanical device or a new sub-division of labour. The point, therefore, is an important one. Nor can it be met by the formula of " equal pay for the same job," or even that of " the same occupational rates," for no job or occupation can be so nicely defined that, intentionally or unintentionally, this definition may not be upset by a readjustment of process. No

less a matter, indeed, than the whole problem of fixing wages is involved. Broadly speaking, it is probably true to say that the rate of wages paid for a job, or in an occupation, is high or low in proportion to the ability of the worker, or group of workers concerned, by means of natural or artificial monopoly, to maintain this "job" or "occupation" as a close preserve Under conditions of competitive industry, wages follow, in fact, the same law as profits; and, from the point of view of employers, a readjustment of process, which breaks down the men's monopoly of physical strength or expert training, seems the most obvious reason for a reduction of wages. The reason appears a less obvious one to trade unionists, who are seeking for other principles of fixing wages than those of the mere "pull" of rival forces in the labour market. A readjustment of process, which brings the job within reach of a less skilled or robust class of worker, does not necessarily entail any disadvantage in production; it is probable, on the contrary, that it involves a positive advantage, or else it would not be adopted by employers. Although women are employed on only a part of men's work, yet they may be doing other work, which is equally skilled or laborious, or at least as productive and valuable to employers as that which was previously done by men. New mechanical methods of production have notoriously the effect of enormously increasing output, and their adoption would seem to give the opportunity for a rise and not a fall of wages. New classes of semi-skilled and unskilled workers may even claim that some compensation is due to them because of the undesirable character of a "purely automatic" or a "simple repetition" job. There is, truly, no just principle of fixing wages except that of "equal pay," not only as between men and women, but as between various groups of workers. For who can measure in terms of wages the efforts and pains, or the real worth, of the skilled craftsman, the semi-skilled mechanic, and the unskilled labourer, the manager and the operative, the technical expert and his clerk, the capitalist and the wage-earner?* The value of human labour, indeed, is infinite, and the claims of each worker are unlimited except by the equal claims of all. Trade unionists are coming to be more and more opposed to variations in the standard wage on account of readjustments of process. Old inequities cannot be redressed in a day, but there is no reason why employers should create new ones, or depart from practices of which the need has been proved by past generations of trade unionists. Within the *men's* field of employment—which on the principle advocated in a previous chapter would cover all doubtful or new processes to

---

* Any special expenditure of physical or nervous energy would be most appropriately compensated for by shorter hours of work or longer holidays

which either sex had a claim—women should follow the *men's*
practice, or not depart from it without the *men's* consent. This
is to say that, in the case of readjustments of process, no deductions from wages should be allowed which would not have been
allowed had men and not women been employed, whilst new rates
should be fixed on the basis of a men's and not a women's standard. Under no circumstances should women receive less than
the minimum wage for men in the industry, or branch of industry,
in question. There is, however, no reason why working conditions should not be adapted so far as possible to the needs of
either sex. Men rightly insist that conditions of female labour
should not drive them from employment, nor restrict them to
unduly laborious or disagreeable parts of the work, but women
similarly may claim that terms ought not to be imposed without
reference to the separate needs of their sex, or even deliberately devised so as to exclude them from employment. Equal
opportunities for men and women in industry do not necessarily
imply identical working conditions; the achievement of true
equality, on the contrary, may require definite divergencies of
practice. Any deduction from wages on account of special assistance or reliefs which are provided to women and not to men are
opposed by trade unionists of either sex. This right is claimed
by employers on the ground of extra cost of labour, but trade
unionists maintain that, not only may such extra cost be insignificant,
or actually nil, but its amount can only be estimated by employers, whose estimates they have no means of checking nor can
they make other ones of their own. The experience of the war
aggravated rather than allayed suspicion amongst the workers that
the least concession of this kind would be liable to instant abuse
by employers who are apparently constitutionally incapable of
resisting temptation to cut wages. Under conditions of competitive industry, however, some elasticity of method may be
required so that women who are granted necessary assistance of
reliefs should not be unfairly handicapped. In this connection, the
various practices of men and women cotton operatives are not
without significance. Thus, in the case of women " twisters "
and " drawers-in " who are assisted by men in lifting the heavy
" beams," the " list " rate of wages must be paid in full, but
the women pay the men for this assistance a small sum of about
1/- a week. On the same principle, when labourers are employed
in cotton mills to assist the operatives in carrying the full
" spools " to the warehouse, the wages of these labourers are
directly paid by or are charged against the operatives, but no deductions on this account are allowed from the " list." In the latter
case, as a matter of fact, any payment made by the operatives is
more than compensated by the increased earnings on the looms.

Nor is the practice of the " sick worker," by which one woman arranges with another to take her place on emergency in the factory, a fundamentally different one in principle. Women provide by this means against their liability to irregular time-keeping, which is a common reason given by employers for deductions from wages. In order to show the advantage to the workers in practices of this kind, it is enough to compare the small cost for assistance incurred by women who adopt them, amounting to seldom more than 2 per cent. or 3 per cent. of their total earnings, with the large sums of ten times that amount deducted from wages by employers for the same or similar purposes. Provided that the workers on either side are well-organized and their interests adequately represented through their trade unions, the system would seem to be capable of useful extension to other industries. As further safeguards, all payments made by one worker, or group of workers, to another should be mutually agreed upon, and enforced by the trade union or trade unions concerned; whilst the wages received by any worker in this way should be based on a standard not lower than that of the worker by whom such payment is made. Between persons of a different standard of living, just dealing is so difficult as to be almost impossible. The present trade union claim is, however, that workers of either sex should be relieved from unnecessarily laborious or injurious conditions; and, as this claim takes effect, the need of women for special provisions will for the most part cease to exist.

In conclusion, it may be said that the case against " equal pay " breaks down, and that a difference, real or supposed, in the needs of men and women, in the market price of male and female labour, in men's and women's output, in their qualifications, or in the job done by them, may, and ought to, be met by other means than those of deductions from wages. The root problem of women in trade unions is a wages problem. Its solution will directly lead to the solution of others, and will finally banish from industry the old suspicions and prejudices which set men and women in antagonism and retard the growth of labour solidarity.

TABLE I

FEMALE MEMBERSHIP OF ALL TRADE UNIONS

1876—1918

	1876	1885	1896	1906	1914	1918	Percentage of all Trade Unionists	Percentage of all Female Workers [3]
Miners' Unions	—	—	—	—	140	10,000	1 0	8 3
Metal Unions	—	—	290	484	1 041	11,000	1 0	3 1[4]
Textile Unions								
Cotton	15,000[1]	30,100[1]	102,847	124,697	210,272	260,000	64 6	74 3
Wool	1,000	1 000	1,728	2,393	7,695	53,000	57 6	30 5
Linen and Jute	—	2,500	9,588	12,651	18,492	55 000	80 0	54 4
Hosiery	3,000	1,000	1,050	1,465	3,657	22,000	78 6	31 9
Other Textile	—	—	962	1,232	6,254	10,000	41 7	11 1
Textile Dyeing, etc , Warehousing	—	—	—	701	7,260	23,000	28 1	82 1
(All Textile)	(19,000)	(34,500)	(106,540)	(143,139)	(253,630)	(423,000)	(60 3)	(52 0)
Clothing Unions								
Tailoring, etc (including Royal Army Clothing Operatives)	50	1,000	944	2,024	11,353	88,000	78 0	54 0[5]
Boot and Shoe	—	50	1,692	893	10,915	28,000	30 8	41 2
Hat and Cap	50	250	2,495	2,265	3,590	3,000	42 9	10 0
(All Clothing)	(100)	(1,300)	(5 131)	(5 082)	(25 858)	(119 000)	(56 4)	(21 3)
Transport Unions (excluding Clerks)	—	—	—	—	650	54,000	6 0	66 7
Printing Unions	300	300	833	977	8,285	39,000	27 5	27 3
Wood working and Furnishing Unions	100	100	131	139	568	5,000	5 2	6 0
Chemical Unions	—	—	—	—	325	3 000	13 7	4 0
Pottery Unions	—	—	546	530	1,804	20,000	60 6	59 0
Food and Tobacco Unions	—	—	1,848	2,447	3,317	7,000	15 8	28 9
Distributive Unions	—	—	500	4,920	18,357	62,000	41 9)	
Clerical Unions								7 6[6]
Commercial (including Insurance Agents)	—	—	70	180	1,703	13,000	20 0)	
Railway	—	—	—	—	100	14,000	14 1	56 0[7]
Civil Service	—	—	850	5,135[2]	13,656	56,000	29 2	24 2
(All Clerks)	—	—	(920)	(5 315)	(15 459)	(83 000)	(24 3)	—
Various Unions	—	500	536	996	4,987	34,000	4 2	—
General Labour	100	200	903	2,674	23,534	216,000	19 6	
All Trade Unions (not including Teachers or Professional Workers)	10 600	36 900	117,888	166,803	357 956	1 086 000	17 0	19 9[8]

[1] Figures for 1876 and 1886 are rough estimates taken from statements made by trade union officials and investigators in contemporary reports and journals of the Women's Trade Union League

[2] The figures for postal assistants relate to 1907, no separate figures for male and female workers being given for 1906 The figures also include telephone operatives

[3] The estimates for all female workers, upon which the percentages are based, are taken from the Board of Trade Report on the State of Employment for January 1919

[4] It must be borne in mind that large numbers of women belonging to semi organised trades are enrolled in general labour unions notably in the case of metal workers so that the percentage for each separate industry is only a more or less approximate one (See text, p. 111)

[5] In the estimate for all workers, tailoresses and clothiers operatives are included, but not dressmakers or various clothes makers

[6] No separate figures are available for commercial clerks and shop assistants, who are, therefore, both included in this column

[7] The estimate for all workers relates to July 1918

[8] The Board of Trade figures for all workers do not include domestic servants or dressmakers in very small shops The number of domestic servants was 1,359,000 in 1911, but is known to have decreased by many thousands during the war A round figure of 1,000,000 has therefore been added to the Board of Trade total, and the percentage must be taken as only a rough one

TABLE II—Analysis of Princip.

Name of Union	Established	Women first admitted	Membership			Contributions		Uses. Benefits.	Women on Executive Committee.	Are men Organisers	Committees on of Branches.	Disqualifications of Female Members.	Main
			Total Membership Dec. 1914	Female Membership Dec. 1918.	Total Membership Dec. 1918.	Men	Women						
Miners Unions													
Lanarkshire Miners County Union	1897	1897	Unknown	2 049 (2 500 Dec 1919)	48 000	2/	4d	Trade ** cotton men s	Nil	Nil.	Mixed	Nil	Pithead coal ers-off
Metal Unions													
Iron and Steel Trades Con federation	1886	1,	10	2 080	79 500	3.—1/6	3d.—1/6	Do men's list with alternativ of uar type down in lieu of half unemploy benefit.	Nil	Nil. (Ten women branch secretaries.)	Mainly all-women o	Nil	Tin plat cold rol
Textile Unions—Cotton.													
Northern Counties Amalgama ted Association of Cotton Weavers (Including local associations)	1884 (Earliest associations date from 18)	1884	50 000	105 500	25	4.—1	4d.—1	Trade breakdown funeral	Nil (Women on local committees)	Nil	Mixed.	Nil	Weavers winders
Amalgamated Association of Beamers Twisters and Drawers (Including 39 local associations.)	18 0 (Earliest associations date from 1861)	1890	300	5	7 50	1/—	1/— 2	same as men.	Nil (Women on district committees)	One	Mixed	Nil	Twisters ers-in
Amalgamated Association of Card and Blowing Room Operatives (Including 14 local associations.)	1866 (Earliest associations date from 1858 being admitted about 1875)	1886	5 000	6 000	9 000	6d—1 4d/ard ing to wages	4d 3 ard ing to wages	Trade and list breakdown funeral	Nil (Women on local committee)	Nil	Mixed.	Nil	Card room ring spi
Amalgamated Cotton Spinners Association. All women but one half men members belong to Piecers' Section only.	187 (Bolton Amalga)	187	2,440	8 440	5 7	2d—3d	3d.— 6	Time l down f eral	Nil	Nil.	Mixed	Disqualified for manage ro se nce as m en piecers.)	Piecers.
Textile Unions—Wool and Worsted Unions													
General Union of Textile Workers.	188	1881	4 000	47 841 (66 000 Dec 1919)	59 500 (100 000 Dec 1919)	2½d—3d	2½d—3d	Trade unemploy ment compensation	Three	Two	Mixed	Nil	Weavers winders, menders knitters
National Society of Woollen so ers and allied Trades	8 0	1 00	1 0	0	11,000	6d	4d	Trade accident fun al	Nil	Nil	Mixed	Nil.	each of frade s
Textile Unions—Textile Dyeing Bleaching Finishing, and Ware housing Unions													
Amalgamate Society of Dyer Bleachers Finishers, Kindred Trade	1878	1 .	1 800	0	8 0	9d.	2	Trade funeral	Nil (Women on district committees	Nil	Mixed	Nil	Light p warehou process labo ing d
National Society of Dyers and Finishers	851	1	45	3 000	5 50	4d—3d	4d	Trade funeral	Nil (Women district committees	Nil	Mixed. One all women dist-ict let el	Nil	Light p warehou ters and F101
Bolton Amalgamation of Blea chers Dyers and Finishers	1866	1900	2 850	7 600	20,8	3d.	3d	Trade funeral infirmions dis ease accident mittee	Nil (Women on local committee	Nil	Mixed	For represen ta tion at dele gate meetings, women members in proportion to contribution	Light p warehou
Female Workers in the Shipping Industry	1908	1908	13 000	1 04	1		3d.	Trade out of work, sickness 5 May) funeral	All except President and Secretary.	Nil	—	—	Stitcher m kers orders, and stit
Textile Unions—Hosiery													
Leicester Amalgamated Hosiery Unions	1885	1885	5 000	0	2 000	3d 3d extra s employ nent bat	1 3d extr unemploy b t	Trade funeral unemploy ment.	One	Nil	Mixed	Nil.	auttere etc
Textile Unions—Flax and Jute.													
Dundee and District Jute and Flax Workers		1906	3 800	6 0	20 000	4½d 5d	2d. 5d	Trade break down	Ten.	Nil	Mixed	Nil.	Spinners parers warpers reelers
Dundee and Distric Mill and Factory Op atives	88	1885	300	4	4 5	4.—£1	3d—1.	Trade break down funeral	Twelve out of twenty	Woman secre tary)	Mixed	Nil	
Textile Operatives of eland	18	1893	1 327	10, 45	10 3,0	1d—4d	1d—4d.	Trade break down	All	All women of c als	Mixed	Nil.	Spinners Makers house w
Other Textile Unions.													
Kidderminster Power Loom Carpet Weavers	1866	18	Nil	3 00	4 50	3d	3d	Trade sick ess funeral unemploy ent	Four	Four women assistant e retaries	Mixed.	One vote to 25 female mem b rs	Weavers textile
Newmills and District Textile Workers Union	1890	1890	Unknown	500	4 000	9d—1	2d	Lack un m ploy ent funeral.	Nil. Women auxiliary co mittees	Women branch secretaries	Some mixed other all women's	Nil	are at workers
Amalgamated Society of Textile Workers and Kindred Trades (Leeds)	1919	191	4 3009	9 00t 12319	10 500t 11010	5d. (t a e only)	3d (t al only)	Trade only Out of work sickness a e funeral a e	Three	One	Mixed	Nil.	Silk sort weavers finishers a o

sis of Principal Trade Unions

...on	Disqualifications of Female Members	Main Occupations of Female Members	Trade Union Restrictions on Female Labour: Normal	Trade Union Restrictions on Female Labour: War Period	Wages: Women's Standard July 1914	Wages: Women's Standard, Nov. 1918	Wages: Men's Standard Nov., 1918	Wages: Substituted Women Nov. 1918
	Nil	Pithead labourers coal pickers drawers-off, saw millers	Campaign to abolish female labour about collieries	Campaign postponed	Average earnings 1/9 to 3/ a day	+ 3/ a day (+ 2/ basic rates fixed, making total wage 6/3 a day for ordinary work, 6/7 to 8/6 for coal pickers, 8/ to 9/1 for drawers-off Dec., 1919)	Saw millers 15/6 a day including bonuses	Saw millers average, 8/ a day including bonuses.
wo-	Nil	Tin plate workers cold rollers, etc.	Prohibition in smelting processes.	Relaxation in regard to labourers and crane drivers	Minimum rates 1/6 to 2/2 a day (Cold rollers.	+ 80% on earnings up to 20/ a week, and + 95% on earnings from 20/1 to 30/ Also increase on basic rates	Labourers 46/6 a week + 12½% Crane drivers 5/ a day + 23 a week + 12½%	Labourers men's full rates + men's war advances Crane drivers men's rates less cost of assistance + men's war advances
	Nil	Weavers, warpers winders	Nil	Nil	Piece work list (same as men's) Average earnings 2[illegible] to 32/	+ 110% + 210% May 1920)	Same as women's	Same as men's
	Nil	Twisters and drawers-in	Prohibition as twisters and drawers-in in certain districts.	Relaxation in certain districts.	Piece-work list (same as men's) Average earnings 40/ to 50/	+ 110% (+ 210% May, 1920.	Same as women's	Same as men's
	Nil	Card and blowing room operatives *ring-spinners*	Definite line of demarcation between men's and women's department	Relaxation on subordinate work	Piece-work is Average earnings card and blowing room workers, 20/ to 24 ring-spinners 16/ to 22/	+ 110% (+ 210% May 1920	Average earnings about 67/ a week including war bonus)	About 60% of men's earnings
	Disqualified for management (same as men piecers)	Piecers	Prohibition as spinners or as piecers in most districts	Relaxation in regard to piecers	Average earnings 10/ to 2[illegible]	+ 110% + 210% May 1920)	Same as women's	Same as men's (Maximum wage of 15/ during period of probation..
	Nil.	Weavers, warpers winders condenser minders, menders knitters burlers	Men and women mostly employed in different departments excepting weavers	Relaxation on scheduled list of suitable men's occupations	No general standard Piece work list or Huddersfield woollen weavers Women's rates 10% less than men's	Piece workers — 89% time workers + 104½%, National basic wage of 17/ a week of 48 hours amounting with war advances to 39/11 Dec. 1919.)	26/ + 37/. Piece worker + 83⅓%, time-worker 104½%	Men's rates on whole job Minimum wage of ⅔ men's standard
	Nil	Machine minders and feeders	Prohibition on men's machines and night work	Relaxation on suitable men's machines and night work.	14/6 to 1[illegible]/6 2/3 men's standard for corresponding work)	+ 20/ a week	46/6 to 52/[illegible]	Men's full rates on night work 4/5 men's standard on day work
	Nil	Light processes in warehouse (Dyeing processes in Scotland.)	Prohibition on wet processes and on men's dry processes	Relaxation on suitable dry processes.	No general standard Bradford, 12/- a week Piece-workers Yorkshire 16/ to 18/ Lancashire 12/ to 15/6	+ 18/10 a week Lancs and Yorks 18/ a week of 48 hours Scotland 1[illegible] + 120% Dec 1919)	28/ to 40/ + 30/	Men's rates regard being had to quantity of work done women's war advances
One ...en's ...ted	Nil	Light processes in warehouse Knotters and burlers in Huddersfield	Prohibition on wet processes and on men's dry processes	Relaxation on suitable dry processes	Piece workers Yorkshire 16/ to 18/6 Lancashire 12/ to 15/6	Do	Do	Do
	For representation at delegate meetings membership in proportion to contribution	Light processes in warehouse.	Prohibition on wet processes and on men's dry processes	Relaxation on suitable dry processes	Piece-workers 12/ to 16/6	Do.	Do	Do.
	—	Stitchers cutters markers-off parcellers etc Hookers and stampers	Prohibition on men's processes	Relaxation on suitable dry processes	Minimum wage 12/ to 1[illegible] a week of 52½ hours	+ 16/10 week (Minimum wage 29/6 to 31/6 a week of 40½ hours, Dec. 1919)	53/11 to 65/5	Men's rate for equal work Minimum wage 8d an hour
	Nil	Knitters menders etc	Prohibition on Cotton's patent frames	Relaxation on Cotton's patent frames	Piece work list broadly estimated to work out at 4d an hour	+ 6½d in 1/ (+ 3½d in 1/ + ½%, + 6/ a week, Dec 1919)	Piece work list, broadly estimated to work out at 8d an hour + 6½d in 1/	Men's rates for equivalent quantity of work done
	Nil	Spinners and preparers Weavers warpers winders and reelers	Prohibition as tenters and mechanics	No change	Spinners 13/11 to 23/6 a week of 5[illegible] hours Preparers 13/ to 19/[illegible]	+ 18/ a week (Minimum wage of 32/ a week of 48 hours proposed under the Trade Board Act Feb 1920)	30/ to 35/ + [illegible]	Men's rates + women's war advances
	Nil	Do	Nil	Nil	Average earnings Preparers, 14/6 Spinners, 16/ Winders 18/ Weavers 2[illegible]/	+ 38%	—	Do
	Nil	Spinners and weavers Makers-up and warehouse women	Nil (Prohibition in roughing processes by men's society	Nil	No standard Average earnings, 11/[illegible]	Factory operatives + 130% warehouse women + 43%	—	—
	One vote to 25 female members	Weavers and other textile workers	Prohibition on Jacquard looms	No change	—	+ 105% (Average earnings 30/ to 50/ Dec. 1910)	No substitution agreements	No substitution agreements
...ed ...ll	Nil	Lace and madras workers	Men and women employed on different machines	Relaxation on such operations as women are physically fit to perform	—	+ 80% to 160%	—	Men's rates for equivalent amount of work done
	Nil	Silk sorters spinners weavers, winders finishers, makers up etc Various other textile workers	Prohibition in some districts as weavers and twisters	No change	12/6 a week.	26/ a week (36/ May 1920)	26/ (18 years) to 44/ 34/6 to 6[illegible] May 1920.)	Practically no substitution

Name												
National Society of Woolcombers and Kindred Trades	1890	190.	1,730	...	11,000	6d	4d	Trade accident, funeral	Nil	Nil	Mixed	Nil
Textile Unions—Textile Dyeing, Bleaching, Finishing and Warehousing Unions												
Amalgamated Society (Dyers, Bleachers, Finishers, and Kindred Trades)	1878	1891	18,00	9,000	28,000	6d	4d	Trade, funeral	Nil (Women on district committees.)	Nil	Mixed	Nil
National Society of Dyers and Finishers	1891	190.	430	3,400	13,500	5d—7d	5d	Trade funeral	Nil. Women on district committees.	Nil	Mixed. One all women's branch Huddersfield.	Nil
Bolton Amalgamation of Bleachers, Dyers and Finishers	1866	1901	2,800	7,000	28,800	5d	4d	Trade funeral, infectious disease, accident	Nil. Women on local committees.	Nil	Mixed	For representation to delegate meetings, membership in proportion to contributions
Female Workers in the Slipping Industry	...08	1901	13,000	19,000	13,000	—	3d	Trade out of work, sickness (3 days) funeral	All except President and Secretary	Nil	—	Nil
Textile Unions—Hosiery Leicester Amalgamate Hosiery Union	1885	1905	500	9,000	12,000	6d ½d extra unempl ment benefit	3d. ½d extra unemployment	Trade funeral, unemployment	One	Nil	Mixed	Nil
Textile Unions—Flax and Jute Dundee and District Jute and Flax Workers	1.00	1906	900	15,000	6,000	4d 5d 8d	4½d 5d 8d	Trade break down	Two	Nil	Mixed	Nil
Dundee and District Flax and Factory Operatives	1885	1885	1,500	3,40	4,5	3d—6d.	3d—4d	Trade, breakdown, funeral	Twelve out of twenty	Women as secretary	Mixed	Nil
Textile Operatives of Ireland	189.	1893	1,5	10,345	6,40	3d—4d	3d—4d	Trade breakdown	All	All women officials.	Mixed	Nil
Other Textile Unions Huddersfield Power Loom Carpet Weavers	1806	1917	Nil	3,000	1,5	1,d	d	Trade sick, general unemployment	Four	Four women assistant secretaries	Mixed	One vote to 1½ female members
Nelson and District Textile Workers Union	1890	1800	Unknown	2,30	..000	½d—1	1n	Trade unemployment, funeral	Nil. Women's auxiliary committees	Women branch secretaries	Some mixed, others all-women's	Nil
Amalgamated Society of Textile Workers and Kindred Trades, Leeds	191?	191?	4,380?	7,10 t 1,907 £,919 (1919)	5, (trade only)	d (trade only)	Trade only. Out-of-work sickness and funeral are optional	Three	One	Mixed	Nil
Clothing Unions. United Garment Workers' Trade Union	1.15	1915	6,380	74,00 (,2,.00 Dec. 1919)	5,000 (Dec. 1919)	6d—11d	2d—a	Dispute, sickness (and funeral)	One (Majority of women on local committees)	Sixteen (most 1½ local)	Mixed except myWest London Women's Branch	Nil
Amalgamated Society of Tailors and Tailoresses	1866	1900	1,030	10,000	30,0	4s—8d	d—4d	Trade, sickness, funeral.	Nil. Women on local committees.	One	Mixed and some all-women's	Women count as half-members at delegate meetings (same as men, ½d contribution)
National Union Boot and Shoe Operatives	1874	1885	14,000	50,000	50,000	6d	1½d	Trade, out-of-work, funeral, sickness	One	Nil	Mixed and one all-women's	Nil
Amalgamated Felt Hat Trimmers and Wool Formers	1886	1883	347	...0	2,370	—	3d	Trade, fire, funeral, sickness, funeral	Eleven and four men (branch officials)	Nil. Man secretary	—	Hat, wool
Transport Unions National Union of Railwaymen	1.15	1915	—	30,000 (Few thousands remaining Dec. 1919)	440,000	4d—5d.	3d	Trade only	Nil	Nil	Mixed	Nil
London and Provincial Licensed Vehicle Workers	1894	1916	8,000 (Few remaining Dec. 1919)	62,000		13 conductors 7d drivers	4d (conductors) 5d drivers	Trade, accident, funeral	Nil	Nil	Mixed.	Nil
Amalgamated Tramway and Vehicle Workers	1889	1915	—	12,000 (Few remaining Dec. 1919)	40,560	4d	4d	Do	Nil	Nil	Mixed	Nil

					rates 10% less than men s	week of 48 hours amounting with war advances to 39/11 Dec. 1919)		
ixed	Nil.	Machine minders and feeders	Prohibition on men s machines and night work	Relaxation on suitable men s machines and light work	14/6 to 19/6 (2/3 men s standard for corre sponding work)	+ 20 a week	56/6 to 62 6.	Men s full rates on night work 4/5 men s standard on day work.
lixed	Nil	Light processes in warehouse. Dyeing processes (in Scot land)	Prohibition on wet processes and on men s dry processes	Relaxation on suit able dry processes.	No general standard Bradford, 17/ a week. Piece-workers Yorkshire 16/ to 18/6 Lancashire 12/ to 16 6	+ 18/10 a week (Lancs. and Yorks, 16/ a week of 48 hours Scotland 15 - + 120% Dec 1919.)	28/ to 40 + 30/	Men s rates regard being had to quan tity of work done + women s war ad vances
Mixed One all women s branch Hud dersfield	Nil	Light processes in warehouse knot te s and burlers in Huddersfield	Prohibition on wet processes and on men's dry p ocesses	Relaxation on suit able dry processes	Piece workers York shire 16 - to 18/6 Lancashire, 12 to 16 6	Do	Do	Do
Mixed	1 or representa tion at dele gate meetings, membership in proportion to contribution	Light processes in warehouse	Prohibition on wet processes and on men s d y processes	Relaxation on suit able dry processes	Piece workers 12 to 16 6.	Do	Do	Do
—		Stitchers cutters markers-off par cellers, etc. Hookers and stampers.	Prohibition on men s processes	Relaxation on suit able dry processes	Minimum wage 12 to 14/- a week of 52½ hours	+ 16/1 a week (Mini mum wage, 29 0 + 34 6 a week of 46½ hours, Dec 1919)	53/11 to 65/5	Men s rates for equal work Minimum wage 8d an hour
Mixed	Nil	Knitters, menders, etc	Prohibition on Cotton's patent frames.	Relaxation on Cot ton's patent frames	Piece-work list broad ly estimated to work out at 4d an hour	— 6½d in 1/ (+ 6½d in 1 + 8% + 6 a week, Dec 1919)	Piece-work list broad ly estimated to work out at 8d. an hour + 6½d in /	Men s rates for equivalent quantity of work done
Mixed	Nil	Spinners and pre parers. Weavers, warpers winders and reelers	Prohibition as tenters and mechanics	No change	Spinners. 13/11 to 15/5 a week of 55 hours Preparers 13/- to 13/	+ 18/ a week (Mini mum wage of 32/ a week of 48 hours pro posed under the Trade Board Act Feb 1920)	30/ to 3 + 25/	Men's rates + women s war ad vances
Mixed	Nil	Do	Nil	Nil	Average earnings Preparers 14/6 Spinners 16/ Winders 18/ Weavers 20 -	+ 98%	—	Do
Mixed	Nil	Spinners and weavers Makers-up and ware house women	Nil Prohibition in rougher' pro cesses by men s soci ety	Nil	No standard Aver age earnings 11	Factory operatives + 130% warehouse women + 13%	—	—
Mixed	One vote to 25 female mem bers	Weavers and other textile workers	Prohibition on Jac quard looms	No change	—	+ 105% (Average earnings 30 to 50/ Dec 1919	No substitution agreements	No substitution agreements
Some mixed, others all women s.	Nil	Lace and madras workers	Men and women em ployed on different machines.	Relaxation on such operations as women are physically fit to perform	—	+ 80% to 160%	—	Men rates for equivalent amount of work done
Mixed	Nil	Silk sorters spinners. weavers winders. finishers. makers up etc Various other textile workers	Prohibition in some districts as weavers and twisters	No change	12 6 a week	20/ a week (Dec - May 1920)	26/ (18 years) to 44/ (34 0 to 61 May 1920)	Practically no sub stitution
Mixed except ing West London Women s Branch	Nil	Tailoresses factory operatives, dress makers milliners corset makers.	None provided that women receive men s rates of wages	Relaxation with re gard to equal time rates	3½d per hour T B. rate 3½d proposed	5d per hour T B. rate — 3d I U rate 8½d T B. rate piece work basic time-rate 9½d Jan 1920)	1/ per hour	Minimum rate 6d per hour. Average earnings 50% to 70% men s wages
Mixed and some all wo men's	Women count as half mem bers at dele gate meetings (same as men 4d contribu tors)	Do.	Prohibition on best cutting and pressing	Relaxation	Do	Do	Do	Do
Mixed and one all-women s	Nil	Closing and stock room operatives	Prohibition in click ing press lasting and finishing de partments	Relaxation	Minimum wage, 17 — 18/ a week of 53½ hours	+ 8, Piece-workers up to 30/ + 8 (Minimum wage 30 a week of 48 hours Feb 1919)	Piece - workers up to £3 + 15, bonus	Men s piece-rates + women s war bonus.
—	—	Hat trimmers and wool formers	Prohibition by allied men s union in felt ing processes	No change	Piece-work statement. Average earnings 15/ to 20/	+120% Dec. 1919	—	—
Mixed	Nil	Porters cleaners ticket collectors etc	Prohibition on rail ways except as cleaners or char women	Relaxation except in manipulating traf fic	Carriage cleaners 15/ a week	+ 20/6	10/ to 32/ — 33/	10 to 28/ + 20/6.
Mixed.	Nil.	Conductresses (1/8) women drivers	Prohibition on public conveyances and as van drivers	Relaxation in regard to conductresses and small van drivers	—	—	Conductors London 4?/ + 20 Manchester 6d to 7½d per hour + 34/	Conductresses London and Leicester men s rates + men s advances provinces generally men s rates + 2 3 men s advances Yorkshire men s rates less grade in creases + propor tion of men s ad vances — Commercial drivers no standard
Mixed.	Nil	Do.	Do.	Do.	—	—	Do.	Do.

TABLE II—Analysis of Principal Trad

Name of Union	Estab-lished.	Women first adm tted.	Membership			Contributions		Women Benefits	Women on Executive Committees.	Women Organisers.	Constitution of Branches.	Disqualifica-tion of Female Members.
			Female Membership Dec 1914	Female Membership Dec., 918.	Total Membership. Dec. 1918	Men.	Women.					
Printing Unions. National Union of Printing and Paper Workers	1840*	1904	6 850	37 000 (37,000, Dec 1919)	73 000	3d —2/	4d —6d	Trade unem ploy ment funeral (in cluding mem ber s hus band) mar riage dowry	Three (Two place reser ved to Lon don Women's Branch)	Five (Also f nancial sec retary)	Mixed except ng London Wo men s Branch	Nil
National Union of Bookbinders and Machine Rulers	1836	1917	—	2 800 (11 000 Dec 1919)	11 700	12/6 per q'ter	2d 3d	Trade, unem ployment funeral mar riage dowry	Nil (Places reserved to women in pro portion to membership)	Nil (Women local offi ials	All-women's.	Nil.
Woodworking Unions National Amalgamated Furnish ng Trades Association.	1902	1911	130	2 000 (2 500, Dec., 1919)	12 410	6d — 1 4	6d	Trade unem ployment fu neral.	Nil	Nil	Mixed and all women's	Nil
Chemical and Pottery Unions Amalgamated Society of Male and Female Pottery Workers	1906	1906	2 110	20 000 (23 000, Dec 1919)	37 000	6d	2d 3d (Extra 1d for unem ployment benefit)	Trade Extra unemploy ment benefit.	Nil (four wo men on district committees	One.	Mixed	Nil
Food and Tobacco Unions Amalgamated Union of Opera tive Bakers.	1861	1919	—	2,000	20 000	1 — 1 3	3 1 —7d	Trade, sick ness out of work, mar riage dowry	Nil	One	Mixed, and all- women.	Nil.
National Union of Cigar Makers	1835	1895	2 000 (1 000 be longing to Notting m Female Cigar Mkrs)	2 750	3 500	1/3	3d (London) 4d (Provinces)	Trade, out-of work, lost time funeral	Three	O ne (Notting ham)	Mixed	Nil.
Distributive Unions National Amalgamated Union of Shop Assistants Ware housemen and Clerks.	1891	1891	5 000	22 200 (135 300, Dec 1919)	51,690 (80,000, Dec 1919)	Trade 4d provident 2d —2/2	Trade 3d provident 3d — 2/2	Trade mem ploy ment sickness fu neral mar riage dowry	One	Four whole time women district secre taries	Mixed (Wo men's Advi sory Council)	Nil
Amalgamated Union of Co operative Employees and Commercial Workers	1891	1891	000	17 000 53 700 Dec 1919)	75 000 (87 000 Dec 1919)	£1 —9d.	4d —7d	Trade, unem ployment sickness fu neral, mar iage dowry	Nil	One (three in 1919)	Mixed	Nil
Clerks National Union of Clerks	1890	1890	1 000	9 670 (10 800 Dec 1919)	36 302	8d	8d	Trade unem ployment sickness, dis tress, old-age, funeral	One	Nil.	Mixed	Nil
Railway Clerks Association	1897	1897	100	13 000†	85 000	4d —6d according to salary	4d —6d according to salary	Trade unem ployment disablement retirement convalescence	Nil	Nil.	Mixed.	Nil
Union of Post Office Clerks	1920	1920	6 500‡	20 100‡ (17 000 May 1920)	11,000 1920	3d 4d or 3d according to salary	3d. 4d or 3d according to salary	No benefits other than those of mem bership.	Five	One.	Mixed.	Nil

Trade Unions.	Constitution of Branches	Disqualifications of Female Members	Men's Occupations or Female Members	Trade Union Restrictions on Female Labour		Wages.			
				Normal	War Period	Women's Standard July 1914	War Advances Nov. 1918	Men's Standard Nov. 1918	Substitutes. Women. Nov. 1918
(Also ... tal ...)	Mixed except in London Women's Branch	Nil	Folders, sewers, stitchers, ... ppers, etc. Increase or assistants. War ... those women... Paper makers. Paper bag and box makers	Discouragement on cutting machines. Prohibition by T... graphical Association ... as ... junctors or machine operatives.	Relaxation	No standard. Average earnings, 12/- ... workers ... claim 17/- a week or 7 hours. 2d an hour T.B. rate	+ 20/- time workers + 100 120% piece workers (London (Min. rate London 45/- a week of 48 hrs ... 6 Dec. 1919. 4½d an hour T.B. rate 8d Nov. 1919)	£6 6	Men ... rates ... sa jobbers, men's full rate of London
Women (Local)	All-women	Nil.	Folders, sewers, stitchers, pagers etc.	Prohibition in skilled branches of book binding.	Relaxation	—	Same as Union and P.W.	Practically no substitution.
	Mixed and all women's	Nil.	French polishers and upholsterers. Aircraft and other munition workers during the war	Prohibition on edge tool and wood... cutting machines.	Relaxation on small parts in aircraft manufacture	No standard. 1 on ... average earning 1/- to 1/- ... High ... combe 2½d. (window chair maker)	According to district London ... on ... chester ... 1½d an hour ... London ... polishers 4½ ... window ... 1/2 May 1920	According to district London 1 to ½ on hour Manchester 1/3 (London 1 13 May 1920	Aircraft wood workers: 6½ an hour + 11/- a week (London 13 May 1920
	Mixed	Nil	Transferers decorators potters and head ... flat-makers, warehouse women	Prohibited as dippers, placers as in making or casting large pieces	Relaxation	No standard. Average earning 11/- to ... a week to 9½d to 1/- per ... piece paid women up to 34/-	+ ... + 3 ... on gross earnings ... (2½ to 25/- a week of 4 hours + 0% transferrers and decorators 9d and 4½d per ... 20% Dec. 1919)	North piece-workers either in full or best 1/3. Placers 20, a week of 33¼ hours 33½% (Flat pressers men's piece rates either in full or less 20% Dec. 1919.
	Mixed and all women's	Nil	Confectioners bakeresses tea cakers etc.	Prohibition in bread-making.	Relaxation	—	45/- Aug. 1919.	... Aug. 1919	... men's wages.
Heating Mixed		Nil	Cigar makers	None, provided women receive men's wages.	No change	No standard. ... piece work rates ... (London 20/- to 1/- ... 20% less for men for identical work Average earnings 13/- to 17/-	+ 20% on rates + 20% bonus. Average earnings, 30/- to £ + 1 2½% London + 3 3% pro... on pre-war rates Dec 1919 c)	Piece work rates limited ... + ... 10/- ... Average earnings 43/- to £3 10/- a week + ... a week + 8½ on pre-war rate. Dec 1919)	Men's rates ... a bonus
... whole women workers ...	Mixed (Women's Advisory Council)	Nil	Shop assistants	Nil	Nil	No standard. 1 union claim minimum rate of 18/- a week or 3½ men's standard London 11/- ... Dressmakers No standard. 8½d. an hour T.B. rate, or 94/3 piece work base rate amount Feb 1920	Roughly + ... 5% + ... during ... 35/- Min rates from 30/- to 33/- a week of 48 hrs. ... to 28 years London ... agreed in the large number of cities.	45 to 60/- from 18 years London + 5 (1919)	+ 5 men's standard
...are in Mixed		Nil.	Shop assistants factory workers	Nil.	Nil	1/- a week	+ 5 ... to 10/- ... Min and district ... Averages ... est as 1st + 5 ... week (48 hours est ... assistants + ... to ... agreements. ... Dec 1919	Various district rates About 60 to £76 ... to ... managers 5 (Dec 1919)	Equal pay in many districts
	Mixed	Nil.	General clerks, typists shorthand typists book keepers secretaries, etc. Municipal clerks	Nil.	Nil	No standard. Average earning 13/- to 15/- a week	+ about 2/6 to 2/- a week	No standard. Average earnings 55 to 85 ... municipal clerks £70 to £125 per annum + civil service bonus ... see below same rates as for men June 1920	Both ... men's rates of wages
	Mixed	Nil	Buying clerks account invoicing and general clerks	Nil	Nil	No normal standard London 12/- to 8/- a week provinces 7/- to 20/-	+ 20/-	30 to 40/- a week + 33/-	Men's minimum rates in each grade + on men's war advances.
	Mixed	Nil.	Telegraphists telephonists sitting clerks	Nil	Nil	London, £8, 10 10 a week small towns 12 to 16 a week	+ 15/- (+ 130% on pre-war salary up ... 6 ...	49/- to 88/- (talk graphists)	3/- to 55/- (tele graphists)

Union	Founded		Members				Benefits		Officials	Organisers	Type	
DISTRIBUTIVE UNIONS. National Amalgamated Union of Shop Assistants, Warehousemen and Clerks	1891	1891	3 000	3 000 (33 300, Dec 1919)	51 690 (80 600, Dec 1919)	Trade 4d provident, 2d.—3	Trade 3d provident, 1d—2½	Trade, unemployment, sickness, funeral, marriage dowry	One	Four whole time women district secretaries	Mixed. (Women's Advisory Council)	Nil
Amalgamated Union of Co-operative Employees and Commercial Workers	1891	1891	2 000	22 000 (33 700, Dec 1919)	7 000 (47 000 Dec 1919)	6d—9d	4d—9d	Trade, unemployment, sickness, funeral, marriage dowry	Nil	One (three in 1919)	Mixed	Nil
Clerks. National Union of Clerks	1890	1890	1 000	9 670 (10 800 Dec 1919)	30 302	8d	8d	Trade, unemployment, sickness, distress, old-age, funeral.	One	Nil	Mixed	Nil
Railway Clerks Association	(8)	189	100	13 000†	8 000	4 1.—6d according to salary	1d—4d according to salary	Trade, unemployment, disablement, retirement, convalescence	Nil	Nil	Mixed	Nil
Union of Post Office Clerks	1910	1920	6 500†	20 100‡ (17 000 May 1920)	115 000 (1920)	3d 4d or 3d according to salary	3d 4d or 2d according to salary	No benefits other than those of membership	Few	One	Mixed	Nil
Small societies affiliated to Civil Service Federation and Civil Service Alliance	—	—	—	1 500‡	50 000	—	—	—	Women on executive committees of Civil Service Federation and Civil Service Alliance.	—	—	—
General Labour Unions National Federation of Women Workers	1906	1906	10 000	80 000† About the same Dec 1919	80,000	—	3d—8d	Trade, unemployment, sickness, benevolent, funeral, marriage dowry	Nil	Fifty	—	—
National Union of General Workers	1889	1889	4 000	80 000† 40 000 Dec 1919	350,000	3d	½d.	Trade, unemployment, disablement, funeral	Nil	One (Women temporary staff in addition)	Mainly mixed. Some all women	Nil
Workers' Union	1898	1898	1 500	80 000† (60,000§ Dec 1919)	400 000 (491 000, Dec 1919)	4d	2d—3d	Trade, accident, disablement, funeral, marriage dowry or part dowry (4s members only))	Nil	Sixteen	Mixed. Few all women s	Nil

Mixed. (Women's Advisory Council)	Nil.	Shop assistants.	Nil	Nil	No standard. 3 L claim minimum rate of 18 a week or 3/4 men's standard London, +	Roughly 25% (Members + 80% during 1919. Min rates from 3[illegible] to 35 a week of 48 hrs from [illegible] to 28 years London + 5 agreed with large numbers of firms	45 to 60/ from [illegible] to 28 years, London + 5 (1919)	4/5 men's standard.
		Dressmakers		—	No standard	8½d an hour T B rate or [illegible]d piece-work basis time-rate Feb. 1920		
Mixed	Nil	Shop assistants, factory workers	Nil	Nil	1[illegible] a week	+50 % to 100% (Various district rates Average 45 - a week of 48 hours 1st assistants. + 3/- to 5 manageresses, 5/ Dec. 1919)	Various district rates About 60 - to [illegible] 1st assistants, + 3 to 5 managers 75 (Dec. 1919)	Equal pay in many districts
Mixed	Nil	General clerks typists short-hand typists, book-keepers secretaries etc. Municipal clerks	Nil.	Nil.	No standard. Average earnings 15 to [illegible] a week	+ about 2/6 to 5 - Municipal clerks £[illegible] to £325 per ann + civil service bonus (see below). Same rates as for men, June 1920	No standard Average earnings, 55, to 85/	Mostly women's rates of wages
Mixed.	Nil.	Booking-clerks account invoicing and general clerks	Nil	Nil	No general standard London 22 to 28, a week provinces [illegible] to 26/	[illegible] 20 6	30 to 40 a week + 3[illegible]	Men's minimum rates each grade + women's war advances
Mixed	Nil	Telegraphists telephonists sorting clerks	Nil	Nil	London 18 to [illegible] a week small town 12, to 28, a week	+ 15 + 130% on pre-war salaries up to [illegible] 60% on amount between [illegible] and [illegible] per ann and 4[illegible]% on amount between £200 and £1 000 per ann. May 1920	40 to 88 telegraphists)	35 to 55 (telegraphists
—	—	—	—	—	18 a week to £2[illegible]0 per annum	Same as above	—	Women's rates of wages.
—	—	**Metal Workers** Engineering (mainly substituted women) asbestos brass foundry electric lamp cable, fishing tackle and needle, nail nut and bolt optical instrument and small tool makers	Prohibition by men's engineering unions in skilled processes	Relaxation	No general standard Midlands district, 12/ a week of 54 hours	½d + 11, a week (+ 5 Jan 1919 + 6 Dec. 1919)	Rates according to district Roughly labourers 26 skilled tradesmen 40 - a week of 52 54 hours + 16 6 + 12½% on earnings.	6d an hour + [illegible] week Higher rates for special work Women employed in place of fully-skilled tradesmen men's basic rates less 10% + women's war bonus
		Chain makers	—	—	2¾d. an hour T B rate	5d an hour T B rate (7¾d Nov 1919)	—	—
Mainly mixed some all women's	Nil	Hollow-ware workers	—	—	10, a week of 54 hours	18, a week T B rate (30/, T B rate + 6/ T U rate, Dec 1919)	—	—
		Textile Workers Cotton, wool hosiery workers dyers, etc., employed in outlying districts	—	—	(See under respective industrial headings)	—	—	-
Mixed Few all-women's	Nil.	Rope and net workers	—		No standard Average earnings, 8/ to 12 a week.	5¼d an hour + 11/- a week (8¼d T B rate April 1920)	—	-
		Lace finishers	—	—	¾d an hour T B rate	4d an hour T.B rate (5¼d June, 1920)	—	—
		Clothing Workers. Dressmakers and women's light clothing makers	—	—	No standard	No standard (8½d an hour T B. rate, Feb 1920)	—	—
		Shirtmakers	—	—	No standard	6d an hour T B rate (8d Nov 1919)	—	—
		Glove makers	—	-		—	—	—
		Button makers	-	—	No standard Average earnings, 8 a week, time 1[illegible] - piece	20 time 23 to 21 piece (8½d an hour T B rate March, 1920)	-	—
		Wood Workers. Aircraft (mainly substituted women)	—	—	No standard Average earnings, [illegible] a week	6d an hour + 11 (+ 5, Jan 1919)††	—	-
		Chemical Workers Heavy explosives (mainly substituted women	—	—	—	5½d an hour + 11/ week (+[illegible] Jan 1919)	—	6d an hour + 11 a week (+ - Jan 19)
		Fine drugs etc	—	—	12 6 to [illegible] a week.	2[illegible] 6 to 35 - a week (35, to 42 6, Jan. 1920	11d an hour T B rate (March, 1919).	—
		Food Workers Cocoa and chocolate, sugar confectionery and jam workers	—	—	No standard Average earnings 11/ to 12/ a week.	5d an hour T.B rate 6¼d T B rate + 1½d to ¾d T.U rate, Jan 1920 ††	—	11d an hour T B rate Dec 19)
		Tin-box makers.	—	—	9/ to 11/, a week	4½d an hour T B rate (¾d Nov 1919)	—	—
		Various. Rubber workers	—	—	No standard.	5¼d an hour + 11 - (+5 - Jan. 1919)	—	6d an hour + 11/-
		Fire-brick workers	-	—	No standard Average earnings, 13 [illegible] a week.	30/9 a week (4 May 1920.	—	—
		Laundry workers	—	—	No standard Average earnings 9/ to 12/	1[illegible] to 2[illegible] a week according to district 30/ to 35, a week of 48 hours, T B rate June 1920.)	—	—
		Domestic workers.	—	—	—	No standard (Roughly 50-100% advance, Dec. 1919)	—	—
		Agricultural workers (substituted women)	—	—	—	—	32 a week minimum (42/ May 1920)	5d to 6d an hour (National 7d Somerset 8d Yorks 10d May 1920)

TABLE III

State of Employment in the United Kingdom during and after the Great War *

		July 1914	Nov 1918	Oct 1919	Increase (+) or Decrease (−) Nov 1918, to Oct 1919	Increase (+) or Decrease (−) July 1914 to Oct 1919
Industries—Building	M †	920,000	438 000	692 000	+ 254 000	− 228,000
	F †	7,000	31 000	9,900	− 21 000	+ 2 900
	Total	927,000	469,000	702,000	+ 233,000	− 225,000
Mines and Quarries	M	1 266 000	1,039,000	1 272 000	+ 233,000	+ 6 000
	F	7 000	13,000	9 900	− 3 000	+ 2 900
	Total	1,273,000	1,052,000	1,282,000	+ 230,000	+ 9,000
Metal Industries	M	1,634,000	1 876,000	1 936 000	+ 60,000	+ 302,000
	F	170,000	596,000	303,000	− 293,000	+ 133,000
	Total	1,804,000	2,472,000	2,239,000	− 233,000	+ 435,000
Chemical Industries	M	159 000	161 000	185,000	± 24,000	+ 26,000
	F	40,000	103,000	74 000	− 29,000	+ 34 000
	Total	199,000	264,000	259,000	− 5,000	+ 60,000
Textile	M	625,000	408,000	511,000	+ 103,000	− 114 000
	F	863,000	818,000	851,000	+ 33,000	− 12 000
	Total	1,488,000	1,226,000	1,362,000	+ 136,000	− 126,000
Clothing Industries	M	287 000	181 000	235,000	+ 54 000	− 52 000
	F	612 000	557,000	578,000	+ 21 000	− 34,000
	Total	899,000	738,000	813,000	+ 75,000	− 86,000
Food, Drink and Tobacco Industries	M	360,000	247 000	344,000	+ 97 000	− 16 000
	F	196,000	231 000	259,000	+ 28 000	+ 63 000
	Total	556,000	478,000	603,000	+ 125,000	+ 47,000
Paper and Printing Industries	M	261 000	158 000	225 000	+ 67,000	− 36 000
	F	148,000	141 000	151 000	+ 10,000	+ 3,000
	Total	409,000	299,000	376,000	+ 77,000	− 33,000
Wood Industries	M	258 000	173 000	227 000	+ 54 000	− 31 000
	F	44,000	83 000	59,000	− 24 000	+ 15 000
	Total	302,000	256,000	286,000	+ 30,000	− 16,000
Other Industries (including Gas Water and Electricity under Local Authorities)	M	456 000	305,000	415,000	+ 110 000	− 41 000
	F	90,000	156,000	143,000	− 13,000	+ 53,000
	Total	546,000	461,000	558,000	+ 97,000	± 12,000
Government Establishments (Dockyards Arsenals, National Factories etc)	M	76,000	275,000	146,000	− 129 000	+ 70,000
	F	2,200	246,000	16 000	− 230,000	+ 14,000
	Total	78,000	521,000	162,000	− 359,000	+ 84,000
Total Industries (including Government Establishments)	M	6 302 000	5 261 000	6 188 000	+ 927,000	114,000
	F	2 179,000	2 975,000	2 454 000	− 521 000	+ 275 000
	Total	8,481,000	8,236,000	8,642,000	+ 406,000	+ 161,000
Agriculture (permanent labour) in Gt Britain	M	800,000	578 000	654,000	+ 76,000	− 146,000
	F	80 000	95,000	81 000	− 14,000	+ 1 000
	Total	880,000	673,000	735,000	+ 62,000	− 145,000
Transport (including Municipal Tramways)	M	1 161 000	858 000	1 188 000	+ 330 000	+ 27 000
	F	18,000	115 000	56,000	− 59 000	+ 38 000
	Total	1,179,000	973,000	1,244,000	+ 271,000	+ 65,000
Finance and Commerce	M	1 401 000	846,000	1 172 000	+ 326,000	− 229,000
	F	506 000	955 000	881 000	− 74 000	+ 375,000
	Total	1,907,000	1,801,000	2,053,000	+ 252,000	+ 146,000
Professional Occupations (employed persons, i.e except in the case of hospitals mainly clerks)	M	127 000	69,000	95,000	+ 26,000	− 32 000
	F	51,000	120,000	74 000	− 46,000	− 23,000
	Total	178,000	188,000	169,000	− 20,000	− 9,000
Entertainment—Hotels Theatres etc	M	199,000	116 000	158,000	+ 42 000	+ 41,000
	F	181,000	222,000	234 000	+ 12,000	+ 53,000
	Total	380,000	338,000	392,000	+ 54,000	+ 12,000
Civil Service	M	243,000	180 000	249 000	+ 69 000	+ 6 000
	F	66,000	225 000	163 000	− 62 000	+ 97 000
	Total	309,000	405,000	412,000	+ 7 000	+ 103,000
Local Government (including teachers but excluding Municipal Tramways and Gas Water and Electricity)	M	376,000	251 000	357,000	+ 106 000	− 19 000
	F	196,000	229,000	218,000	− 11,000	+ 22 000
	Total	572,000	480,000	575,000	+ 95,000	+ 3,000
Total for above Occupations	M	10 609 000	8 159 000	10,061,000	+ 1 902 000	− 548 000
	F	3 277 000	4 936 000	4,161,000	− 775,000	+ 884,000
	Total	13,886,000	13,095,000	14,222,000	+ 1,127,000	+ 336,000

GENERAL INDEX

Addison, Dr 75
Admiralty, 45, 77
Agricultural Societies, 91, 181.
Agriculture : substitution, 91
Agriculture : wages, 91
Aircraft workers, 81-3, 158, 187
Arbitration Tribunal for Women, Special, 79, 81, 93, 94, 227

Benefits, Trade Union, 210-11 (see particular unions)
Besant, Mrs Annie, 26.
Birtwistle, Mr, 9, 17.
Black, Miss Clementina, 20, 26
Bondfield, Miss Margaret, 41, 58-9, 64, 105, 113
Bookbinders, Early Disputes of, 6-8
Bookbinding (see Printing)
Boot and Shoe Societies, 30, 143-6
Boot and Shoe Trade : substitution, 81, 144-5.
Boot and Shoe Trade : wages, 84, 144-5
Broadhurst, M P., Mr, 16, 19.
Brushmaking substitution, 45.
Brushmakers' Societies, 180
Burrows, Mr. Herbert, 26.

Carpet Societies, 134
Charwomen, Revolt of, 47.
Chainmakers, Revolt of, 47-8
Cigar-making substitution, 38, 163
Cigar-making : wages, 53, 89, 163
Civil Service Societies, 98, 175-9
Civil Service : wages, 90, 178
Clerks' Societies, 29, 39, 171-9.
Clerks : substitution, 39, 90, 172-3, 175
Clerks : wages, 44, 53, 90, 95, 172-4, 175
Clothing Societies : miscellaneous, 156.
Combination Act, 5.
Committee on Production, 86, 92, 95.
Conductresses, Strike of, 92-3
Constitution, Trade Union, 203-209 (see particular unions).
Contributions, Trade Union, 66, 210-12 (see particular trades)

Co-operative Workers : substitution, 90, 168-70
Co-operative Workers wages, 56, 90, 168-70
Cotton Associations, 4-5, 8-9, 11, 17, 23, 29, 41-2, 61, 85, 99, 118-26.
Cotton Industry : substitution, 4-5, 23, 29, 84-5, 122, 126, 221
Cotton Industry : wages, 5, 44, 51, 52, 94, 109, 121-3, 125-6, 235-6
Cross, Mr, 30.

Davis, W J, 25, 66-7
Dilke, Sir Charles, 20, 27, 60
Dilke, Lady, 17, 37
Dressmakers' Societies, 12, 22, 28.
Domestic Workers' Societies, 22, 29, 180, 181-7.
Domestic Workers : wages, 96
Dunning, Mr., 7-8

Eight Hour Bill, 109
Ellis, Mrs, 13-14, 21.
Employment, State of, 68-9, 108
Endowment of Dependent Persons, 228-9
Engineering Employers' Federation, 69-70, 73, 106, 222.
Engineering Trades (see Metal Trades)

Factory and Workshop Acts, 16, 17, 18-19, 27-8, 38, 60, 65, 66, 74, 101, 152
Fair Wages Clause, 45, 86.
Faithfull, Miss Emily, 8, 33.
Felt Hat Trade : substitution, 40, 146.
Felt Hat Trade : wages, 146.
Flax and Jute Societies, 29, 129-32
Flax and Jute Trade substitution, 130-2
Flax and Jute Trade wages, 130-2.
Food Workers' Unions, 28, 162, 181-7
Food Workers : wages, 46, 57, 109, 162, 186
Ford, Miss I. O., 41.

Gavin, Mr., 31, 42.
Gee, Mr. Allan, 31, 42.

George, Right Hon. David Lloyd, 71, 72, 78
General Labour Unions, 22, 28-9, 39, 181-8.

Hat Societies, 12, 30, 39-41, 146
Health Insurance Act, 60
Health of Munition Workers, 73, 77, 101-2.
Health Protection (see Factory and Workshops Act and " Unsuitable " Occupations).
Hendry, Mr., 42
Hicks, Mrs , 28.
Hollow-ware Workers, Revolt of, 48-9
Home Work, Select Committee on, 57.
Hosiery Societies, 14-15, 132-3.
Hosiery Trades · substitution, 45, 133
Hosiery Trades . wages, 10, 45, 133

Industrial Courts Act, 109
International Labour Movement, 105.

James, Miss, 28.
Joint Committee on Women's Wages, 94-185
Jones, Mr , 42
Juggins, Mr., 20

Keegan, Mr., 42.
King, Mr,, 11, 18

Labour Commission, 28
Labour Party, 105
Labour Supply Committee, 76, 77
Lace Societies, 134
Lace Workers, Early Agitation of, 3
Laundresses, Agitation of, 27-8
Laundresses' Societies, 27-8, 180, 181-7
Laundresses · wages, 96, 109, 187
Lawrence, Miss Susan, 47, 79, 102, 105.
Leather Trades substitution, 45-6.
Leeds Trades Council, 27
Leicester Spinners, Petition of, 3
London County Council, 47.
London Trades Council, 11, 15, 26, 28, 39.

Macarthur, Miss Mary, 31, 45, 46, 50, 57-8, 63, 74, 76, 79, 93, 104, 105, 199, 233, 234.
Mallon, Mr J J., 58, 102.

Management, Trade Union, 61-5, 212-5 (see particular unions).
Mason, Mrs , 14-15, 16.
Matchmakers, Strike of, 26-7.
Marsland, Miss, 31.
Mawdsley, Mr., 31
Membership, Trade Union, 22, 30, 50-1, 98-9, 108-9, 111-13 (see particular unions).
Metal Societies, 29, 115-7, 181-7
Metal Trades substitution, 19-20, 38-9, 69-83, 116-7
Metal Trades · wages, 19, 39, 44, 47-9, 57-8, 77-81, 116-17, 186
" Millwall " Strike, 46-7
Miners' Societies, 30, 91, 114.
Mines : substitution, 20-1, 91, 114.
Mines · wages, 114.
Minimum Wage Bill, 109.
Montagu, Right Hon Edwin, 86
Mothers' Pensions Bill, 201
Mullin, Mr., 31.
Municipal Workers, 178, 181-7
Munitions of War Act, 71, 75, 76, 78-9, 93
Munition Workers (see Metal Workers)

National Industrial Council, 110
Net Workers, 187

Output, Comparative, 72-3, 89-90, 91-2, 190, 191-2, 193, 195-6, 231-2. (see particular trades)

Pankhurst, Miss Sylvia, 71.
Paterson, Mrs Emma, 10-12, 15-16, 21, 23-5
Post Office Societies, 98, 175-9
Post Office wages, 53, 90, 176-9
Pottery societies 6, 37-8, 159-61.
Pottery Trades · substitution, 6, 36-8, 159-60
Pottery Trades : wages, 53, 95, 159-61
Printing and Bookbinding Societies, 8, 12, 28, 32-5, 150-6.
Printing and Bookbinding · substitution, 8, 32-5, 45, 85-6, 150-3
Printing and Bookbinding : wages, 6-7, 32-3, 34, 44, 52-3, 155-6

Railway Societies, 147-8
Railway Clerks, 174-5
Railways substitution, 91, 147-8
Railways wages, 91, 147-8
Railway Women's Guild, 104

Representation of People's Act, 104.

Restoration of Pre-war Practices Act, 106-7, 221, 223-4.

Restrictions, Trade Union, 220-6 (see particular trades)

Rowntree, Mr Seebohm, 228.

Rope Workers, 28, 187

Samuel, Right Hon. Herbert, 90, 227.

Shackleton, Sir David, 41

Shells and Fuses Agreement, 70

Shipton, George, 11, 15, 41

Shop Assistants' Societies, 29, 39, 164-70

Shop Assistants · substitution, 39, 89-90, 165-7.

Shop Assistants : wages, 44, 53-6, 89, 95, 109, 165-7.

Shop Hours Act, 60

Short Hours Bill, 9.

" Sick Worker," 195, 236

Silk Workers, 134-5

Standing Joint Committee of Industrial Women's Organizations, 96, 103, 104, 113, 208, 209, 228.

Statutory Orders, 77, 79-83

Strikes, 11, 26-7, 46, 201

Substitution of Men and Women, 10, 17-18, 31, 44, 69, 86-7, 189-90, 193, 194

Symons, Miss Madeleine, 100

Tailoresses, Strikes of, 21-2, 27.

Tailoring Societies, 4, 5, 12, 21, 22, 27, 29, 30, 141-3.

Tailoring Trade : substitution, 4, 31-2, 44, 84, 143.

Tailoring Trade wages, 21-2, 44, 57, 58, 95, 109, 143, 187.

Talbot, Miss, 64, 165

Teachers' Salaries, Departmental Committees on, 229

Textile Dyers, 29, 137-9.

Textile Societies, Miscellaneous, 28, 133-5

Textile Warehouse Workers, 139-40.

Thorne, Mr. Will, 42

Tobacco Societies, 30, 38, 162, 163, 181-7.

Trade Boards Act, 20, 47, 57-8, 95, 109, 143, 156, 163, 167, 187, 231.

Trade Boards (Amendment) Act, 100-1

Trades Union Congress, 15-16, 18-21, 65-7, 99, 100, 101, 113, 186.

Trades Union Congress, Parliamentary Committee, 105, 113

Trades Union Council, Scottish, 47

Training, Technical, 108, 195, 196, 234

Transport Workers, 91-3, 147-9.

Treasury Agreement, 71-2.

Truck Act, 58-9.

Tuckwell, Miss Gertrude, 17, 46, 182.

Tynan, Miss A , 64.

Unemployment, 69, 107, 108.

Unemployment Insurance, 101, 224

" Unsuitable " Occupations, 16, 17-18, 21, 23, 65, 66, 67, 76-7, 87, 91, 99-100, 220-1

Upholstresses' Societies, 12, 157

Wages, 10, 44-5, 51-8, 87-9, 100, 109-110 (see particular trades).

Wages (Temporary Regulation) Act, 109

War Cabinet Women in Industry Committees, 93, 107, 227, 228, 231.

War Emergency Workers, National Committee, 74.

Ward, Mrs Bessie, 64-5, 89, 167

Watkins, Miss, 7.

Webb, Mr. Sidney, 44

Webb, Mrs Sidney, 228, 231

Welders, Women, 82-3

Welfare Supervision, 102, 103

" Whitley " Councils, 102, 109

Whyte, Miss, 13, 21, 65.

Wilkinson, Miss Ellen, 97, 168

Women's Co-operative Guild, 56, 104, 113, 168.

Women's Employment Committees, 231.

Women Officials, 64-65, 215-9 (see particular unions).

Women's Protection and Provident League (see Women's Trade Union League)

Women's Societies, 12-13, 22, 26-9, 113, 203

Women's Suffrage Movement, 104

Women's Suffrage Society, 9, 10.

Women's Suffrage Society, London, 82, 91, 97, 104.

Women's Trades Council, 24

Women's Trade Union Council, Manchester, 36, 62, 113, 119, 153.

Women's Trade Union Journal, 10, 22, 23, 43

Women's Trade Union League, 10-21, 22-5, 45, 47, 59, 74, 104, 113, 182, 209-10

Women's Trade Union League Conference, 16-18

Woodworkers, 45, 81-2, 157-8, 187.

Wool and Worsted Societies, 13-14, 29, 126-9.

Wool and Worsted Trades · substitution, 84, 127, 129.

Wool and Worsted Trade wages, 51, 89, 94-5, 127-9.

Zugg, Miss Mary, 8

INDEX OF TRADE UNIONS

Agricultural Labourers, National Union, 181.

Beamers, Twisters and Drawers-in, Amalgamated Association, 123-4

Blind, National League of, 180.

Bonnet Makers, Grand Lodge of Operative, 5

Bookbinders and Machine Rulers, National Union, 151-2, 154-6.

Bookbinders, London Union of Journeymen, 6-8, 11, 21, 35-6

Boot and Shoe Operatives, National Union of, 30, 50, 52, 62-3, 145

Boot, Shoe and Slipper Operatives, Rossendale, 145-6

Brassworkers and Metal Mechanics, National Union, 18, 38, 66-7, 99, 115.

Brushmakers, National Society, 180

Card and Blowing Room Operatives, Amalgamated Association, 31, 123-5.

Carpenters, Cabinet Makers and Joiners, Society of, 81, 97

Carpet Trades Association, Northern Counties, 134

Carpet Weavers' Union, Kidderminster, 21, 99, 134

Catering Trades Union, United, 164-5

Chain Country Workers' Union, 30

Cigar Makers, National Union, 18, 30, 38, 53, 162-3.

Civil Servants, Society of, 177.

Civil Service Alliance, 177-8

Civil Service Federation, 177-8

Civil Service Sorting Assistants' Association, 176

Civil Service Union, 178.

Clerks, National Union, 53, 90, 95, 171-3, 175.

Clothiers' Operatives, Amalgamated Union, 30

Compositors, London Society, 8, 30, 52, 85-6, 150-1, 155

Confectionery Workers' Society, 28.

Co-operative Employees, Amalgamated Union, 51, 56, 90, 97, 164, 167-70, 176, 184, 185

Core Makers, Amalgamated Society, 116.

Cotton Weavers, Accrington Association, 9, 17.

Cotton Weavers, Blackburn Association, 119, 214.

Cotton Weavers, Chorley Association, 99, 120

Cotton Weavers, Manchester and Salford Association Power-looms, 62, 119

Cotton Weavers, Northern Counties Amalgamated Association, 31, 41-2, 61-2, 118, 119-23.

Cotton Weavers, Oldham Association, 17, 61, 120.

Cotton Weavers, Wigan Association, 119, 120.

Dockers' Union, 116, 142, 147, 181.

Domestic Workers of Gt. Britain, 180.

Drapers' Assistants, Irish Union, 164

Dressmakers, Milliners and Mantle Makers' Society, 12.

Dyers, Bleachers and Finishers, Amalgamated Society, 49, 136

Dyers, Bleachers and Finishers, Bolton Amalgamation, 29, 137

Dyers and Finishers, National Society, 136.

Electrical Trades Union, 115

Engine and Crane Drivers, National Union, 116, 185

Engineers, Amalgamated Society, 11, 18, 38, 69-73, 74-81, 97, 115, 200

Fawcett Association, 175, 176.

Felt Hatters, Society of Journeymen, 30, 40-41, 146

Felt Hat Trimmers and Wool Formers, 30, 40-41

Female Biscuit Operatives, Dublin Guild, 162

Female Bookfolders, National Union, 42

Female Cigar Makers, Nottingham Society, 38, 162, 163

Female Gardeners' Lodge, 5.

Female Lace Workers, Nottingham Society, 134.

Female Machinists and Electrical Workers, 39, 115

Female Tailors' Lodge, 5

Female Workers in the Shipping Industry, 87, 139-40

File Trades, Amalgamated Union, 117.

File Cutters, Hand, 30.

Flax and Yarn Spinners' Union, 132.

Furnishing Trades Association, National Amalgamated, 157-8.

Gardeners' Union, British, 180

Garment Workers' Union, United, 95, 141-4, 185

Gas Workers' and General Labourers National Union, 39, 42, 116.

General Workers, National Federation, 98, 126, 184.

General Workers, National Union, 97, 182, 183, 185, 188, 207, 209, 213.

Gold, Silver and Kindred Trades, Amalgamated Union, 117

Grand General Union of the United Kingdom, 4.

Grand National Consolidated Trades Union of Gt Britain and Ireland, 5.

Grocers' Assistants, National Union, 164.

Hat Makers, United, 21

Hosiery Menders' Union, Hinckley and District, 132

Hosiery Union, Leicester Amalgamated, 15, 29, 132-3

Hot Pressers' Union, Hanley, 21

India Rubber Cable and Asbestos Workers' Union, 180

Jute and Flax Workers' Union, Dundee and District, 63, 130-1

Labour, Amalgamated Union, 184

Lace Makers, Long Eaton and District, 134.

Laundry Workers, National Union, 180

Machine Woolcombers, National Union, 126, 128-9

Matchmakers, Society of, 26-7

Mill and Factory Workers' Association, Scottish, 29, 42, 43

Mill and Factory Workers' Union, Dundee and District, 29, 130, 131

Miners' Association, Cumberland, 30

Miners' Association, Lanarkshire, 114

Municipal Employees' Association, 185

Nailers' Union, Old Swinford, 19.

Nut and Bolt Makers, 20

Operative Bakers, Amalgamated Union, 162

Operative Cotton Spinners' Amalgamation, 31, 84-5, 118, 125-6

Operative Printers' Assistants, National Union, 152-3, 154-6, 204

Packing Case Makers, London, 157, 185.

Parasol and Umbrella Makers' Union, 10

Patent Cop Winders, Bobbin and Hank Winders, Gassers, Doublers, Reelers and Preparers, Manchester Association, 119.

Pen Makers, Birmingham, 42

Postal and Telegraph Clerks' Association, 175, 176.

Postal Workers' Union, Temporary, 176

Postmen's Federation, 98, 176.

Post Office Workers, Union, 175-7, 178.

Pottery Workers, Society of Male and Female, 53, 159-161.

Printers and Transferers' Union, 37

Printers' Warehousemen and Cutters, National Union, 30, 35, 36, 51, 52, 63.

Printing and Kindred Trades Federation, 36, 45, 153-4, 156

Printing and Paper Workers, National Union, 51, 152, 154-6, 185, 204.

Railway Clerks' Association, 174-5
Railwaymen, National Union, 91, 147-8
Ring Spinners' Association, Manchester and Salford, 119
Rotary Power Framework Knitters' Society, 132
Rope Makers, Society of, 28
Royal Army Clothing Department Employees, 22, 141

Seamers and Stitchers, Society of, 14
Shop Assistants, National Amalgamated Union, 39, 41, 51, 53-6, 58-9, 89, 95-6, 99, 164, 165-7.
Steel Smelters, British, 30, 116.

Tailors and Tailoresses, Amalgamated Society, 21, 30, 141-3
Tailors and Tailoresses, Scottish Society, 21, 31, 141
Tailors, Society of Journeymen, 4
Textile and Kindred Workers (Leek) Amalgamated Society, 134-5
Textile Operatives of Ireland, 29, 132.
Textile Workers', General Union, 14, 29, 31, 42, 51, 126-7.
Textile Workers, Newmilns and District, 134
Theatrical Employees, National Union, 180
Tin and Sheet Millmen's Union, 30
Typographical Association, 32, 150
Typographical Association, Scottish, 33-5, 86, 150-1, 154
Typographical Society, Edinburgh, 33-5, 53, 86, 150-1

Upholsterers, Amalgamated Union, 49, 157
Upholstresses, Liverpool Society, 157.
Upholstresses, London Society, 12

Upholstresses, Manchester Society, 157

Vehicle Workers, United, 91, 106, 148-9

Warehouse and General Workers, National Union, 164, 181, 184.
Women Bookfolders' Union, 36.
Women Bookfolders, National Union, 36.
Women Civil Servants, Federation of, 176
Women Clerks and Secretaries, Association of, 171, 173-4, 203
Women Employed in Bookbinding, London Society, 12.
Women Employed in Printing and Bookbinding, Manchester Society, 153, 154-6, 203.
Women Employed in Printing Trades, Edinburgh Society, 8.
Women's Engineering Society, 115
Women Hosiery Workers' Union, Nottingham, 132.
Women Motor Drivers, Society of, 92, 148
Women Post Office Clerks' Association, 176
Women's Typographical Society, 10
Women Welders, Society of, 82-3, 97, 115.
Women Workers, Irish Union, 184.
Women Workers, National Federation, 45-6, 47-50, 65-7, 74-82, 94 97-8, 107, 116, 141, 165, 181, 182-3, 185, 200, 205-8, 213, 218, 220, 225, 232, 234
Woollen Weavers, Dewsbury, 13-4
Workers' Union, 57, 78, 97, 126, 146, 157, 181, 183-4.
Working-women, National Union, 12,15
Workwomen, Leeds Society, 27, 41

GARDEN CITY PRESS, LETCHWORTH, HERTS.

9 781176 276444